THE ETHNIC I

THE ETHNIC I

A Sourcebook for Ethnic-American Autobiography

JAMES CRAIG HOLTE

Greenwood Press

NEW YORK • WESTPORT, CONNECTICUT • LONDON

Library of Congress Cataloging-in-Publication Data

Holte, James Craig.
  The ethnic I.

  Bibliography: p.
  Includes index.
  1. American prose literature—Minority authors—
History and criticism. 2. Autobiography. 3. Minorities—
United States—Biography—History and criticism.
4. Ethnology—United States. 5. United States—Ethnic
relations. 6. Immigrants—United States—Biography—
History and criticism. I. Title.
PS366.A88H65   1988   818′.08   87–23650
ISBN 0-313-24463-4 (lib. bdg. : alk. paper)

British Library Cataloguing in Publication Data is available.

Library of Congress Catalog Card Number: 87–23650
ISBN: 0–313–24463–4

First published in 1988

Greenwood Press, Inc.
88 Post Road West, Westport, Connecticut 06881

Printed in the United States of America

The paper used in this book complies with the
Permanent Paper Standard issued by the National
Information Standards Organization (Z39.48–1984).

10 9 8 7 6 5 4 3 2 1

Copyright Acknowledgment

Grateful acknowledgment is given for material appearing in the Introduction
which originally appeared in slightly different form in James Holte, "The
Representative Voice: Autobiography and Ethnic Experience," *MELUS* 9, 2:
25–46 (Amherst: University of Massachusetts, 1983).

Contents

Acknowledgments

Nothing of substance is created alone, and this book would never have been possible without the help of a number of people. My thanks and appreciation go to Wayne Charles Miller, a mentor in the best sense of the word; William Bloodworth, who encouraged and supported the project; the staff of the Department of English at East Carolina University, who spent hours helping put the manuscript together; and especially Patsy Collier, who processed so many of the words here.

Finally, this book is dedicated to Gwyn, who was there in the beginning, and Molly, who came near the end.

THE ETHNIC I

Introduction: Personal Voices from the New World

American writing has always been personal. From the first letters and reports from the colonies to contemporary nonfiction novels and new journalism, Americans have drawn on their own experiences as the primary source for much of their writing. Much of traditional American literature is a direct expression of personal experience. Franklin's *Autobiography*, Thoreau's *Walden*, and Twain's *Life on the Mississippi*, for example, present personal experience in such a way that both the authors and their cultures are defined in the narratives.

The American literary tradition is not a catalogue of isolated masterpieces; it is an almost obsessive inquiry into what it means to be an American. Every generation asks this question and comes up with its own answers, but the way the answers are discovered is influenced by literary perceptions as well as individual concerns. Perceptions are influenced by conventions; we often discover what we set out to find. For some, the tradition of frontier millennial evangelicalism imbues every act with religious significance; others see every event as part of a class struggle or mythic pattern; and others view their life stories as part of a process of assimilation or rejection. To be aware of the literary conventions that influence us is to be aware of both our perceptions and our literary history. In answering the question of what it means to be an American, our writers, in a relatively fluid society, have put little emphasis on class or manners. Cooper, Hawthorne, and James, among others, have noted that this society lacks a cultural tradition. Thus our writers have had to look to themselves and their own experiences as the primary source of value and meaning, and as a result we are constantly attempting to define who and what we are.

To understand how writers have answered the question of identity, we must understand some of the conventions of the autobiography. From the reports of the earliest explorers to the writings of Maxine Hong Kingston, Jerre Mangione, and Theodore White, there exists a continuity of conventions and concerns as well as radical differences in the social contexts from which the literature emerged.

Critical and popular attitudes toward a literary genre can reveal significant cultural attitudes. Every genre exists within a specific framework of textual forms, functions, materials, authorial intentions, and reader expectations. The development and popularity of a literary form are of more than academic interest; they have wider cultural implications. The popularity of such "non-traditional forms" as the occasional essay, the novel and the sermon in the seventeenth century, and the western and the proletarian novel in our more recent past reveals not only the interests of those who produced this literature but also the concerns of those who read it.

Understanding the conventions of a genre is essential for a writer as well. This knowledge enables writers to draw on a wide range of forms and structures. For example, an awareness of traditional hagiography and the seventeenth-century sectarian narrative not only provided John Bunyan with the structure for *The Pilgrim's Progress* and *Grace Abounding to the Chief of Sinners* but also enabled his readers to make meaning from those texts.

Adaptations to a genre are also bound by the same conventions. The success of Benjamin Franklin's *Autobiography*, for example, is due in part to his deliberate secularization of the earlier religious conversion narrative and mirrored the growing secularization of American culture at the end of the eighteenth century. His themes, images, and references not only looked back to a familiar body of literature but also reflected contemporary cultural concerns. The reasons for the continued popularity of the *Autobiography* are many, but a major one must be its establishment of a new set of conventions that have been adopted by American writers since Franklin's time. In a sense, all success narratives, including those of Andrew Carnegie, Edward Bok, and Frank Capra, owe something to Franklin's *Autobiography*.

The conjunction of literary choice and cultural influence is especially evident in autobiography. As Stephen Butterfield observes in *Black Autobiography in America* (Amherst: University of Massachusetts Press, 1974):

The genre of autobiography lives in the two worlds of history and literature, objective fact and subjective awareness.... In response to a particular historical period, the autobiographer examines, interprets, and creates the importance of his life. He may also affect history by leaving the work behind as a model for other lives. Autobiography asserts, therefore, that human life has or can be made to have meaning, that our actions count for something worth being remembered, that we are conscious agents of time, that we not only drift on the current of our circumstances but we fish in the stream and change the direction of its flow. (1)

Art in general and the autobiography in particular transform history through the creation of a special ritual, and in the process of coming to terms with the disorder they observe and experience, artists create what M. K. Blasing in *The Art of Life: Studies in American Autobiographical Literature* (Austin: University of Texas Press, 1977) called "a temporary center around which the accumulated facts of history may be organized" (xxiv). This created temporary center may then become a fact of its own, a perceptual convention, influencing the perceptions of others to the degree that actual experience is transformed by the imagined construct. The *Autobiography of Andrew Carnegie*, for example, has become such a significant cultural fact that it is almost impossible to discuss immigration, success in America, or immigrant American writing without reference to it.

Autobiography is a complex literary form. At first glance it would appear simple, since in its most basic structure it is a record of a person's life, and because all of us have some kind of life it would seem that the autobiography would be accessible to all. And the sheer number of autobiographies is overwhelming. Lewis Kaplin, in *A Bibliography of American Autobiographies* (Madison: University of Wisconsin Press, 1961), lists over 6,000 published American autobiographies.

In creating an autobiography, however, a writer transforms the complex interaction of self and society into a literary form. Raw experience must be shaped. The question of whether this imposition of form on experience takes place during the actual activity or is an act of literary imposition that occurs during the construction of a narrative may be unanswerable, but there is evidence that many writers use the autobiography as a means of imposing order on experiences that are disruptive and confusing. *The Autobiography of Malcolm X* and Maxine Hong Kingston's *The Woman Warrior*, for example, are excellent examples of literary form imposing order on chaos.

Two fundamental questions are raised by all autobiographers: Who am I and how did I become what I am? In addressing themselves to these questions, writers can choose among a variety of autobiographical forms to organize their experiences. Some of the forms are relatively simple. Exploits and memoirs, for example, are related objective forms in which the autobiographer chronicles his life and records famous events witnessed and famous people encountered. In this kind of autobiographical writing chronology is the primary organizing principle; little attempt is made to examine the motivations and thoughts of characters, and as a result these kinds of narratives often reveal more about an autobiographer's time than about the autobiographer. Sections of the autobiographies of Andrew Carnegie and Carl Schurz, men who accomplished much in their lifetimes, conform to this pattern.

Other forms are more complex. In the defense, the confession, and the conversion narrative, for example, a single significant experience or an overriding idea controls the entire narrative, dictating what is included and what is emphasized. The autobiography of Nicky Cruz, *Run, Baby, Run*, is a good example. Cruz writes a traditional religious conversion story, and as a result only those parts of his life that emphasize the conversion experience are included. Similarly, Carlos Bulosan's *America Is in the Heart* is essentially a defense of Filipino immigrants; Bulosan organizes his narrative around the struggle faced by Filipinos on the West Coast in the 1930s.

An even more subjective and complex form than these narratives is the developmental autobiography, a form discussed at length by Wayne Shumaker in his excellent study of the autobiography, *English Autobiography: Its Emergence, Materials, and Form* (Berkeley: University of California Press, 1954). In this form, which employs many of the techniques of fiction, the primary purpose is to show how the writer lived and thought, not just what he or she accomplished or observed. In writing this kind of personal narrative an autobiographer creates a complex character within a realistic social setting, and the narrative moves around a central, well-developed theme. Maxine Hong Kingston's *The Woman Warrior*, Piri Thomas' *Down These Mean Streets*, and Richard Wright's *Black Boy* are examples of successful developmental autobiographies.

The foundations of all American personal writing can be found in the spiritual narratives of the Pilgrims, Puritans, and Quakers. As Daniel Shea has observed in *Spiritual Autobiography in Early America* (Princeton, N.J.: Princeton University Press, 1968) these narratives are not original literary forms, but were borrowed from religious practices:

The explicit arguments of early spiritual narratives were highly conventional. A Puritan sought to assemble the evidence for divine favoritism toward him, and many Quaker journals recount the protracted search of the narrator for truth, which he inevitably finds in the doctrine of the Society of Friends. (12)

Implicit in these narratives is an integration of personal experience and inner evaluation, and the result is neither mere history nor mere personal observation, but rather a reordering and reevaluation of personal experience within a specific literary framework, or the beginnings of true autobiography.

Sacvan Bercovitch has traced the continuation of this kind of writing from colonial America to the present in *The Puritan Origins of the American Self* (London: Cambridge University Press, 1974) and *The American Jeremiad* (Madison: University of Wisconsin Press, 1978). He argues convincingly that Puritan thought, as seen in the development, continuation, and adaptation of a number of rhetorical models, including the spiritual narrative, has had a major influence on the transformation of American culture and the way its citizens view themselves, the nation, and even the world.

Perhaps the single most famous and influential American autobiography is Benjamin Franklin's *Autobiography* (New York: New American Library, 1961). Franklin's narrative is both a culmination of the colonial spiritual narratives that precede it and the first modern American autobiography. The Puritan and Quaker narratives were records of the inquisition of the soul. Franklin's work is the record of an inquisition of the self, a self that is created in the narrative, which is both the story of Benjamin Franklin and an expression of a changing culture. Franklin is, of course, well aware of the tradition he is adapting. He borrows directly from his Puritan forebears, opening his narrative with a statement of purpose in which he addresses his posterity, his son and other "spiritual descendants," and begins to outline his particular journey through life. Franklin's journey through life was a secular one, however, and rather than marking a movement from inherent depravity to a state of grace, the typical Puritan movement, Franklin observes a different course:

From the poverty and obscurity in which I was born and in which I passed my early years, I have raised myself to the state of affluence and some degree of celebrity in the world. (16)

Salvation is thus transformed into wealth and notoriety.

Autobiographies provide models for readers, and Franklin's "efficacious advertisement" for himself and his country became the primary model for the growing commercial nation. It was adapted and transformed into hundreds of other versions, including the related homilies of Horatio Alger. Franklin's optimistic story of freedom and progress in a new land became one of the favorite American stories, and his secular conversion became a national obsession. Many immigrant and ethnic writers acknowledge a debt to him, and behind every narrative of success stands the figure of Benjamin Franklin. Mary Antin's *Promised Land*, for example, is one Jewish immigrant girl's version of Franklin's story, and Edward Bok's *Americanization of Edward Bok* tells a Dutch immigrant's version.

Franklin did more than define the proper transformation for Americans; he transferred the moral implications from private spirituality to public success and gave the ideas of progress and change a validity by describing them in the language of salvation. Progress, mobility, and change became American traditions, but in addition to denoting worth, they also created a sense of dislocation and dissatisfaction.

No one chronicled the dislocation and dissatisfaction of his age better than Henry Adams. In his famous autobiography, *The Education of Henry Adams* (New York: Random House, 1931), Adams attempts to "run order through chaos," unity through multiplicity, as he charts the development of modern, urban, industrial America. Adams' world is the reverse of Franklin's; Franklin's virtues produced Adams' horrors, and writers who chart the failure of American society write with a debt to Adams. Richard Rodriguez' *Hunger of Memory*, Jerre Mangione's *Ethnic at Large*, and Emma Goldman's *Living My Life* all emphasize the multiplicity that exists, often destructively, within American culture.

The autobiography is one way of imposing order on change, and perhaps one reason for the popularity of this form in the United States is the feeling of rootlessness felt by so many Americans. It is no surprise to find that those

Americans who have experienced this uprootedness most dramatically, immigrant and ethnic Americans, have produced a large body of autobiographical writing. Some, like Mary Antin, Andrew Carnegie, and Jacob Riis, have followed the tradition of assimilation, but others, like Piri Thomas, Malcolm X, and Black Elk, seeing themselves as outsiders, have used the autobiography, and often the conventions of the conversion narrative, as a way of pointing out the defects in Franklin's vision (which has become the official standard vision of the nation), which assumed the absence of class, racial, or sexual discrimination, the essential good will of all men, the ameliorative effects of public education, and the continued abundance of natural resources.

The very language used to describe ethnic and immigrant experience underscores the notion of change and conversion. The image of the melting pot, used as a symbol of adaptation and assimilation and popularized in 1908 by Israel Zangwell's play, *The Melting Pot*, is both complex and confusing. The ideology behind the image, whether used by the proponents of assimilation or those opposed, as well as the ideology of those who put forward the concept of cultural pluralism as the correct way to describe the ideal relationship among the various cultures in the United States, suggests some kind of transformation. While scholars have debated whether this transformation was to take place in the culture at large or just in the ethnic community, the idea of transformation or conversion on the part of someone has been central to the debate. Ethnic writers themselves have taken both sides of the issue. Edward Bok and Richard Rodriguez argue that the throwing off of ethnic behaviors and the assumption of white, middle-class values are beneficial for ethnic Americans, while Maya Angelou and Maxine Hong Kingston assert that ethnic diversity enriches American culture. Along with the language chosen to describe the experience—language that not only describes the experience but prescribes the perception of it—there was, of course, the actual unsettling experience of migration. In her dissertation on immigrant personal narratives, "The Foreign-Born View America" (New York University, 1962), Cecyle Neidle notes that the autobiographical impulse arose among immigrants because of the shock and disillusionment occasioned by a prolonged state of crisis that they experienced upon their arrival in the United States.

This reality is fully confirmed by people who differed in personality, background, and educational preparation. It can be asserted that the emotional impact of the experience was not dissipated though decades lay between the time of arrival and the writing of one's experience. (VII)

This echoes Oscar Handlin's observation in *The Uprooted* (Boston: Little, Brown, 1951) that this period of shock and resulting crisis came about as a consequence of the disorientation caused by the failure of American reality to match immigrant expectations. Even a brief survey of ethnic narratives would confirm this. A common element in almost all ethnic autobiographies, whether the writer ultimately comes to succeed in the United States or not, is a description of the disappointment and trials and tribulations faced when first confronting the reality of American social and economic structures. The autobiographies of such diverse writers as Emma Goldman, Jacob Riis, Monica Sone, and Mary Anderson all emphasize this point.

Ethnic writers often assume the role of outsiders when they write about their experiences in America. Ethnic writers and other ethnic Americans recognized the pluralistic nature of American society from daily experience, while official American ideology continued to proclaim the unitary nature of the culture. Facing the pressures of Americanization—pressures to abandon a language, a religion, a community, a tradition—many felt confusion and anger, while others accepted the need to adapt to a majority culture. The ethnic autobiography, the outsider's story, takes many forms, but two major approaches can be seen. Starting from outside the culture, some writers chronicle the transformation from outsider to insider, from immigrant to American. The narratives of Mary Antin, Edward Bok, Andrew Carnegie and Frank Capra are excellent examples of this kind of success story. Some other writers, however, beginning at the same point, observe and record the opposite lesson; it is the dominant culture that keeps them out for reasons of race, sex, class, or language, and their narratives record the failures of a society as much as the inability of an individual to rise in the world. The autobiographies of Emma Goldman, Black Elk, and Malcolm X present this kind of analysis of American experience. Even in these narratives some of the conventions of the conversion story are employed, for in failing or electing not to enter "mainstream" culture, the writer is still transformed. One of the conventions of the conversion narrative is that the writer becomes a spokesperson for the community at the end of the story, and often in narratives where a writer rejects assimilation, the representative voice of the narrator is one of the major themes of the autobiography. The development of a self takes place in a community apart from middle-class America, and the writer becomes, in the narrative, the voice of that community.

Whether affirming their experiences in America or chronicling rejection, ethnic-American writers have left a large and diverse record of their observations. Some of the observations are famous. Andrew Carnegie's *Autobiography, The Autobiography of Malcolm X*, and Maxine Hong Kingston's *Woman Warrior* are all well-known and popular works. Some of the narratives are obscure. Few readers are familiar with Zora Neale Hurston's *Dust Tracks on a Road* or *The Autobiography of Mary Jane Hill Anderson*. The autobiographies, however, whether famous or forgotten, provide an overview of significant aspects of American culture from a unique perspective. Ethnic and immigrant writers saw America with new eyes. Beginning at the edges of American culture, these writers, whether they moved toward the cultural center or remained at the outside, perceived and recorded life in America as few native-born writers could. Jacob Riis' depictions of tenement life in nineteenth-century New York, Black Elk's story of prereservation life, and Emma Goldman's account of the anarchist movement in the ethnic community are just three examples of the important observations contained in these works.

No single volume can examine the entire subject of ethnic American autobiography, but the following pages attempt to provide an overview of the genre and an examination of the work of representative writers from a variety of ethnic backgrounds and historical periods. The autobiographies of Carl Schurz, Mary Jane Hill Anderson, and Andrew Carnegie, for example, describe the experiences of immigrants who came to the United States prior to the mass migrations of the late nineteenth century, and as a result their stories are substantially different from the works of Mary Antin and Edward Corsi, who came at the height of immigration to the United States. Richard Rodriguez and Maya Angelou, on the other hand, document the complexities of ethnic life in contemporary American society.

These and other writers included in this volume have left a large body of literature that is just beginning to be studied. The work of ethnic-American writers demands further analysis—a task that is being undertaken by more and more scholars and students concerned with American ethnic cultural identity. Through such examinations we can continue to study the process of cultural evolution in the United States and gain additional insights into the question that lies at the heart of our literature: What does it mean to be an American?

NOTE

Some of this material appeared, in slightly different form, in "The Representative Voice: Autobiography and the Ethnic Experience," *MELUS* 9, 2 (1983): 25–46. In addition to the critical works mentioned in this Introduction, readers interested in the study of American ethnic autobiography will find the following works helpful: Elizabeth Bruss, *Autobiographical Acts: The Changing Situation of a Literary Genre* (Baltimore, Md.: Johns Hopkins University Press, 1976); James Olney, *Metaphors of Self: The Meaning of Autobiography* (Princeton, N.J.: Princeton University Press, 1972); and Karl Weintraub, *The Value of the Individual: Self and Circumstance in Autobiography* (Chicago: University of Chicago Press, 1978).

MARY ANDERSON
(1873–1964)

Woman at Work

BIOGRAPHY

Mary Anderson was born in Lidköping, Sweden, 1873. The daughter of a Lutheran farmer, Anderson emigrated to the United States in 1889, following her older sister, who had come two years before. She began working as a cook and maid in Ludington, Michigan, before moving to Chicago to take a job making buttonholes in a shirtwaist factory. Working in the clothing industry in Chicago, Anderson became actively involved in the trade union movement. She was elected president of her local of the Boot and Shoe Workers Union and later was named to the Executive Committee of the Chicago Federation of Labor.

In 1917 Anderson became an advisor to Samuel Gompers, president of the American Federation of Labor, for women's interests in the union movement. In 1919 President Wilson appointed her director of the Women's Bureau of the Department of Labor, a position she held under four presidents for twenty-five years. Anderson retired in 1944 and died in January 1964.

THE AUTOBIOGRAPHY

Mary Anderson called herself a militant trade unionist, and it is not surprising that her autobiography, *Woman at Work*, records a life dedicated to the union movement. Like thousands of other immigrants who came to the United States at the height of American immigration, 1880–1910, Anderson found herself forced to work long hours for low pay in unsafe and unsanitary conditions; she also found that the union movement provided her with both a cause to believe in and emotional security. Anderson devoted her life to service, allowing little time for personal concerns, and as a result *Woman at Work* is an autobiography of public achievement. Anderson is aware of this:

I thought as a young girl that I would get married too, but somewhere I lost myself in my work and never felt that marriage would give me the security I wanted. I thought that through the trade union movement we working women could get better conditions and security of mind. (65)

In a number of ways *Woman at Work* is a traditional immigrant narrative. Anderson recalls her childhood in the homeland, her transatlantic journey, her first work experiences, and her eventual success in the New World. Unlike such famous success narratives as *Autobiography of Andrew Carnegie* and *The Americanization of Edward Bok, Woman at Work* celebrates public service rather than personal success. Anderson defines achievement as helping others, and while *Woman at Work* is the story of one working woman, it is also a history of working women in the United States.

Anderson describes her childhood in Sweden briefly. She writes that she was the youngest of seven children. Her father owned a small farm, and the family lived in a five-room wooden house with a red tile roof, a typical rural farmhouse. She was educated at the local Lutheran parsonage and recalls that she was a good student. She also remembers that she had a good time as a child. She fondly describes working on the farm, playing in the snow, and making candles during the long Swedish winter. The family farm was a poor one, and eventually her father lost it. As a result, her life changed. Anderson remembers:

My mother and father could not support us any longer and we knew that we had to get out and do something to earn a living, but we could not think what to do because there was no opportunity for anything except housework in our neighborhood. The solution came when my sister Anna, who had gone to America the year before, sent for Hilda and me to join her. (9)

The Andersons were not alone facing hard decisions in the 1880s. Tens of thousands of Swedes left their homes for the United States during that decade, and in 1889 sixteen-year-old Mary Anderson and her sister Hilda joined the exodus.

Anderson describes her passage and arrival in New York quickly, commenting only that her ship was a "good boat" and that she and his sister attended a band concert when they landed in New York. Her life in Sweden and her immigration are only background information for her main theme, however, and Anderson begins to explore the subject of working in the second chapter of her autobiography, "A Casual Worker in the Promised Land."

Like many other immigrants, Mary Anderson came to the United States looking for economic opportunity. She writes that she had heard of the success of others and had read the glowing accounts earlier Swedish immigrants had sent home. Her first job was a disappointment. She found work at a lumberjacks' boardinghouse washing dishes for two dollars a week. For six years Anderson worked at a variety of domestic jobs in rural Michigan until finally she and her sister moved to Chicago to find what Anderson calls "real work in a factory." She worked at Schwab's, making buttonholes for shirtwaists for $14 a week. Looking back, Anderson sees her move to Chicago and factory work as her initiation into American life:

Although I did not know it at the time, this was to be the real beginning of life for me in America. For six years I had been a casual worker, going from one job to another, doing what I could to earn a living. I was independent. If I did not like a job, I quit and got another. But after I went to Schwab's and joined the union I found that it was not always necessary to change jobs to get better working conditions. Sometimes we could improve conditions through union negotiations with the employer. That was a better way, because then conditions were improved for a great many people and not just for the one person who changed to a better job. (20)

In this passage Anderson moves from "I" to "we," and this change reflects her attitude through the rest of her narrative. The experiences she selects to include are illustrative of more than one woman's adventures in the New World; they represent the struggles of organized labor and the discrimination faced by working women. Mary Anderson, who served as the official representative of working women in the Department of Labor for twenty-five years, uses her autobiography to chronicle the battles fought and won by working women. Her story becomes their story.

In describing her life in Chicago, Anderson provides a comprehensive picture of working conditions—long hours, low pay, piecework, and a system of fines that kept many workers impoverished. In the autumn of 1910, when the great Chicago garment workers strike broke out, Anderson, as a representative of the Women's Trade Union League, assisted in establishing a network to help in the relief of the strikers and their families. She writes proudly that she helped find food, clothing, and coal for the strikers, as well as working with local newspaper reporters to get balanced coverage of the strike. The strike was finally settled when Hart, Schaffner, and Marx, the largest employer in the clothing industry, agreed to collective bargaining and the right of arbitration of grievances, setting a model for the entire industry. Because of her successful work during the strike, Anderson was asked to leave her work at the factory and become the Women's Trade Union League representative with the United Garment Workers Union. She accepted.

From 1911 to 1917 Anderson was involved in a wide variety of union activities throughout Illinois. She remembers organizing a variety of different workers, such as broom makers, miners, and state employees at the Illinois institutions for the insane. In addition, she lobbied for labor legislation and such social welfare projects as health benefits and aid to immigrants. She also helped to establish worker education programs, including a series of classes in economics for union members at the University of Chicago and Northwestern University.

In January 1918 Mary Anderson began working for the federal government, serving in the Women's Division of the Ordnance Department. On the rec- ommendation of Samuel Gompers, Anderson was assigned to develop stan- dards for women working in munitions plants. Later in the same year, after the establishment of the Women in Industry Service division of the Depart- ment of Labor, Anderson transferred there. In both positions she was re- sponsible for establishing safe working conditions for the women called to serve industry during World War I. Anderson toured plants and inspected working conditions. She made recommendations to President Wilson, and in the process she became the administration's spokesperson for women's rights in general.

Anderson's advocacy made her enemies as well as friends. She argued that women could work as well as men in nearly all situations, and she refused to draw up a list of "men only" occupations. She also angered employers by demanding that women receive equal pay for equal work, a radical suggestion then as now. Anderson fought against sexual discrimination throughout her government service, and it came as a shock to her that she was attacked by the Women's Congressional Committee.

In 1921, after the passage of women's suffrage, the Women's Congressional Committee proposed an equal rights amendment to the Constitution that read, "Men and women shall have equal rights throughout the United States and every place subject to its jurisdiction." Anderson, a member of the Wom- en's Bureau of the Department of Labor, was asked to support the amendment, but after study and consideration she declined. She was joined in her refusal by the National Women's Trade Union League, the Consumer League, the League of Women Voters, the General Federation of Women's Clubs, and the National Council of Catholic Women. Anderson argued that the amendment was merely a symbol and that such special legislation would be a hardship to women since there was no way of telling the effects of such sweeping language. In addition, Anderson believed that the amendment would inval- idate much of the labor legislation designed to protect women in the work- place. The real rights of women, she believed, were too important to be lost for a symbolic gesture.

Anderson writes that the attack from the Women's Congressional Com- mittee that followed her decision hurt, but she adds that the attack from more conservative quarters did not. In 1924 the *Dearborn Independent* published an article that accused Anderson and other prominent women in government of being part of a "spider web of subversive organizations trying to further bolshevism" (188–89). The paper went on to assert that women's organiza- tions and the Women's Bureau supported Communist programs throughout the United States. Anderson remarks that for ten years following the publi- cation of that article she was called a dupe of the Communists, but she didn't mind since almost every liberal and progressive in the country was branded as a subversive or a socialist. She thought she was in good company.

Anderson's response to these attacks from the Left and the Right shows her to be a pragmatic trade unionist. She fought her battles for immediate results rather than ideological gains. She believed that women's rights would be secured when workers' rights were protected and that the government had a duty to regulate those areas of life in which the health and security of its citizens might be in jeopardy.

Anderson's pragmatism can also be seen in the accomplishments she selects to include in her autobiography. For example, she records her establishment of a summer school for women in industry at Bryn Mawr. She details her meetings in 1921 with the college's president that led to a program to bring potential women leaders to Bryn Mawr to study. She writes that she would have preferred schools run by women workers themselves, but admits that the Bryn Mawr experiment was a success. She also lists her efforts to establish safety standards for domestic workers and her fight to end racial discrimination in the workforce as major accomplishments.

At the outbreak of World War II President Roosevelt asked Anderson to assist in the industrial development of the workforce. Her task was to show employers what women were doing and could do in industry. Using the experience she had gained during World War I, Anderson established standards for the influx of women into industry.

In 1944, after twenty-five years of government service, Mary Anderson resigned. She received many awards and citations, and she includes one from the General Federation of Women's Clubs in her autobiography. It reads, in part,

The paths you have opened will become broad avenues leading to the goal of social justice, for no one can stop the cavalcade you have started marching onward and upward. (256)

With typical modesty Anderson ends her autobiography by stating that she did not start the cavalcade; she was but "one of the thousands of others and if I got to the front it was only because there were so many pushing from behind" (257).

CRITICISM

Mary Anderson is better known for her union work and government service than for her writing. A short biography appears in James B. Olson's *Historical Dictionary of the New Deal*, and study of her life and work can be found in Susan Ware's *Beyond Suffrage: Women in the New Deal*.

Despite its relative neglect, *Woman at Work* is an important narrative. It provides a firsthand account of the impact of women in the trade union movement and of the influence unionism had on the lives of ethnic men and women. In addition, Anderson's autobiography documents some of the contributions made by American working women in war and peace.

BIBLIOGRAPHY

Anderson, Mary. *Woman at Work*. Minneapolis: University of Minnesota Press, 1951.

Bernstein, Irving. *Turbulent Years: A History of the American Worker, 1933–1941*. Boston: Houghton Mifflin, 1970.

Olson, James B., ed. *Historical Dictionary of the New Deal*. Westport, Conn.: Greenwood Press, 1985.

Scharf, Lois. *To Work and Wed: Female Employment, Feminism, and the Great Depression*. Westport, Conn.: Greenwood Press, 1980.

Ware, Susan. *Beyond Suffrage: Women in the New Deal*. Cambridge: Harvard University Press, 1981.

———. *Holding Their Own: American Women in the 1930s*. Boston: Twayne, 1982.

MARY JANE HILL ANDERSON
(1827–1924)

The Autobiography of Mary Jane Hill Anderson

BIOGRAPHY

Mary Jane Hill was born in Bailiborough, Ireland, on September 8, 1827. Her family was moderately wealthy. Her father owned several small farms that he rented to tenants and managed to have his daughter educated at a private school. In February 1850 Mary Jane Hill married Robert Anderson, the son of a grist-mill owner, and shortly after the wedding the couple sailed for America to join the several members of the Anderson family who had already left Ireland.

It took six weeks and three days for the Andersons to reach New Orleans. From there the newlyweds sailed up the Mississippi River to Galena, Illinois. In the spring of 1854 the Andersons and their three children moved north to Minnesota and settled in Eden Prairie, where they lived on a frontier farm until 1889. The Andersons then moved to Minneapolis, where Robert Anderson died in 1899. Mary Jane Hill Anderson wrote her autobiography for family members in 1922, when she was ninety-five. She died two years later.

THE AUTOBIOGRAPHY

The Autobiography of Mary Jane Hill Anderson is a privately printed narrative of only thirty-nine pages, written by Anderson for her children in the hope that they would "find in it something more than a mere chronicle of events" (1). Despite the brevity of Anderson's narrative, the autobiography is of interest to contemporary readers for two reasons. First, Anderson sheds light on a relatively neglected aspect of American history, the smaller immigration to the United States that occurred prior to the mass migration of the final decades of the nineteenth century. Not only does her autobiography provide a firsthand account of early Irish immigration to the United States, it also offers readers a personal history of one of the ethnic-Americans who contributed to the settlement of the middle western frontier. Second, *The Autobiography of Mary Jane Hill Anderson* can be seen as a model for the entire genre of immigrant autobiographies. Anderson describes the basic elements of the immigrant experience: life in the home country, the journey to America, struggle and excitement upon arrival, adoption of a new culture, and eventual assimilation. Anderson's narrative provides only highlights— representative events and memories. As a result, her story takes on an almost universal character, becoming at once the story of Mary Jane Hill Anderson and the story of any young immigrant woman confronting the frontier.

Anderson begins her autobiography with a description of her childhood in Ireland. Her recollections of her life there emphasize the picturesque and the romantic: worshiping at cheerful Sunday services at the local Episcopal church, attending singing school, wearing elaborately embroidered dresses, and falling in love. Anderson makes no mention of the famine that was raging throughout Ireland during her childhood and that forced millions of her countrymen and women to emigrate. Hers is not a story of poverty, and since she writes for her own family, she has no ideological argument to make. Her interest is in her own life and experience, not in the state of her native land.

Like many other immigrant writers, Anderson describes her voyage from her old home to the New World as both an adventure and an ordeal. Although admitting that she and her husband faced storms, seasickness, and a shipboard fire, she recalls that "the trip was for the most part pleasant" (13). Less pleasant and more dramatic was the trip upriver from New Orleans. Anderson's account of the three-week voyage portrays the journey as an initiation into the harsh realities of the new land. She recalls seeing blacks for the first time and wondering if all Americans were that color. She also records her discovery of a cholera epidemic in progress and her confinement to her cabin for most of the trip. She mentions in passing that while she and her husband survived, some of her fellow passengers did not.

The Andersons arrived at Beaty's Hollow, twelve miles from Galena, Illinois, on November 7, 1850, after a three-month journey. That same evening Anderson gave birth to a son in a cabin owned by Martha Richie, her sister-in-law. Of that experience she writes:

I can look back and see the Lord's hand leading us and raising up friends in our times of need. I had not even a few hours to spare at the end of a three month's journey until my time of delivery. I had no definite plans and no money; but I firmly believe it was his loving care that directed Martha to Galena. She, of all others, would have been my choice to be with me in my distress. There was no doctor; my husband was not there; but nature and Providence delivered me. (15–16)

Anderson continues to develop her theme of testing and Providence as she recounts her life on the frontier of Minnesota. Upon the family's arrival at Eden Prairie, Robert, the Andersons' second son, drowned, and the family was forced to bury him in a neighbor's field because there were no churches or graveyards. She describes how the family persevered, however, burning trees and clearing land for the homestead. Eventually eight related families from Ireland joined the Andersons near Eden Prairie.

Anderson provides details of the family's settling in, such as the purchase of their first sewing machine, a "Grover and Baker," and their first reaper, a "McCormick Self-Rake." She notes that the family lived in their cabin for eighteen years and that seven of their children were born there. Looking back to the days in the log cabin on the frontier after she moved away, Anderson observes:

Here I think we spent our happiest days. We had a home of our very own, we were young and hopeful, and with our little family and life before us, and always work to do and the strength to accomplish it, what more could we ask? (21)

One of the major themes in the second part of her narrative is the chronicle of the development of civilization on the frontier. Anderson recalls the end of the Indian wars in Minnesota and the family's friendship with one particular Indian who visited them each winter, bringing fresh meat in exchange for dinner and companionship. She notes that the passing of the Indian threat coincided with the coming of the two most significant elements of civilization: the church and the school.

Anderson gives a detailed account of the construction of the first church in Eden Prairie. Her husband was the first treasurer of the Presbyterian church, and she recounts discovering the church's original account book as she was writing her autobiography. The pasteboard book revealed that the church cost $1,057 to build in 1867. The front door cost $17, and the lock and hinges cost an additional $6.40. Anderson recalls that most of the contributions for the construction were in produce, and she estimates that the door, lock, and hinges cost 160 pounds of beef.

Frontier education was also a volunteer affair. Anderson remembers that the local teacher was paid $25 a month and "boarded around" with each family sending a young scholar for education. She remarks that living with the families of the students was hard for the teacher but good for all the families, since "it brought new life into the home, and in those days few things of interest or profit happened" (34–35). Anderson observes that eventually the school, like the church, became one of the centers for social and civic life on the prairie.

In 1889 the Andersons left the frontier and their cabin to live near their children and grandchildren in Minneapolis. Writing from this remove, Anderson gives a final overview of her pioneer life:

And so we left the old life and the scene of many happy years. It was hard for us to give up the old home with all its tender memories, but we built a comfortable house next door to Agnes [her daughter], and with our children and grandchildren around us, and with the leisure we had earned, lived a life of contentment. (37)

CRITICISM

The Autobiography of Mary Jane Hill Anderson is not a well-known work. There is a reference to it in the *Gopher Historian* (Spring 1967), and it is listed in *A Comprehensive Bibliography for the Study of American Minorities*. Because Anderson's autobiography is short and was privately printed, it has been overlooked. This is a mistake. Anderson's narrative is a charming story. Writing at the age of ninety-five, Anderson left a concise but moving testimony to the courage and faith of the immigrants who settled along the frontier during the nineteenth century. In addition, her autobiography, because of its simplicity and brevity, serves as an accessible introduction to the study of ethnic autobiography.

BIBLIOGRAPHY

Anderson, Mary Jane Hill. *The Autobiography of Mary Jane Hill Anderson*. Minneapolis, 1934.

Anderson, M. J. "From an Irish Farm to a Minnesota Homestead." *Gopher Historian* 21 (1967): 21–26.

Miller, Wayne C., ed. *A Comprehensive Bibliography for the Study of American Minorities*. New York: New York University Press, 1976.

Piggot, Michael. "Irish Pioneers in the Upper Mississippi Valley." *American Irish Historical Society Journal* 9 (1910): 301–30.

MAYA ANGELOU
(1928–   )

I Know Why the Caged Bird Sings

BIOGRAPHY

Maya Angelou was born on April 4, 1928, in St. Louis, Missouri. Her parents divorced when she was three and sent her and her brother to live with their material grandmother in Stamps, Arkansas. She remained in Stamps, except for one extended visit to St. Louis, for nearly a decade. Her grandmother, Annie Henderson, raised her two grandchildren while running the town's only black-owned general store. In 1940 Angelou's mother moved the two children from Stamps to San Francisco, where she was then living. While Angelou was growing up in San Francisco, she attended public school and began to study drama and dance at the California Labor School.

In the 1950s Angelou turned her talents to dance and soon achieved international success. She appeared to *Porgy and Bess* on a twenty-two–nation tour sponsored by the U.S. Department of State. Later she appeared both on and off Broadway in a variety of productions. At the same time she began to develop a growing interest in writing and civil rights. From 1961 to 1966 she lived and worked in Africa, serving as a teacher, editor, and free-lance writer in Egypt and Ghana. In 1966 Angelou returned to the United States to become a lecturer at the University of California, Los Angeles. Since then she has been a teacher and writer-in-residence at a number of American universities, including the University of Kansas and Wake Forest University.

Although Angelou has written a number of dramas and screenplays, she is best known for her autobiographical prose and poetry. *I Know Why the Caged Bird Sings*, the first and most famous of her autobiographical works, appeared in 1970 and was nominated for the National Book Award. Other volumes followed quickly: *Just Give Me a Cool Drink of Water 'fore I Diiie* (1971), *Gather Together in My Name* (1974), *Oh Pray My Wings Are Gonna Fit Me Well* (1975), *Singing' and Swingin' and Gettin' Merry like Christmas* (1976), *And Still I Rise* (1978), *The Heart of a Woman* (1981), *Shaker, Why Don't*

You Sing? (1983), and *All God's Children Need Traveling Shoes* (1986). Today, Angelou is one of the best-known women writers and one of the best-known black writers in the United States.

THE AUTOBIOGRAPHY

Maya Angelou opens her autobiography with a description of herself as a small child reciting a poem in the Colored Methodist Episcopal Church in Stamps, Arkansas. She recalls her own embarrassment and laughter from the children's section of the church, and then her retreat into her own private comfort:

Wouldn't they be surprised when one day I woke out of my black ugly dream, and my real hair, which was long and blond, would take the place of the kinky mass that Momma wouldn't let me straighten? My light blue eyes were going to hypnotize them. . . . Then they would understand why I never picked up a Southern accent, or spoke the common slang, and why I had to be forced to eat pig's tails and snouts. Because I was really white and because a cruel stepmother, who was understandably jealous of my beauty, had turned me into a too-big Negro girl, with nappy black hair, broad feet and a space between her teeth that would hold a number-two pencil. (2)

From this early moment of displacement and confusion, Angelou describes her growth into a mature, proud, young black woman. *I Know Why the Caged Bird Sings* is a dramatic narrative structured around confrontations with racism, poverty, and sexual abuse, but it is also a triumphant one because the confrontations lead to self-awareness and strength. Angelou knows of the pain involved in self-awareness, and she informs her readers early as she establishes the position from which she will grow.

In the early chapters of *I Know Why the Caged Bird Sings* Angelou recreates her early life in Stamps, Arkansas, a town that, she recalls, was a typical Southern segregated society. The center of her life in the poor, small town was her grandmother, Annie Henderson, who owned and operated the Wm. Johnson General Merchandise Store, the main structure and social focal point for the black community of Stamps. Angelou describes the Store, always spelled with a capital letter, as a "Fun House of Things" where she and her brother could watch sawmen and seedmen come by for lunches and townspeople stop in to buy cloth, food, feed, and even balloons. Playing and living in and around the Store, Angelou had the opportunity to observe the entire community, and in her narrative she provides portraits of Stamps' black citizens.

While the Store provides Angelou with the focal point for the early sections of the narrative, the fields around Stamps serve as a significant backdrop for the interaction of her characters. Throughout the autobiography Angelou presents vivid descriptions of the farmlands and fields around Stamps turning colors to mark the passing seasons. In *I Know Why the Caged Bird Sings* nature is a constant source of support and wonder, providing Angelou with the standard by which to measure the actions of the people she meets.

In describing her childhood in Stamps, Angelou emphasizes two themes: the stultifying effects of poverty and racism on the members of the black community and the heroic struggle of her grandmother to overcome the hostility she encountered and her efforts to raise Angelou and her brother properly.

Angelou writes that her grandmother's rules for behavior were simple: she was to be clean and she was to be obedient. Keeping them was not as simple. As Angelou describes the poverty in Stamps and the meanness and insensitivity of some of the people there, she establishes the problem all intelligent children face: how to be clean when dirt is all around and how to respect those who don't appear to deserve it.

Angelou reserves her hostility for those people who threaten the stability of her family. First, of course, are the openly racist whites like the members of the Klan who threaten Angelou's uncle because "a crazy nigger messed with a white woman" (14). While this kind of direct confrontation is rare, the narrative is full of the effects of segregation and racism. Angelou comments that in Stamps the segregation was so complete that for black children whites did not exist as people, only as a hostile force. Even white children could induce that dread, and Angelou includes a scene in which a "troop of po-whitetrash kids" ridicule her grandmother while she is forced to watch helplessly.

Not all the villains in Stamps are white, however. Angelou remembers her hatred for the Reverend Howard Thomas, the district presiding elder of her church, who visited every three months and stayed with the family. He was, she writes, "ugly, fat, and laughed like a hog with colic" (27). His looks were not the most offensive thing to Angelou and her brother, however; his selfishness was. He never bothered to learn their names, but more important, when he arrived he ate the best parts of the chicken served for the Sunday meal. To Angelou, Thomas was as much of a threat to the family's dignity as the Klan riders or the "powhitetrash."

When Angelou was eight, she and her brother returned to St. Louis to live with their mother. In describing St. Louis Angelou contrasts the peace and security of Stamps with the chaos and violence of the big city, referring to the black section of St. Louis as having the "finesse of a gold-rush town." It is in this environment that Angelou is confronted with personal violence when she is raped by the mother's boyfriend, Mr. Freeman.

Angelou's description of her rape and the resulting trial marks the depths from which she must climb in order to survive. Angelou describes the events quickly, letting the horror of the situation rather than rhetorical excess convey her shock. First she describes the rape itself, and then the equally painful disclosure and trial. She records that she was embarrassed on the stand by her attacker's attorney and that although Mr. Freeman was convicted, he was sentenced to only one year and one day. He never served any time, however. The day after the trial he was found dead next to the St. Louis slaughterhouse.

Angelou recalls that she was stunned by these events. Feeling both abused and guilty, she drew into herself and refused to speak, believing that her rape and the subsequent death were somehow her fault and that she had given up her place in heaven for these sins. Angelou was sent back to Stamps, perhaps because her "St. Louis family got fed up with my grim presence" (74).

For the next five years Angelou recuperated in Stamps. Little was demanded of her, and she found the quiet barrenness of Stamps comforting. She remembers that she was "without will or consciousness," and that she learned to withdraw, going into a protective cocoon. She writes that her eventual healing was aided by Mrs. Flowers, an educated black woman and friend of Angelou's grandmother. Mrs. Flowers provided Angelou with literature and conversation, urging her to read, think, and recite. After spending many long afternoons with Mrs. Freeman, Angelou felt that she could take pride in her blackness and joy in literature and the arts. These were valuable lessons, especially in Stamps, where she and her brother still had to face indignities at the hands of whites and the hardship of inferior segregated schools. Angelou includes two specific incidents in this section of her narrative to illustrate the totality of the segregation in Stamps. The first is her graduation from the Lafayette County Training School, where the white superintendent praised the class for its athletics. Listening to his speech, Angelou remembers thinking:

The white kids were going to have a chance to become Galileos and Madame Curies and Edisons and Gauguins, and our boys (the girls weren't even in on it) would try to be Jesse Owens and Joe Louis.... We were maids and farmers, handymen and washerwomen, and anything higher that we aspired to was farcical and presumptuous. (151–52)

The second example involves Dr. Lincoln, the town's only dentist, a white man who had borrowed money from Angelou's grandmother. Angelou had a toothache, so her grandmother took her to him. Even after she reminded him of the loan, he refused to treat Angelou, saying, "Annie, my policy is I'd rather stick my hand in a dog's mouth than in a nigger's" (160). Angelou and her grandmother then had to take a bus to Texarkana to get treatment.

Despite the constant reminders of segregation, Angelou thrived on her family's love, and by 1940, when she graduated first in her eighth-grade class, she was able to look forward to moving from the cocoon of Stamps when her mother sent for her and her brother to join her in San Francisco.

Angelou fell in love with San Francisco quickly. She was thrilled with the beauty and the freedom she found there. Angelou's mother ran a fourteen-room boardinghouse in the Fillmore district of the city, and the final sections of *I Know Why the Caged Bird Sings* are full of descriptions of the gamblers, prostitutes, and dockworkers who strayed and stayed in the boardinghouse. Angelou found the diversity of people and scenes in San Francisco a joyful relief after the sameness of Stamps, and she uses the city effectively as a background for her description of her transformation from girl to woman.

Angelou presents her maturation in two forms, public and private. While in high school she decided she needed a job, and since she had fallen in love with the streetcars, she applied for a position as a conductor. She discovered that there were no black conductors in the city, and despite advice to apply elsewhere, she was determined and continued to apply for the job until she was accepted. She eventually succeeded, becoming the city's first black streetcar conductor.

She was also becoming aware of her own sexuality. Angelou writes that she decided she needed to become a woman and set out to find a boyfriend. She remembers that she confronted a neighbor and offered herself to him. She describes the act itself as disappointing—no shared tenderness, no words of love—and three weeks later she discovered that she was pregnant.

Angelou ends *I Know Why the Caged Bird Sings* with the birth of her son. She had grown into adulthood, surviving St. Louis and enduring Stamps, now faced with the responsibilities of motherhood. The life she presents in her autobiography has been hard, and in the end of her narrative she moves from her particular situation to generalize about the situation of black women in the United States:

The Black female is assaulted in her tender years by all those common forces of nature at the same time she is caught in the tripartite cross of masculine prejudice, white illogical hate and black lack of power.

The fact that the adult American Negro female emerges a formidable character is often met with amazement, distaste, and even belligerence. It is seldom accepted as an inevitable outcome of the struggle won by survivors and deserves respect if not enthusiastic acceptance. (231)

CRITICISM

Maya Angelou has been praised for her work in a variety of fields. She is a member of the American Film Institute, Equity, the Directors Guild of America, and the American Federation of Television and Radio Artists. Her work has been nominated for a Pulitzer Prize, a National Book Award, and a Tony Award. She was named Woman of the Year in Communication by *Ladies' Home Journal* in 1976, and she has received numerous honorary degrees and fellowships.

Most of the serious literary criticism of her work has focused on her autobiographical works, of which *I Know Why the Caged Bird Sings* is considered the best. Writing in the *Dictionary of Literary Biography*, Lynn Z. Bloom asserts that Angelou is performing for contemporary black American women—and men, too—many of the same functions that escaped slave Frederick Douglass performed for his nine-teenth-century peers through his autobiographical writings and lectures. Both become articulators of the nature and validity of a collective heritage as they interpret the particulars of a culture for a wide audience of whites as well as blacks. (4)

Stephen Butterfield, in *Black Autobiography in America*, agrees that Angelou's is part of mainstream black-American autobiography:

Part of Maya Angelou's work overlaps the themes of the male autobiographies—her attitude toward education, her conscious adoption of pride in blackness as a defense against white condescension—but she also speaks of the special problems encoun-tered by black women and affirms life in a way that no male author could duplicate. (212)

Throughout her successful career as a writer, dancer, and teacher, Angelou has been one of the most visible and most outspoken representatives of black America. Her work, especially *I Know Why the Caged Bird Sings*, has been recognized for its honesty and courage. Angelou remains one of the most influential writers in America.

BIBLIOGRAPHY

Angelou, Maya. *I Know Why the Caged Bird Sings*. 1970. New York: Bantam, 1971.
———. "Nina Simone: High Priestess of Soul." *Redbook* 136 (November 1970): 132–34.
———. *Just Give Me a Cool Drink of Water 'fore I Diiie*. New York: Random House, 1971.
———. *Gather Together in My Name*. New York: Random House, 1974.
———. *Oh Pray My Wings Are Gonna Fit Me Well*. New York: Random House, 1975.
———. *Singin' and Swingin' and Gettin' Merry like Christmas*. New York: Random House, 1976.
———. "Cicely Tyson: Reflections on a Lone Black Rose." *Ladies' Home Journal* 94 (February 1977): 40+.
———. *And Still I Rise*. New York: Random House, 1978.
———. *The Heart of a Woman*. New York: Random House, 1981.
———. "Why I Moved Back to the South." *Ebony* 37 (February 1982): 130–34.
———. *Shaker, Why Don't You Sing?* New York: Random House, 1983.
———. *All God's Children Need Traveling Shoes*. New York: Random House, 1986.
Arensberg, Liliane. "Death as a Metaphor of Self in *I Know Why the Caged Bird Sings*." *College Language Association Journal* 20 (December 1976): 273–91.
"*The Black Scholar* Interviews Maya Angelou." *Black Scholar* 8 (January–February 1977): 44–53.
Bloom, Lynn. "Maya Angelou." *Dictionary of Literary Biography* 38. Detroit: Gale, 1985.
Butterfield, Stephen. *Black Autobiography in America*. Amherst: University of Mas-sachusetts Press, 1974.

Cameron, Dee Birch. "A Maya Angelou Bibliography." *Bulletin of Bibliography* 36 (January–March 1979): 50–52.

Demetrakopoulos, Stephanie A. "The Metaphysics of Matrilinearism in Women's Autobiography." In *Women's Autobiography: Essays in Criticism*, edited by Estelle C. Jelinek. Bloomington: Indiana University Press, 1980.

Kent, George E. "Maya Angelou's *I Know Why the Caged Bird Sings* and the Black Autobiographical Tradition." *Kansas Quarterly* 7 (Summer 1975): 72–78.

McMurry, Myra K. "Role Playing as Art in Maya Angelou's *Caged Bird.*" *South Atlantic Bulletin* 41 (May 1976): 106–11.

Smith, Sidonie A. "The Song of a Caged Bird: Maya Angelou's Quest after Self-Acceptance." *Southern Humanities Review* 7 (Fall 1973): 365–75.

Stepto, R. B. "The Phenomenal Woman and the Severed Daughter." Review of *And Still I Rise*, by Maya Angelou, *The Black Unicorn*, by Audra Lorde. *Parnassus: Poetry in Review* 8 (Fall/Winter 1979): 312–20.

MARY ANTIN
(1881–1949)

The Promised Land

BIOGRAPHY

Mary Antin was born in Polotzk, Russia, in 1881. Her father, Israel, studied to become a rabbi but eventually rejected the strictures of religious orthodoxy. Faced with czarist anti-Semitism and the problem of supporting his wife and six children, Israel Antin left Russia for "the land of opportunity" in 1891. The following year the rest of the Antin family joined him in Boston.

Although he was convinced that there were no barriers to economic success in America, Israel Antin was not successful. He continually moved his family about Boston, finally settling in the immigrant slums of the South End. The older children worked to help support the family, but Mary, who was a failure as a millener's assistant, was encouraged to concentrate on her education. She became an outstanding student, winning literary awards in grammar school and attending Boston's elite Girls' Latin School. Her poetry appeared in the Boston *Herald* and *Transcript*, and in 1899 her series of autobiographical letters, *From Plotzk to Boston*, was published.

Antin was offered a scholarship to Radcliffe, but turned it down to marry geologist Amadeus Grabau in 1901. She moved to New York and attended Teachers College, Barnard, and Columbia. In 1911 the *Atlantic Monthly* began publishing installments of her most famous work, *The Promised Land*, which was published by Houghton Mifflin the following year. In 1914 she published *They Who Knock at Our Gates*, an appeal for open immigration.

In 1919 she and her husband separated, and she then moved to Winchester, Massachusetts. She lived quietly, dying of myocarditis and cancer in a New York nursing home in 1949.

THE AUTOBIOGRAPHY

The publication of *The Promised Land* in 1912 coincided with an increase in nativistic hostility toward immigrants in the United States. The bitter strike at Lawrence, Massachusetts, involving 22,000 workers of sixteen nationalities, was seen as an alien threat, and such xenophobic organizations as the Junior Order United American Mechanics and the Guardians of Liberty recruited thousands of members with appeals to stem the flow of dangerous aliens. *The Promised Land* was a passionate defense of the immigrants; Antin saw herself as a spokesperson for the recently arrived Americans. Early in her autobiography she writes, "Should I be sitting here, chattering of my infantile adventures, if I did not know that I was speaking for thousands? Should you be sitting here, attending to my chatter, while the world's work waits, if you did not know that I spoke also for you?" (88).

She spoke persuasively. The publishers of her autobiography quickly issued a special edition, *At School in the Promised Land*, intended for classroom use, and the editors announced the lessons to be learned from Antin's life:

> That education and social influence may triumph over the obstacles of heredity and the circumstances of environment . . . that besides explaining to Americans the experiences, the hopes, and the problems of immigrants, the author reminded the native-born of their priceless heritage of liberty and opportunity, and stirred new inspiration for its preservation by the present generation. (iii)

The Promised Land provides readers with an example of a model assimilation. In her autobiography Mary Antin records how a young Jewish girl from Russia came to the United States, took advantage of the opportunities she discovered, worked hard, and prospered. She narrates a conversion, a throwing-off of an old culture and an acceptance of a new one.

Like many popular immigrant autobiographies, Antin's *The Promised Land* is a narrative of success. What sets it apart from such other popular narratives of the turn of the century as the autobiographies of Andrew Carnegie and Edward Bok is that the success is intellectual rather than material. For Antin, America is the land of opportunity not because it offered a way to wealth, but because it offered the chance to acquire an education.

The Promised Land is also a narrative of transformation, and Antin divides her text into two carefully balanced sections—the restrictive life in czarist Russia and the possibilities offered in democratic America. Many other immigrants have written about being made over in the new land, but few have described the process with such boundless optimism as Antin.

Antin's interest in education is evident in the earliest chapters of her autobiography. Like all autobiographers, she is influenced by later directions in her life when she selects details to include in describing her beginnings. One of the first images she provides is that of two little girls, dressed in their finest clothes, walking to school in Polotzk. The girls, Mary and her sister, were on the way to the one-room schoolhouse of Isaiah the Scribe, who taught Hebrew, Yiddish, Russian, and German. Antin describes the tiny school as a "new world" for her, and from this first reference, schools will become landmarks on her journey. Throughout her narrative, Antin contrasts her success at school with the economic hardships suffered by her family.

Antin begins to develop this structural tension in her narrative as she presents the institutional discrimination faced by Jews in czarist Russia. The most pervasive fear was of the pogrom, an organized and often state-sponsored persecution of Jews. Antin describes peeking from a shuttered window at a Christian parade, fearful lest she be seen and provide an excuse for the marchers to enter the house and attack her family. She recalls that her father had hung a picture of the czar prominently in the house so that if an officer entered he would not have an excuse to fine the family. She also mentions a less immediate but still pervasive form of discrimination—only ten out of one hundred Jewish children could expect any kind of education, only three out of one hundred had any hope for a university education, and there were no free schools for girls.

In addition to official repression, the Antin family faced economic hardships. As a very young child, Antin lived in comparative comfort, but her father proved to be an inept businessman, and soon the family was reduced to living on the money Antin's mother brought in selling teas and spices. Antin's father was forced to apply to a Jewish community organization to provide funds for his trip to America. The final Russian sections of *the Promised Land* describe a year of poverty waiting for news and passage money from a father far removed from his waiting family. Only the vision of America, a land of boundless opportunities, provided the family with any hope, and when her father sent the money for the family's third-class passage, Antin writes, "So at last I am going to America! Really, really going at last! The boundaries burst. The arch of heaven soared. The winds rushed in from outer space, roaring in my ears, 'America! America!' " (*At School* 13).

In many immigrant autobiographies, the passage from the Old World to the New is described as both an ordeal and a dramatic transition, a literal rite of passage in which the immigrants undergo hardships that will make them appreciate the life they are about to discover on the other side of the ocean. Antin, recalling her enthusiasm about coming to America, describes her passage as a grand adventure.

While Antin continues to contrast educational opportunities and economic deprivations in the American sections of her autobiography, the balance soon shifts. In the first section of her narrative the opportunities are only hopes, and the limitations of life under the czarist regime confine the family. In the second half of the autobiography Antin appears to triumph over every obstacle. The result is a narrative full of optimism and joy that reads, at times, like a testimonial for the American educational system. *The Promised Land* becomes a record of those teachers and social workers who dedicated their lives to the education of the children of the immigrants.

Antin's description of her life in the New World begins with an idyllic recollection of a summer spent with her family at Crescent Beach, Massachusetts, where her father opened a refreshment stand. She recalls the beauty and the ease of the summer and then the disappointment as her father lost his business and the family moved to a tenement in Chelsea.

Despite the continual struggle to feed, house, and clothe his family, Antin's father saw the importance of education, and in her autobiography Antin records her first day at school as a sacramental initiation for both herself and her father:

This foreigner who brought his children to school as if it were an act of consecration, who regarded the teacher of the primer class with reverence, who spoke of visions, like a man inspired, was not like other aliens . . . not like the native fathers, who brought their unmanageable boys, glad to be relieved of their care. I guess Miss Nixon guessed what my father's best English could not convey. I think she divined that by the simple act of delivering our school certificates to her he took possession of America. (205)

Antin's use of religious imagery here is instructive. *The Promised Land* is, in fact, a conversion narrative. Although most conversion narratives are religious, the conversion experience need not be, and in Antin's case the conversion is secular, from foreigner to American. Nevertheless, her autobiography follows the familiar conversion pattern: testing, transformation, and eventual triumph. In her autobiography Antin emphasizes the triumphant elements of her conversion, and the sacramental entrance into the American school can be seen as her baptism into the faith of Americanism.

The Promised Land is a record of an enthusiastic convert, and Antin describes her physical and intellectual journey in America as a constant progression. Once she has become part of the school system, she succeeds beyond her wildest expectations. She writes that within a week she advanced to the second grade, and within a year she was promoted to grammar school. Throughout her narrative she describes the teachers who arranged extra classes for her and other immigrant children. Eventually she sees that the school made it possible for her, and millions of others, to become part of America, and she uses her autobiography to pay tribute to the public school system:

The public school had done its best for us foreigners, and for the country, when it made us into good Americans. I am glad it is mine to tell how the miracle was wrought in one case. You shall be glad to hear of it, you born Americans; for it is the story of the growth of your country; of the flocking of your brothers and sisters from the far ends of the earth to the flag you love; of the recruiting of your armies of workers, thinkers, and leaders. And you will be glad to hear of it, my comrades in adoption; for it is a rehearsal of your own experience, of the thrill and wonder of which your own hearts have felt. (223)

In depicting her progress through the Boston public school system, Antin provides examples of her successes that serve as mileposts on her pilgrimage to Americanization. Two are particularly noteworthy. The first is the publication of her poem written in honor of George Washington. At the suggestion of her father, Antin took her poem to the *Boston Herald*, where a friendly editor accepted it for publication. Antin recalls her feelings of being part of her adopted country:

I enjoyed being praised and admired and envied; but what gave a divine flavor to my happiness was the idea that I had publicly borne testimony to the goodness of my exalted hero, the greatness of my adopted country. (*At School* 65)

The second is her meeting with Edward Everett Hale, clergyman and author and "Grand Old Man of Boston." The descriptions of both events show how deeply Antin committed herself to the ideals of America and democracy, and by the end of her narrative it is clear that Antin has ceased to be a stranger in the new land and has become an evangelist for it.

CRITICISM

The Promised Land is justly famous. Antin succeeds in grounding her praise of America within the context of economic struggle, and the result is a narrative of considerable depth. Cecyle Neidle, in her dissertation, "The Foreign-Born View America," called *The Promised Land* "a dithyramb to everything in American life" (156). George Stephenson, in *A History of American Immigration*, considers Antin's autobiography to be an expression of "the emancipating mission of America to the oppressed of all the earth" (289).

Jules Chametzky, writing in "Main Currents in American Jewish Literature from the 1880s to the 1950s (and Beyond)," makes the insightful observation that

in the current atmosphere of ethnic celebration, Antin's wonder and sense of liberation in America—Allen Guttmann cites her book as a representative of "the cult of gratitude"—and her delight in the English language may be a source of uneasiness. That it records a genuine strain of immigrant response and was emotionally resonant for many Jews, as well as comforting and reassuring to members of the dominant culture . . . can scarcely be doubted. (90)

The Promised Land remains a compelling and heartwarming narrative. Antin emerges as an energetic and enthusiastic, if somewhat biased, observer of America. While the process of Americanization was both limiting and paternal, it did succeed in many instances, and Mary Antin provides an example of Americanization at its best.

BIBLIOGRAPHY

Antin, Mary. *From Plotzk to Boston*. Boston: Clark, 1899.
————. *The Promised Land*. Boston: Houghton Mifflin, 1912.

————. *At School in the Promised Land*. Boston: Houghton Mifflin, 1912.

————. *They Who Knock at Our Gates*. Houghton Mifflin, 1914.

Chametzky, Jules. "Main Currents in American Jewish Literature from the 1880s to the 1950s (and Beyond)." *Ethnic Groups* (London) 4, 1 and 2 (1982): 87–101.

Guttmann, Allen. *The Jewish Writer in America*. New York: Oxford University Press, 1971.

Liptzin, Solomon. *The Jew in American Literature: From Early Republic to Mass Immigration*. Philadelphia: Bloch, 1966.

Neidle, Cecyle. "The Foreign-Born View America: A Study of Autobiographies Written by Immigrants to the United States." Ph.D. diss., New York University, 1962.

Stephenson, George. *A History of American Immigration, 1820–1924*. Boston: Ginn and Co., 1926.

BLACK ELK
(1863–1950)

Black Elk Speaks

BIOGRAPHY

In August 1930 poet John Neihardt, gathering material for his narrative poem *Cycle of the West*, met Black Elk, an Oglala Sioux *wichasha wakon*, or holy man. Neihardt asked Black Elk to speak to him about the old times, and the result of those conversations is *Black Elk Speaks*, one of the most popular autobiographies of an American Indian.

Black Elk lived during the crucial decades of American Indian history, and the story of his life has influenced several generations of readers, native and non-native American alike. Black Elk was born in 1863 near the Little Powder River in the Dakota Territory. The early part of his life reflects prereservation Sioux culture, while his adulthood was spent on government reservations. Black Elk was a witness to some of the events that marked the end of a way of life for the Plains Indians. Black Elk was present at both the Battle of the Little Big Horn and the massacre at Wounded Knee, and in addition he performed in Buffalo Bill's Wild West Show in both the United States and Europe. After living as a "wild Indian," fighting government troops, participating in the Ghost Dance movement, and enduring life on a reservation, Black Elk provided readers with a native American perspective on over seventy years of American history. He died on August 19, 1950.

THE AUTOBIOGRAPHY

Black Elk Speaks is a work deserving attention. The narrative that Neihardt recorded is more than a story of the adventures of a man who witnessed the passing of a way of life; *Black Elk Speaks* is "the story of a mighty vision" that Black Elk received when he was nine. This vision provided meaning and coherence for Black Elk, and in telling the story of his vision to Neihardt, he insured the transmission of the wisdom he attained, a wisdom as much concerned with a community and a way of life as with an individual.

In telling his life story, Black Elk, like many other ethnic-American writers, speaks with a representative voice. He begins his narrative with a statement of his purpose:

My friend, I am going to tell you the story of my life, as you wish; and if it were only the story of my life I think I would not tell it; for what is one man that he should make much of his winters, even when they bend him like a heavy snow? So many other men have lived and shall live that story, to be grass upon the hills.

It is the story of all life that is holy and is good to tell, and of us two-leggeds sharing in it with four-leggeds and the wings of the air and all green things; for these are children of one mother and their father is one spirit. (1)

Unlike most mainstream American autobiographies, *Black Elk Speaks* is not a celebration of the self; on the contrary, Black Elk sees its significance in its universality, which was the measure of a story's worth in traditional native American cultures.

The conflict between native American and white cultures is a central theme in Black Elk's narrative, and he begins to develop it at the outset of his work, describing how his people were happy in their own country before the whites (Wasichus) came and there was fighting because white men were driven crazy by the gold they discovered in the Indian lands and demanded to build a road through the Sioux territory. Throughout the early sections of his narrative, Black Elk develops the building tension between the cultures. He describes tribal life and buffalo hunting in nostalgic terms, always set against continual encroachments of white civilization and the resulting battles. Black Elk successfully captures a culture in conflict, and he employs this conflict to establish the urgency of his great vision, which becomes the crucial event in his life and the controlling idea of his autobiography.

When Black Elk was nine years old, he heard a voice calling to him saying, "it is time; now they are calling you" (21). He immediately fell unconscious and remained so, unmoving, for twelve days in the grip of his vision. Black Elk describes his vision in twenty-two detailed pages. In this mystical experience Black Elk was addressed by the powers of the world—six grandfathers representing the powers of the North, South, East, West, Earth, and Sky—and taken to the center of the earth to see the future. In the vision he was given the task of restoring the sacred hoop of the Sioux nation and making the whole tree of life bloom again. If he were to succeed in this task, one of the grandfathers promised him that he would see "a good nation walking in a sacred manner in a good land!" (36). If he were successful, he would stop the invasion of the white man and return the land and the people to their original states.

In addition to giving Black Elk wisdom and power, the vision compelled him to act. In order to function as a holy man, Black Elk needed to act out in a ritual manner portions of his vision, to relive parts of the dream for those he was attempting to help. The vision became a psychological imperative for Black Elk, and his autobiography, which tells for the first time his entire vision, is another kind of ritual reenactment.

Black Elk's autobiography is concerned with history as well as mysticism. Black Elk sets the need to restore his land and his people within the framework of the Indian wars. He presents the Sioux attitude succinctly:

We were in our own country all the time and we only wanted to be left alone. The soldiers came there to kill us, and many got rubbed out. It was our country and we did not want to have trouble. (105)

Black Elk provides a detailed description of the Battle of the Little Big Horn as a turning point in the life of the Sioux. The trouble began in 1874 when General Custer led his troops into the Black Hills. Black Elk's position is clear: He recalls the treaty of 1868 that gave the land to the Sioux forever. He also writes that the cause for all the troubles was General Custer's discovery of gold.

Although the Sioux won the battle with Custer, they lost the war. Despite heroic resistance and numerous acts of personal bravery, the Sioux nation was decimated by soldiers, hunger, and disease. Black Elk's account of the aftermath of the battle with Custer is told with resignation, as if in looking back at that period of his life he realizes that the outcome was inevitable. In contrast to his vision of a good people in a good land, the end of the hostilities left the Sioux scattered on reservations and depending on the white man for food.

Black Elk did not exercise his power during the wars, but in 1882, when he was nineteen, he performed his first cure. Black Elk's success as a healer is ironic; his vision commanded him to heal his land and people, to restore the sacred circle of the Sioux nation, but he began to heal sick individuals only after the entire nation had been broken.

Once Black Elk begins to describe his experiences as a healer, the nature of the autobiography changes. The early sections can be seen as a narrative of native American life prior to the coming of the reservations. In the second section of his autobiography, however, Black Elk moves from a story of a man to a story about the environment. In these passages *Black Elk Speaks* becomes the story of "all that is holy," a story of the relationship between the good earth and a good people. In telling of the powers of the bison and the elk, for example, Black Elk places himself in a symbiotic relationship to the land, the animals, and his people. As a holy man becoming aware of his powers and the responsibilities of his vision, he is compelled to understand the "powers" of all of creation so that he can call upon them successfully. Black elk provides an example and an explanation of the elk ceremony, which he performed as part of his growth in wisdom. After finishing his description, he explains that the ceremony was so significant that it gave meaning to his life and put him in harmony with the Power of the World. The Power of the World was changing, however, and the same year that Black Elk performed his ceremony the last of the bison herds was slaughtered. The environment itself had been transformed by the white man, and Black Elk prepared himself to learn another lesson.

The next section of *Black Elk Speaks* is called "Across the Big Water," and in it Black Elk describes the fate of the Sioux. "The nation's hoop was broken, and there was no center any longer for the flowering tree. The people were in despair" (214). Black Elk continued to heal for three years, but in 1881 he joined a band of Sioux to perform in Buffalo Bill's Wild West Show. He remembers thinking that he should go to learn the white man's secret so that he could use it to help his people.

Black Elk's journey with Buffalo Bill becomes an empty pilgrimage. He learns that there is no "secret," and he grows continually more alienated as he moves farther from his homeland. Black Elk describes performing in New York, England, France and Germany. He even provides an account of a special performance before Grandmother England (Queen Victoria) and remembers both her warm welcome for the performing Indians and the sanctuary her land (Canada) provided many Sioux after the Dakota wars.

Black Elk returned to the Sioux in 1889 and discovered that his "people were pitiful and in despair" (231). He seemed to have lost his vision, and at first he refused to heal. But the people were weak from hunger, and the outbreaks of measles and whooping cough were severe. He again began to work cures. At that time the Ghost Dance revival reached the Sioux.

The Ghost Dance originated among the far western tribes and quickly spread throughout the native American communities. It was a messianic faith, taught by Wovoka, also called Jack Wilson. Known as the Wanekia (One Who Makes Live), Wovoka, who was considered to be the son of the Great Spirit, had a vision of another world about to come that would save the Indian people, make the whites disappear, and return all the bison to a richly reborn earth. The attraction of such a faith is obvious. To a people facing cultural extinction, it offered a possibility of a return to the old days and an eradication of the hated enemy. At first Black Elk was skeptical, but the more he learned about the Ghost Dance the more he saw in it a re-creation of the nation's hoop similar to that of his own vision. Eventually he decided to add his energies to the growing movement and began to participate in the dances. He soon had another vision, this one compelling him to make Ghost Shirts for the dancers.

The dancing spread throughout the Dakota reservations during the spring and summer of 1890. Watching the ritual, government officials saw the beginnings of a potential uprising and condemned it. Nevertheless the dancing continued until the confrontation of Wounded Knee on December 19, 1890.

At Wounded Knee over 500 soldiers supported by artillery and rapid-fire wagon guns attacked the Sioux at the Pine Ridge Reservation. Black Elk was there and took part in the battle, which quickly became a massacre. His account of the famous slaughter is moving, but his recollection of the aftermath of Wounded Knee is even more powerful:

Men and women and children were heaped and scattered all over the flat at the bottom of the hill where the soldiers had their wagon guns, and westward up the dry gulch all the way to the high ridge, the dead women and children and babies were scattered. When I saw this I wished that I had died too, but I was not sorry for the women and the children. It was better for them to be happy in the other world, and I wanted to be there too. (260)

Both the Ghost Dance movement and the Indian resistance died at Wounded Knee. In the final chapter of his autobiography, "The End of the Dream," Black Elk recounts the wanderings of the Wounded Knee survivors through the Dakotas until they returned, starving and freezing, to the Pine Ridge Reservation to lay down their arms in front of the waiting soldiers. In his final paragraph Black Elk depicts himself as a "pitiful old man who has done nothing, for the nation's hoop is broken and scattered. There is no center any longer, and the sacred tree is dead" (270).

CRITICISM

Black Elk Speaks is a powerful lament. In combining the history of the Indian wars, the training and practice of a holy man, and a vision of a nation lost, Black Elk has given his readers an invaluable insight into native American culture. This, as well as the firsthand accounts of the battles at the Little Big Horn and Wounded Knee, helps to explain the autobiography's continued popularity.

The genre itself is significant, as William Bloodworth observed in "Varieties of American Indian Autobiography":

Indian autobiographies deserve our attention not only because they are truly and indisputably American or because, as Luther Standing Bear has said about his own story, "No one is able to understand the Indian race like an Indian." They also represent a diverse and complex literary genre, one that obliges us to consider the nature of autobiographical expression in traditional Indian cultures, the role of outside white influence in the recording of personal experience, and the ultimate aesthetic as well as documentary value of the work. (67)

Several important considerations remain for the student of *Black Elk Speaks*. First, Black Elk's life is filtered through the consciousness of John Neihardt, and even the most faithful recorder alters the information he transcribes. While the words are those of Black Elk, does the structure of the narrative, emphasizing the loss of innocence and the deterioration of the environment because of the onslaught of the white man, belong to Black Elk as well, or has it been imposed by Neihardt? In addition, as William Blood-worth has noted in "Varieties of American Indian Autobiography," Black Elk had converted to Catholicism prior to his meeting with Neihardt, and his recollections of both his visions and his life may be colored by Christian theology or New Testament apocalyptic thought. Does some of the imagery in Black Elk's vision, for example, come from a native tradition or from the Book of Revelation?

Despite these potential problems, however, *Black Elk Speaks* is a significant American autobiography. It is more than a personal chronicle of an eyewitness to great battles. *Black Elk Speaks* is an articulate and moving personal history of an Indian holy man, and in combining communal history with individual vision, Black Elk speaks eloquently for the Sioux nation.

BIBLIOGRAPHY

Black Elk, as told to John G. Neihardt. *Black Elk Speaks*. New York: William Morrow, 1932. Reprint. Lincoln: University of Nebraska Press, 1979.

Bloodworth, William. "Varieties of American Indian Autobiography." *MELUS* 5, 3 (1978): 67–81.

———. "Neihardt, Momaday, and the Art of Indian Autobiography." *Teaching English in the Two-Year College* 4 (1978): 137–43.

McKluskey, Sally. "Black Elk Speaks and So Does John Neihardt." *Western American Literature* 6 (1972): 238.

Neihardt, John G. *The Sixth Grandfather: Black Elk's Teachings Given to John G. Neihardt*. Lincoln: University of Nebraska Press, 1984.

O'Brian, Lynn Woods. *Plains Indian Autobiography*. Boise: Boise State University, 1973.

Sayre, Robert. "Visions and Experience in *Black Elk Speaks*." *College English* 32 (1971): 509–35.

EDWARD BOK
(1863–1930)

The Americanization of Edward Bok

BIOGRAPHY

Edward Bok was one of the most prominent and influential immigrant-Americans of his generation. He was born in Den Helder, the Netherlands, in 1863 and emigrated with his family to the United States in 1870. The family settled in Brooklyn, and Bok, without knowing any English, began attending public school and working in a bakery. At the age of thirteen Bok quit school to work as an office boy at the Western Union Telegraph Company. While working there he wrote for the *Brooklyn Magazine* and the *Daily Eagle*. By 1884 Bok was the editor of the *Brooklyn Magazine*.

In 1887 Bok took charge of advertising for the recently established *Scribner's Magazine*. In 1889 he was named by publisher Cyrus Curtis to become editor of the *Ladies' Home Journal*. For thirty years he remained in that position and became one of the most influential journalists in America. For three decades Bok shaped public opinion in the United States from his editorial desk.

In 1920, shortly after stepping down from the *Journal*, Bok published his autobiography, *The Americanization of Edward Bok*, which won the Pulitzer Prize for biography and went through over thirty editions in four years. Bok devoted his years after retiring to public works and writing. He died, an honored and wealthy man, in 1930.

THE AUTOBIOGRAPHY

The Americanization of Edward Bok, written in the third person, is an unabashed narrative of success, one of a long list of books written by and about successful self-made men in the late nineteenth and early twentieth centuries. In almost textbook terms, Bok's autobiography describes the rise of a boy of humble beginnings to a position of wealth and power. It chronicles the activities of a man who became the friend of presidents and the advisor to millions of American women. Bok saw in his success a model for others to emulate, and his autobiography is full of righteous advice. While Bok actively sought wealth and success throughout his life, he also saw himself as a steward whose mission, in the *Journal* and in his autobiography, was to mold and shape the morality of his readers. While some modern readers might see his combination of capitalism and Christianity as a compromise of both, Bok provides a clear example of the moral philosophy behind America's Gilded Age.

The Americanization of Edward Bok is a carefully crafted sermon on the virtues of capitalism and the work ethic. Like Benjamin Franklin before him, Bok charts the way to success in America. Like numerous other immigrant writers, Bok assumes the role of a representative figure, a spokesman for all American immigrants. He even includes a specific defense of the foreign-born American in the conclusion of his narrative:

How good an American has the process of Americanization made me? That I cannot say. Who can say that of himself? But when I look around me at the American-born I have come to know as my close friends, I wonder whether, after all, the foreign-born does not make in some sense a better American—whether he is not able to get a truer perspective; whether his is not the deeper desire to see America greater; whether he is not less content to let its faulty institutions be as they are; whether in seeing faults more clearly he does not make a more decided effort to have America reach those ideals or those fundamentals of his own land which he feels are in his nature, and the best of which he is anxious to graft into the character of his adopted land. (451)

Despite the representative tone and the allusion to the possibilities of cultural pluralism in this passage, Bok's book remains a highly personal document, and despite the fact that it was widely read, it was more likely to produce astonishment than recognition. Few immigrants led lives anything like Edward Bok's.

Bok uses a narrative pattern employed by many other immigrant auto-biographers: immigrant's arrival, struggle to assimilate into a new culture, setbacks, and eventual triumphs. Bok devotes only 29 pages to his arrival and struggle, while presenting his assimilation and rise to fame and fortune in 423 pages. His purpose is clearly edification, not criticism.

The Americanization of Edward Bok is about education, but it is not about schools. Bok believed in self-education and the lessons of the marketplace, and he writes that although the public schools taught him English, he learned about industry and self-reliance on the streets of Brooklyn. Bok emphasized initiative as the essential virtue for success throughout his narrative. By the time he was thirteen Bok had risen from window cleaner and lemonade salesman to cub reporter and office boy. Bok's early initiatives created further opportunities. He describes himself as an addicted letter writer, delighting in writing to famous people to ask their opinions on public issues and re-questing their autographs. Bok fills the early pages of his autobiography with reminiscences of communication and later meetings with such famous Americans as President Garfield, President Hayes, General Grant, General Sherman, Henry Wadsworth Longfellow, and Ralph Waldo Emerson. Bok includes this list of "famous friends" to illustrate his rapid transformation from outsider to insider. The primary focus of his autobiography, and a more convincing argument for his successful assimilation, is his career as editor of the *Ladies' Home Journal*.

In 1889, when Bok assumed the editorship of the *Journal*, its circulation was 440,000; by 1903 the circulation had surpassed 1,000,000, making Bok's *Journal* the most widely read periodical in the United States. Although it was read by many men, the *Journal's* readership was predominantly female and solidly middle class. Bok directed his editorial efforts at that audience and placed his faith in it. As Salme Steinberg observes in *Reformer in the Marketplace: Edward Bok and The Ladies' Home Journal*, Bok believed that

the middle-class woman was the stabilizer between "the unrest between the lower classes and the rottenness among the upper classes." To preserve the character of the middle classes, he solicited an article urging girls not to marry "below their position in life...." His job, as he conceived it, was to reinforce the good features of middle-class life while he exposed its weaknesses. (44)

Throughout his autobiography Bok refers to himself as a reformer and a progressive, and while his attitude and interests reflected those of his readers, he was no radical. Bok believed in the gospel of success and the triumph of virtue, and he consistently emphasizes the cheerful side of life in both the *Journal* and the autobiography. When he commissioned features on prison reform and life in urban tenements, for example, he made certain that the *Journal* presented them in an uplifting context. His view of ethnicity was also narrow; in describing his tenure as editor of the *Journal* in his auto-biography he remarks that he seldom commissioned stories about blacks because they would be of no interest to his readers. *The Americanization of Edward Bok* reflects many of the prejudices and stereotypes that Bok shared with his middle-class readers. He recounts warning mothers not to place their children in the hands of "illbred" immigrant Irish girls and exposing the supposedly evil sexual practices of immigrant Greek males.

Bok describes how his attitude toward a multiethnic America began to change during his final years at the *Journal*. He writes that the increase in the number of immigrants coming to the United States and the success of the multiethnic American army in World War I caused him to rethink some of his positions and to accept a series of articles for the *Journal* that em-phasized the positive elements of immigration and the potential benefits of immigration for the United States.

Throughout the *Americanization* Bok emphasizes his role as advisor to American women and provides details of his crusades as an advocate in such areas as public health, good taste, the environment, and politics. Bok asserts that women were "morally stronger" than men and that women's chief aim in life was "to improve men by the force of moral power." He writes that his aim, as autobiographer and editor, was to direct that moral power.

Bok admits that his efforts to change the taste of American women were less than completely successful. Although his endorsement of American architecture influenced some home builders, his crusade against European fashions was a complete failure. He was, however, much more successful as an environmentalist.

In his autobiography Bok devotes a large section to chronicling his considerable environmental and public health achievements. He describes with pride his campaigns to remove billboards from the nation's highways and to halt the construction of an enormous electric power plant along Niagara Falls. In addition, he correctly portrays himself as an influential advocate of the establishment of a national park system.

Bok also saw himself as an advocate for improved public health, and he writes enthusiastically about his support for the temperance movement. Bok describes his battle to convince the *Journal*'s publisher, Cyrus Curtis, to prohibit the depiction of any glassware used for beer, wine, or spirits in his advertisements. In addition to commissioning articles stressing the evils of alcohol, Bok led the battle to enact federal laws regulating the sales of patent medicines, which frequently contained high percentages of alcohol, morphine, opium, cocaine, and other drugs.

Bok writes that the most important public health battle he fought as editor of the *Journal* was his effort to make sex education acceptable to American women. Beginning in 1906, Bok risked losing both sales and advertising revenue when he introduced sex education as a *Journal* topic. He became convinced that the high rate of venereal disease in the United States was a result of widespread ignorance of "the mysteries of life." He commissioned a series of articles on the subject from such noted and respected writers as Jane Addams and Helen Keller urging parents to assume their responsibilities for their children's sexual education. Although he and the *Journal* faced an initial wave of indignation and hostility, his crusade was ultimately successful. He writes proudly that by the end of his tenure as editor he discovered serious discussions of the problem in other periodicals.

Bok recognizes that his most controversial decision as editor was his opposition to women's suffrage. Although the *Journal* had printed numerous antisuffrage articles for years, its official policy was neutrality, but in 1912, Bok changed the *Journal's* position. In his autobiography Bok argues that he looked carefully at all sides of the issue and decided, finally, that American women were not ready to be given the vote; he concluded that suffrage was against their own best interests.

This argument from the autobiography captures Bok and his age perfectly. The male editor of the nation's largest and most influential women's periodical opposes giving women the vote. Bok saw himself as the wise advisor to middle-class American women, and he writes as a paternal authority. He assumed that his readers would accept his arguments on that authority. Often they did, but not always.

The picture of Bok that emerges from the *Americanization* is that of a wise patriarch living in a traditional, male-dominated, middle-class world. Bok cheerfully admits this as well as the irony of his editorship of a woman's magazine:

No man, perhaps, could have been chosen for the position who had a less intimate knowledge of women. Bok had no sister, no woman confidant: he had lived with and for his mother. She was the only woman he really knew or who really knew him. His boyhood days had been too full of poverty and struggle to permit him to mingle with the opposite sex. And it is a curious fact that Edward Bok's instinctive attitude towards women was that of avoidance. He did not dislike women, but it could not be said that he liked them. They never interested him. (168)

CRITICISM

Although *The Americanization of Edward Bok* was one of the most popular autobiographies of the early twentieth century, it is not well known today. Salme Steinberg's *Reformer in the Marketplace: Edward Bok and the Ladies' Home Journal* is a comprehensive and scholarly biography of Bok that uses material from the autobiography extensively. Steinberg, like most contemporary students of Bok, sees Bok primarily as a journalist and a reformer. When Bok is mentioned, it is primarily in the context of the rise of mass journalism in the United States.

The exception of this view sees Bok as one of the prime examples of the self-made man in American culture. Irvin Wyllie, in *The Self-Made Men in America: The Myth of Rags to Riches*, and Robert B. Downs, in *Famous American Books*, assert that Bok is one of the best examples of the myth of success because he did succeed so well, he believed in the myth, and he articulated it so forcefully in his autobiography.

The Americanization of Edward Bok, despite its recent neglect, remains an important document. It is one of the best firsthand sources of information on the development of modern American advertising and journalism, and it reflects quite clearly the American fascination with the idea of the self-made man. Finally, it tells the remarkable story of the rise of an immigrant boy to a position high on the American ladder of success.

BIBLIOGRAPHY

Bok, Edward, *Successward*. New York: F. H. Revell, 1895.
————. *The Young and the Church*. Philadelphia: Henry Altemus, 1896.

————. *The Keys to Success*. Philadelphia: John D. Morris, 1900.

————. *The Young Man in Business*. Boston: L. C. Page, 1900.

————. *Why I Believe in Poverty as the Richest Experience That Can Come to a Boy*. Boston: Houghton Mifflin, 1915.

————. *The Americanization of Edward Bok*. New York: Scribner's, 1920.

————. *A Man from Maine*. New York: Scribner's, 1923.

————. *Twice Thirty: Some Short and Simple Annals of the Road*. New York: Scribner's, 1925.

————. *America, Give Me a Chance!* New York: Scribner's, 1926.

————. *Perhaps I Am*. New York: Scribner's, 1928.

Davenport, Walter, and James Derieux. *Ladies, Gentlemen, and Editors*. Garden City, N.Y.: Doubleday, 1960.

Downs, Robert B. *Famous American Books*. New York: McGraw-Hill, 1971.

Drewry, John. *Some Magazines and Magazine Makers*. Boston: Stratford, 1924.

Mott, Frank Luther. *Golden Multitudes: The Story of Best Sellers in the United States*. New York: Macmillan, 1947.

Steinberg, Salme. *Reformer in the Marketplace: Edward Bok and the Ladies' Home Journal*. Baton Rouge: Louisiana State University Press, 1979.

Woodward, Helen. *The Lady Persuaders*. New York: Ivan Obolensky, 1960.

Wyllie, Irvin G. *The Self-Made Man in America: The Myth of Rags to Riches*. New York: Free Press, 1966.

CARLOS BULOSAN
(1914–1956)

America Is in the Heart

BIOGRAPHY

Carlos Bulosan was born in a small Philippine farming village in 1914. He worked while attending school in the Philippines to save enough money for a steerage ticket to the United States, where he intended to join his two older brothers who had left home to work in California. In 1930 the sixteen-year-old Bulosan arrived in Seattle with the intention of becoming a writer. During the 1930s Bulosan worked as a dishwasher and in a bakery while helping to organize Filipino laborers on the West Coast. In addition, he continued to write, especially after he was hospitalized for tuberculosis in 1936.

Although he had achieved a degree of success as a writer during the 1930s, he became famous in the next decade, when his major works–*The Voice of Bataan*, *The Laughter of My Father*, and *America Is in the Heart*—appeared to critical and popular acclaim. The war with Japan had made American readers conscious of the Philippines, and Bulosan's work, which celebrated Filipino courage and industry as well as American opportunity and justice, was seen as a vehicle for cross-cultural understanding.

After the end of the war, however, Bulosan's popularity declined. His union activity and his sympathetic depiction of immigrant workers, blacks, native Americans, and Mexicans made him appear a radical to many readers. In addition, his health, which was never good, began to decline seriously. In 1956, poor and forgotten by most American readers, Bulosan died in Seattle.

THE AUTOBIOGRAPHY

In *Asian American Literature* Elaine Kim makes an important observation about Bulosan's narrative:

Bulosan was primarily a fiction writer, and *America Is in the Heart* is both less and more than a personal history: it is a composite portrait of the Filipino American community, a social document from the point of view of a participant in that experience. (48)

Like many other autobiographical writers, Bulosan uses the techniques of fiction in his narrative, and the reader of *America Is in the Heart* must be aware that the central character in the narrative is a composite figure who undergoes an initiation into American culture similar to, but in some key ways different from Bulosan's. Like many ethnic-American writers, Bulosan's primary concern was to tell the story of his people through his narrative, and while some elements are exaggerated—Bulosan himself was not strong enough to work in the fields as his autobiographical character does, for example—the autobiography does present an accurate picture of Filipino-American life on the West Coast during the 1930s.

Like many other immigrant writers, Bulosan structures his autobiography around a three-part experience—life in the home country, emigration and trials on arrival in the United States, and eventual success. Although the narrative structure is commonplace, the narrative itself is not. Bulosan not only provides a vivid description of economic exploitation and class struggle, he also portrays the effects of racism on America's nonwhite immigrants. In addition, his journey from colonial Philippines to America provides him with the material to construct a story of vivid contrasts.

Bulosan uses the initial chapters of *America Is in the Heart* to establish the basic conflict of his autobiography—the exploitation of the poor by the rich. In describing his early life on the island of Luzon in the Philippines, Bulosan presents a corrupt colonial regime in the process of forcing peasants from their land in order to increase the profits of absentee landlords and large corporations. His theme in the early sections of his narrative is the destruction of the villages and the resulting migration to the cities and beyond. Bulosan writes that his father was forced to sell strips of the family farm to finance his brothers' educations until the farm was too small to provide enough food for the family. He writes that the same process was occurring throughout the island:

Some of my uncles were already dispossessed of their lands, so they went to the provincial government and fought for justice; but they came back to the village puzzled and defeated. It was then that one of my uncles resorted to violence and died violently, and another entered a world of crime and criminals. (23)

Bulosan presents a picture of a society in chaos: anarchist bands roam the countryside, poor farmers sell their land and their seed for food, and the government pretends that nothing unusual is taking place. He also describes his personal degradation, posing nude for tourists in order to eat. Finally he found work as a houseboy.

Bulosan, like many other immigrant writers, credits his interest in education with providing him the opportunity to escape the poverty of the old country. While working as a houseboy, Bulosan continued his education, planning to emigrate to the United States. He writes that he wanted to learn English so that he would not be lost in America, and while he was learning to read English he came across the story of Abraham Lincoln, "a poor boy who became president of the United States." He became fascinated with the story of the rise to fame of a poor boy like himself, and when he learned from his employer that Lincoln "died for a black person" he became even more impressed and worked harder to improve his English.

Like other writers who came to the United States in steerage, Bulosan presents the passage to America as a grim ordeal. He records seasickness and death. He also remembers the comment of a first-class passenger who saw the Filipino immigrants emerge from below decks, "Why don't they ship those monkeys back where they came from?" (99).

Bulosan's depiction of his life on the West Coast after his arrival in Seattle reads like a cross between the novels of John Steinbeck and those of Richard Wright. Bulosan describes the life of immigrant migrant workers, men and women who followed the coastline from jobs in the fish canneries in Alaska to jobs picking vegetables in southern California. He structures the central sections of his autobiography as a personal odyssey during which he comes into contact with a range of people as he moves from job to job and gambling hall to dance hall in search of work and his brothers who left the Philippines before him.

Bulosan's two central themes in this section of the narrative are the economic exploitation of the Filipino workers and the racial discrimination they faced. Like the Chinese laborers who came before them, Filipino workers discovered not only dangerous working conditions and low pay but also social conditions detrimental to community life. The vast majority of Filipino immigrants were men, and several West Coast states had laws prohibiting the marriage of members of Mongolian and Caucasian races. Despite the fact that Filipinos are not Mongolian, the authorities on the West Coast enforced the separation of the races. Bulosan presents a scene in which two policemen raid the apartment of a Filipino living with a white woman:

"Listen to the brown monkey talk," said one of the detectives, slapping Alonzo in the face. "He thinks he has the right to be educated. Listen to the bastard talk English. He thinks he is a *white* man. How do you make this white woman stick with you, googoo?" (136)

In *America Is in the Heart* Bulosan uses interracial relationships as metaphors for his vision of the ideal America, a culture with complete economic and social equality. What he discovers as he moves up and down the West Coast, however, fails to match his vision, and like many other writers of the 1930s Bulosan turns to the political Left for solutions. He eventually finds his older brother Macario organizing Filipino workers, and Bulosan records his brother's statements of beliefs, which are, of course, Bulosan's as well:

We must live in America where there is freedom for all regardless of color, station and beliefs.... It is but fair to say that America is not a land of one race or one class of men. We are all Americans that have toiled and suffered and known oppression and defeat, from the first Indian that offered peace in Manhattan to the last Filipino pea pickers.... America is also the nameless foreigner, the homeless refugee, the hungry boy begging for a job and the black body dangling on a tree.... All of us, from the first Adams to the last Filipino, native born or alien, educated or illiterate—*We are America*! (188–89)

The final sections of *America Is in the Heart* record Bulosan's work with the Filipino Workers Association and his efforts to become a writer. Bulosan worked as a writer and editor for *The New Tide*, a progressive journal that "tried to grasp the social realities and to interpret them in terms of the needs of the decade" (193). Bulosan held to a middle course in the radical politics of the period, and he writes proudly of the establishment and success of the United Cannery, Agricultural, Packing, and Allied Workers of America (UCA-PAWA) and the need to support the antifascists during the Spanish civil war. He is circumspect, however, in his treatment of American Communists. In his narrative Bulosan depicts Communist party workers as sympathetic to the needs of Filipino workers in America; he notes, for example, that "the Communist Party had contributed something definite toward the awakening of Filipinos on the West Coast" (293). Bulosan himself did not join the Party, and while he intended his autobiography to be seen as an exposé of an exploitive economic and social system and a call for social action, he suggests that such traditional measures as education and organization, rather than revolution, would bring about social transformation.

Bulosan ends his autobiography with a patriotic plea for brotherhood in the face of the common enemy. He recalls hearing of the Japanese attack on Pearl Harbor and realizing that both the Philippines and the United States were in danger. He describes helping organize committees to aid in the enlistment of Filipinos in the U.S. armed forces. Bulosan celebrates the unity he sees in both the Anglo and Filipino communities, but he remembers that "it took a war and a great calamity of our country to bring us together" (319).

CRITICISM

America Is in the Heart was once one of the most popular ethnic-American autobiographies, and Carlos Bulosan was once one of the best-known Filipinos in the United States. But as Elaine Kim observes in *Asian American Literature*, "Bulosan's popularity waxed and waned with the political climate" (45). Kim notes that during World War II Bulosan's work appeared in the

New Yorker and the *Saturday Evening Post* and that *Look* claimed that *America Is in the Heart* was one of the fifty most important American books ever published (45).

Bulosan's initial popularity and subsequent neglect reflect popular opinion rather than scholarly study, which recognizes Bulosan's achievement in *America Is in the Heart*. Carey McWilliams, for example, calls the autobiography a "social classic . . . that reflects the collective life of thousands of Filipino immigrants" (quoted in Kim, 49). Kim, whose *Asian American Literature* is one of the most comprehensive examinations of the subject, writes that

America Is in the Heart is in many ways part of that inclusive and characteristically Asian American genre of autobiography or personal history dedicated to the task of promoting cultural good will and understanding. (47)

Bulosan's narrative is also important for several other reasons. First, Bulosan's firsthand account of life in the Philippines and on the West Coast prior to World War II is a compelling critique of American colonial policy and racism. Second, Bulosan's depiction of the efforts to organize Filipino workers adds to our understanding of the history of American labor and its relationship to migrant workers. Finally, *America Is in the Heart* dramatizes the dream of America as a great, good place that may exist in spite of economic and social discrimination. Bulosan, like a number of other ethnic-American writers, places primary value on the America that might be, rather than the actual America he discovered.

BIBLIOGRAPHY

Bulosan, Carlos. *The Voice of Bataan.* New York: Coward-McCann, 1943.
———. *The Laughter of My Father.* New York: Harcourt Brace, 1944.
———. *America Is in the Heart.* 1946. Seattle: University of Washington Press, 1973.
———. "I Am Not a Laughing Man." *The Writer* 59, 5 (May 1946): 143–46.
———. *Sound of Falling Light: Letters in Exile.* Edited by Dolores S. Feria. Quezon City: University of the Philippines, 1960.
———. "My Education." *Amerasia Journal* 6, 1 (May 1979): 113–19.
———. "Selected Letters of Carlos Bulosan. 1937–1955." *Amerasia Journal* 6, 1 (May 1979): 143–54.
———. "Silence." *Amerasia Journal* 6, 1 (May 1979): 57–60.
———. "The Thief." *Amerasia Journal* 6, 1 (May 1979): 83–85.
Castro, Patricia A. "Filipino Writers in America." M. A. thesis, Columbia University, 1951.
Catapusan, Benicio T. "The Filipinos and the Labor Unions." *American Federationist* 47 (1949): 173–76.
———. *The Social Adjustment of Filipinos in the United States.* Los Angeles: University of Southern California, 1940.
Chow, Christopher. "A Brother Reflects: An Interview with Aurelio Bulosan." *Amerasia Journal* 6, 1 (May 1979): 155–66.

DeWitt, Howard. *Anti-Filipino Movements in California: A History, Bibliography, and Study Guide*. San Francisco: R and E Research Associates, 1976.

Epsey, John J. "A Filipino's Triumph of Faith and Spirit." Review of *America Is in the Heart*, by Carlos Bulosan. *New York Herald Tribune Weekly Book Review* 19, 33 (April 11, 1943): 4.

Kim, Elaine H. *Asian American Literature: An Introduction to the Writings and Their Social Context*. Philadelphia: Temple University Press, 1982.

McWilliams, Carey. *Factories in the Field: The Story of Migratory Farm Labor in California*. Santa Barbara, Calif.: Peregrine, 1971.

Morantte, P. C. "The Problem Facing the Filipino Author." *Philippines* 1, 5 (June 1941): 24.

Price, John A. Review of *America Is in the Heart*, by Carlos Bulosan. *Wisconsin Library Bulletin* 42, 3 (March 1946): 45.

————. Review of *America Is in the Heart* by Carlos Bulosan. *Christian Science Monitor* 38, 91 (March 14, 1946): 20.

————. Review of *America Is in the Heart*, by Carlos Bulosan. *Booklist* 42, 13 (March 15, 1946): 225.

————. Review of *America Is in the Heart*, by Carlos Bulosan. *Wilson Library Bulletin* 20, 8 (April 1946): 570.

————. Review of *America Is in the Heart* by Carlos Bulosan. *United States Quarterly Book List* 2, 2 (June 1946): 96.

FRANK CAPRA
(1897–   )

The Name above the Title: An Autobiography

BIOGRAPHY

Film director Frank Capra, whose movies defined Americanism during the 1930s and 1940s, was born in Bisaquino, Italy, on May 18, 1897. Following a brother who came to the United States five years earlier, Capra and his family emigrated to America and settled in Los Angeles in 1903. An outstanding student, Capra was educated at Manual Arts High School and then studied chemical engineering at the California Institute of Technology, graduating in 1918. After graduation he enlisted in the army and taught ballistics for a year.

His work in film began in 1922 when he found a job with Walter Bell developing film for the motion picture industry. Later he worked as a prop man and an editor for Bob Eddy, maker of short comedies. He soon began to combine his talents, working as a writer and then as writer-director for such famous silent filmmakers as Hal Roach and Mack Sennett. He directed comedian Harry Langdon in his earliest and most successful pictures and was then hired by Columbia Pictures.

Capra blossomed at Columbia. During the 1930s he directed such famous films as *Platinum Blonde* (1931), *It Happened One Night* (1934), *Mr. Deeds Goes to Town* (1936), *Lost Horizon* (1937), and *Mr. Smith Goes to Washington* (1939). In 1942 Capra was commissioned as a major in the U.S. Army Signal Corps and produced the famous *Why We Fight* films, which were shown to American soldiers and civilians to counter Axis propaganda and explain the causes of World War II.

After the war Capra established an independent film company, Liberty Films, which he sold to Paramount in 1952. He wrote, directed, and produced four science documentaries for the Bell Telephone Company in the 1950s. His last major film was *Pocketful of Miracles* (1961). Since then Capra has been an active speaker and participant in numerous film festivals. In 1971 he published his autobiography, *The Name above the Title*.

THE AUTOBIOGRAPHY

The title of Capra's autobiography is a boast: It refers to Capra's position as the most successful director at the Columbia studios during the 1930s. Columbia's president, Harry Cohn, permitted only one director, Capra, to place his name above the titles of his films, an admission of Capra's status. Although Capra's reputation has undergone a number of revisions—some critics in the 1950s and 1960s saw his work as overly sentimental and trite— he remains one of the most important directors in film history, and his major works have retained their popularity and critical appeal. His autobiography is about film, but it is also about his success in the film industry, and this permits Capra to tell the story of a poor Italian immigrant child who rose to wealth and a position of power in one of the most significant American industries of the twentieth century. While *The Name above the Title* is the story of a man who made movies, it is also the story of how one man succeeded in the land of opportunity and came to express his love for that land in his work.

Capra begins his autobiography with a statement about his reasons for becoming a filmmaker:

I hated being poor. Hated being a peasant. Hated being a scrounging newskid trapped in the sleazy Sicilian ghetto of Los Angeles. My family couldn't read or write. I wanted out. A quick out. I looked for a device, a handle, a pole to catapult myself across the tracks from my scurvy habitat of nobodies to the affluent world of somebodies. (xi)

He follows this statement with a description of his childhood, a childhood of a poor peasant.

Like many other immigrant writers, Capra uses the immigrant experience to organize his narrative—life in the old country, emigration, and struggle and success in the new land. Since Capra left Italy when he was five, the old country and journey sections of his narrative are brief. Capra concentrates on his struggle and successes in the new land. The depictions of life in Italy are significant, however, for they define the place from which all of Capra's progress starts. Capra's older brother had left Bisaquino five years before a letter arrived from California. No one in the family could read it, so a local priest informed the family that Benjamin Capra had survived shipwrecks, involuntary labor, and deportation before arriving in Los Angeles, where he intended to stay. He invited his family to join him there. Like hundreds of thousands of other southern Italian families in the first decade of the century, the Capras had no prospects in their homeland, so they decided to join Benjamin. After thirteen days of steerage aboard the *Germania*, two days at Ellis Island, and eight days on the transcontinental railroad, the Capra family arrived in Los Angeles. Capra recalls that "Papa and Mama kissed the ground and wept for joy. I cried, too. But not with joy. I cried because we were poor and ignorant and tired and dirty" (5).

Capra writes that the first challenge for an immigrant family in a strange land is to stay alive. Within a month of their arrival, all the family members save Capra found jobs. He continued to go to school; although he had been born a peasant, he remembers thinking, he wasn't going to die one. Like many other young immigrants, Capra saw education as a way to move from poverty and obscurity, and he was willing to work at a series of part-time jobs to pay for his education and assist his struggling family. Capra worked hard; he finished high school in three and a half years so that he could work six months to pay for one year's tuition at the California Institute of Technology.

Capra continued to work hard in college. He records his schedule, emphasizing his ability to juggle his time. He rose at 3 to ride his motorcycle to his night job; from 3:30 to 7:30 he was a night engineer at a Pasadena Power and Light plant; from 8 to 12 he attended classes; from 12 to 1 he waited tables at a college dorm; from 1 to 5 he attended classes; from 5 to 7 he played football or sang with the glee club, and then waited dinner tables; at 7 he rode his motorcycle home; and from 7:30 to 10 he studied. Despite the schedule, he managed to win the Freshman Scholarship Prize.

Despite the death of his father and the loss of the small farm the family had managed to purchase, Capra continued to work and study, and he enjoyed his life. He received his degree in chemical engineering in 1918 and enlisted in the army. He remembers:

Up to that time, in spite of being constantly on the run between classes and jobs, life had been one great big ball for me. Conquering adversities was so simple I began to think of myself as another Horatio Alger, the success kid, my own rags-to-riches hero. (9)

Capra's reference to Horatio Alger here is significant. Like the young heroes in Alger's novels, Capra himself was to become a self-made success. For him hard work, virtue, and luck would provide the ways to wealth. Capra was fortunate to be both bright and ambitious at a time and in a place where those virtues would be rewarded. After being discharged from the army and suffering the effects of severe influenza and the postwar economic downturn, Capra happened upon the film industry, and with a job as a prop man he started his climb to fame and fortune.

Once Capra begins describing his work in the film industry, *The Name above the Title* becomes a chronicle of success. In his preface Capra claims that his book is not an autobiography but that "it is mostly random recalls of what went on in my head during my youth and in my forty-odd years of filmmaking" (xi). Capra's narrative is more carefully designed than that, however, and the recollections of his work in film are controlled by two themes:

his desire to become a director—to be in control of the making of a movie—and his commitment to making populist, patriotic films that celebrate the best in his adopted country.

Capra recalls that even when he was working as a prop man for Bob Eddy, he believed in the idea of "one man, one film," and as a writer for Hal Roach and Mack Sennett he argued for a chance to writer, direct, and edit his own films. Like his idol, D. W. Griffith, Capra realized that film was both a new language and the dominant art form of the twentieth century. He was convinced that the movies were more than a business, and as he describes working in Hollywood, first in the silent period and later during the sound era, he provides a fascinating series of profiles of the people with whom he worked, including Harry Langdon, Barbara Stanwyck, Gary Cooper, Jean Arthur, and Jimmy Stewart. In addition, he describes his own growing control of the process of making movies.

In 1934 Capra's film *It Happened One Night*, starring Clark Gable and Claudette Colbert, won five Academy Awards: Best Picture, Best Actor, Best Actress, Best Writer, and Best Director. Capra's romantic comedy demonstrated his ability as a major filmmaker, a strong director who could stamp his material with a personal vision. In 1935 Capra was elected president of the Academy of Motion Picture Arts and Sciences. He was rich and famous, but he suddenly was struck with a mysterious illness, and upon his recovery Capra decided to make only "committed" films. The result of this decision was a series of movies that define Capra as a director and demonstrate his love for his new homeland—*Mr. Deeds Goes to Town, Lost Horizon, You Can't Take It with You, Mr. Smith Goes to Washington, Meet John Doe*, and *It's a Wonderful Life*.

Benjamin Franklin referred to his autobiography as "an advertisement for a rising nation," and these Capra films are also advertisements for America. In them Capra created vivid images of such all-American values as patriotism, honesty, optimism, and hard work, and in the process he created stories that celebrate the common man. While some critics have seen these films as undigestible pulp, calling them "Capracorn," others see them as idealistic statements about what is best in America. They also demonstrate how grateful a successful immigrant can be.

At the outbreak of World War II, Capra reenlisted in the army. Working in the Army Signal Corps, he planned and produced the famous *Why We Fight* films. These documentaries, using captured Axis footage and Allied news photographs, were intended as a response to German and Japanese propaganda. They were also intended to explain the reasons for the war and rally Allied soldiers and civilians to the support of the embattled democracies.

Both the war films and Capra's social dramas reveal his faith in democracy and love of the United States. The films assert that in America virtue will prevail and the poor can inherit the earth. At the end of his autobiography

Capra makes his faith in humanity and his use of films to spread his faith clear:

I had to return to my roots for a much-needed draught of peasant courage. Out of the refill came a book that is an impertinent try at saying to the discouraged, the doubting, or the despairing what I have been presuming to say in films: "Friend, you are a divine mingle-mangle of guts and stardust. So hang in there! If the doors opened for me, they can open for anyone. (495)

Both Capra's films and his autobiography are works of gratitude. In a sense Capra did live a life out of a Horatio Alger novel, and while his autobiography emphasizes the vehicle for his success, his films, it also documents the distance he traveled.

CRITICISM

Capra's reputation as a filmmaker is secure. While some critics point to his simplistic faith in America and democracy as flaws in his films, almost all film historians rank Capra as one of the major directors of the first half of the twentieth century. Studies of Capra and his work generally emphasize both his subject matter and his sure handling of the elements of filmmaking. Dennis DeNitto, for example, in *Film: Form and Feeling*, writes that Capra's films "share the premise that America's problems can be solved by optimism, integrity, sincerity, and fairness" (273). Gerald Mast, in *A Short History of the Movies*, observes of Capra:

The consistency of material, solid scripts, perceptive comic characterization, the informed understated acting in his films make them sincere and clever statements of the era's conventional optimism and folksy humanism. (293)

Robert Sklar, writing in *Movie-Made America: A Cultural History of American Movies*, praises Capra's films as important American myths and idealized social fables.

Frank Capra is an important American artist, and his work has influenced the culture in significant ways. In his films and in his autobiography Capra provides his audience with an idealized vision of America: He creates a picture of the country as we wish it would be.

BIBLIOGRAPHY

Bergman, Andrew. *We're in the Money: Depression America and Its Films*. New York: Harper and Row, 1972.
Bohn, Thomas. *An Historical and Descriptive Analysis of the "Why We Fight" Series*. New York: Arno, 1977.

Capra, Frank. *The Name above the Title*. 1971. New York: Vintage, 1985.

DeNitto, Dennis. *Film: Form and Feeling*. New York: Harper and Row, 1985.

Glatzer, Richard, and John Raeburn. *Frank Capra: The Man and His Films*. Ann Arbor: University of Michigan Press, 1975.

Griffith, Richard, *Frank Capra*. London: Gordon, 1979.

Maland, Charles. *Frank Capra*. Boston: Twayne, 1980.

Mast, Gerald. *A Short History of the Movies*, 2d ed. Indianapolis: Bobbs-Merrill, 1976.

Scherle, Victor, and William Levy. *The Films of Frank Capra*. Secaucus, N.J.: Citadel, 1977.

Sklar, Robert. *Movie-Made America: A Social History of American Movies*. New York: Random House, 1975.

Willis, Donald. *The Films of Frank Capra*. Metuchen, N.J.: Scarecrow, 1974.

ANDREW CARNEGIE
(1835–1919)

Autobiography of Andrew Carnegie

BIOGRAPHY

Andrew Carnegie seemed larger than life even during his own lifetime. One of the first captains of American industry and the ideal example of a self-made man, Carnegie was a poor immigrant boy who acquired vast amounts of wealth only to spend his final years giving much of it away. He was, and remains, one of the most famous American immigrants.

Andrew Carnegie was born in Dunfermline, Scotland, on November 25, 1835. His father was a linen weaver, and his mother was the daughter of a shoemaker. The Carnegie family became caught up in the social and political upheavals of the industrialization of the Scottish textile industry, which wiped out the long-established home weaving industry that had dominated Scottish economics, and in 1848 emigrated to the United States in search of work. The Carnegies settled in Allegheny, Pennsylvania, and at the age of fourteen Andrew Carnegie began working as a bobbin-boy in a cotton factory for $1.20 a week.

In 1849 Carnegie began working for the O'Reilly Telegraph Office in Pittsburgh, first as a messenger and later as a telegraph operator. From this point in his career, Carnegie's fortunes would be closely associated with the rapidly increasing technology that was transforming American business and industry. In 1853 Carnegie was hired by the Pennsylvania Railroad as a telegraph operator, and by 1861, when he temporarily left the railroad to help establish a military telegraph system at the outbreak of the Civil War, Carnegie had become an accomplished industrial manager with experience in transportation, communications, and manufacturing.

In 1865 Carnegie resigned from the Pennsylvania Railroad to establish his own firm, the Keystone Bridge Company, which, in addition to supplying bridges for the railroads, manufactured iron and steel. From this base Carnegie built his industrial empire. By 1873 he was establishing business relations with English steel manufacturers, and soon thereafter he brought the revolutionary Bessemer process for steel manufacturing to the United States. In 1882 he joined forces with industrialist Henry Frick and acquired vast coal and coke properties. As a result of the merger the Carnegie Company came to dominate the American steel, coal, and metal industries.

In the 1880s Carnegie began to pursue other interests. In 1882 he began his career as a writer, publishing *An American Four-in-Hand*, a narrative of his visit to Europe, and in 1886 his *Triumphant Democracy*, a survey of the social and political progress of the United States, appeared. His most important writing can be seen in "Wealth," reprinted in England as "The Gospel of Wealth." In that essay, which appeared in 1889, Carnegie, defining the accumulation of wealth as a form of stewardship, called on the rich to liquidate their fortunes for the benefit of the larger community.

During his management of his steel company Carnegie had acquired the reputation of a fair employer, but in 1892 five strikers and three Pinkerton guards were killed during a bitter labor struggle at his Homestead plant in Pennsylvania. Carnegie was in Scotland at the time of the strike, but the confrontation and the deaths affected him deeply. In 1901 he sold his interest in his company to the newly formed United States Steel Corporation.

From 1901 until his death in 1919 Carnegie concentrated his energies on divesting himself of his wealth. Although his large gifts to education and libraries remain his most famous philanthropies, Carnegie devoted most of his time and interest to the peace movement, establishing the Endowment for International Peace and enlisting the aid of such figures as Theodore Roosevelt and Kaiser Wilhelm II in trying to avert World War I. He died, after giving away over $350 million, on August 11, 1919.

THE AUTOBIOGRAPHY

The *Autobiography of Andrew Carnegie* was published in 1920, but readers had the opportunity to see the famous man from his earlier writings, such as "How I Served My Apprenticeship," "The Gospel of Wealth," and *Triumphant Democracy*. The *Autobiography* provides, however, the first unified narrative of the many-sided life of Andrew Carnegie. It also tells a story almost too fantastic to be believed, a tale of the rise of a poor immigrant boy to the height of wealth and power in America and the decision of the grown man to give nearly all that wealth away. Carnegie was an enigma to many of his contemporaries, and his autobiography provides the materials of which myths are made.

Carnegie was, of course, aware of the potentially legendary aspects of his life, and he structures his autobiography to emphasize them. Like the earlier mythic American autobiographer, Benjamin Franklin, Carnegie saw his life and rise from poverty and obscurity to wealth and celebrity as part of a specifically American adventure. Throughout his narrative he implies that such a dramatic success could occur only in America. As a result, the *Auto-biography* becomes, at times, as much a narrative about American democracy and economic opportunity as a story of one Andrew Carnegie, Scottish immigrant. On the other hand, Carnegie was aware that he took advantage of the opportunities provided as few others did, and he writes of his life with the assurance of a man who knows that his memory would survive had he not written his own life story. He begins his autobiography with his own confident statement of intentions:

I intend to tell my story, not as one posturing before the public, but as in the midst of my own people and friends, tried and true, to whom I can speak with the utmost freedom, feeling that even the trifling incidents may not be wholly destitute of interest for them. (1)

Like a number of other immigrant American autobiographers, Carnegie writes fondly of his homeland. The first chapter of the autobiography, "Parents and Childhood," is, however, more than a nostalgic description of Dunfermline. Carnegie uses the introductory chapter of his narrative to establish one of his central themes, the relationship between political freedom and economic prosperity.

Carnegie writes proudly that he was born of "poor but honest" parents. He considers himself fortunate in both his ancestors and birthplace, crediting them with giving him a lifelong love of hard work and democracy. In describing his family, Carnegie devotes special attention to his maternal grandfather, Thomas Morrison, and his uncle, Bailie Morrison. Both men were ardent Chartists who advocated sweeping political reforms including universal suffrage and the abolishment of privilege. Politics was a central part of Carnegie's childhood, but so was economic unrest.

Describing the beginning of the industrial revolution in Scotland that affected his family, Carnegie writes that the industrial changes from hand to steam-driven weaving destroyed the family's position, and his father's looms soon became almost worthless. Despite the additional income provided by the small shop of Carnegie's mother, the family began considering emigration; there were no jobs for independent weavers. In 1848 the family sold the looms and furniture to raise money for the passage to America.

The Carnegie family followed a pattern established by earlier immigrants. After their arrival in New York they immediately headed west, joining relatives near Pittsburgh who provided the newly arrived family with a place to stay and with the opportunity to work. Carnegie's father found a job as a weaver, and his mother bound shoes at home for $4 a week. Even though the family struggled, Carnegie remembers this period as a time of warmth and family unity. Writing about his early life in America, Carnegie asserts that his parents provided him and his brother with love and kindness, a heritage far more important than an illustrious name or wealth. Drawing on his own experience,

Carnegie believed that poverty was beneficial, since it taught the poor the necessary lessons about life and hard work. In addition to these and other references in his autobiography, Carnegie provides readers with a more elaborate exposition of his doctrine in "The Advantages of Poverty," which appeared in the journal *Nineteenth Century* in 1891.

Carnegie begins to establish one of the major themes of his narrative, a chronicle of his rise to wealth and celebrity, in his third chapter, "Pittsburgh and Work." In writing his autobiography and such an other occasional piece as "How I Served My Apprenticeship," Carnegie is aware of his acquisition of a vast fortune, and he sets out to create from his own life a model for others to emulate. He depicts himself as the epitome of the self-made man, and he encourages his readers by suggesting that since he succeeded, so can they.

Carnegie's success in business reads like a faerie tale. Beginning as a bobbin-boy in a cotton factory, Carnegie advanced to telegraph messenger, telegraph operator, bookkeeper, railroad manager, and finally railroad superintendent within scarcely more than a decade. He recounts his apprenticeship in a sermonlike manner, alternating his adventures with admonitions. After describing the work of a telegraph operator, for example, Carnegie warns his readers:

It is not the rich man's son that the young struggler for advancement has to fear in the race for life, nor his nephew, nor his cousin. Let him look out for the "dark horse" in the boy who begins by sweeping out the office. (41)

Carnegie describes his rise as if he were a hero from a Horatio Alger novel, and although he emphasizes his hard work and complete dedication to duty, he does admit that luck played some part in his success. Carnegie acknowledges that he was fortunate to recognize the importance of technology and to master the telegraph system. He writes that his adaptation of this new communications technology to the needs of the Pennsylvania Railroad made him a key member of the railroad's management. Carnegie saw opportunities throughout his career, and his autobiography, especially the sections dealing with his rise in business, is a record of opportunities taken. By 1861, when Carnegie left the Pennsylvania Railroad to help create the foundation of the Union's military-industrial complex by establishing efficient rail and telegraph service for the army, Carnegie had become an important industrial manager, had already seen the direction of railroad growth, and was planning to invest in Pullman sleeping cars, rail making, and the steel industry.

The end of the Civil War found Carnegie establishing his own company, the Keystone Bridge Company, which provided bridges and rails for the Pennsylvania Railroad. Carnegie writes of his decision to be his own boss:

I was determined to make a fortune and I saw no means of doing this honestly by any salary the railroad company could afford to give, and I would not do it by indirection. (135)

From 1865 until 1870 Carnegie traveled between the United States and Europe selling bonds of small railroads and iron companies to European investors. While in England he observed the successful adaptation of the Bessemer process and the beginning of the conversion of the iron industry into the steel industry. He immediately saw the advantages of the process and began planning to divest himself of his diversified interests and concentrate on the production of steel. The proper way to master business, he writes, is "to put all good eggs in one basket and then watch that basket" (170). He then elaborates on this maxim:

I believe that the true road to preeminent success in any line is to make yourself master in that line. I have no faith in the policy of scattering one's resources, and in my experience I have rarely if ever met a man who achieved preeminence in money making—certainly never one in manufacturing—who was interested in many concerns. (170)

Carnegie's depiction of his success at establishing the empire of steel is less dramatic than his account of his rise from office boy to millionaire, and although he intends to provide examples for would-be captains of industry from this phase of his life, Carnegie's chronicle of his capture of the steel industry is not the most effective section of his narrative.

Andrew Carnegie captured the imagination of his age for more than his wealth. Carnegie recognizes this and describes in detail his intellectual awakening, which occurred after an around-the-world trip that he first narrated in *Round the World* in 1884. With his business concerns prospering, Carnegie began to travel and read, and the result was dramatic. Carnegie writes that after reading Spencer, Darwin, Confucius, and Buddha his life changed. He remembers that he found order and peace in his life with this intellectual discovery and that he soon grew as secure philosophically as he was financially. This change in the autobiography reflects the change that had taken place in the autobiographer. No longer does the narrative record just business and financial successes; instead it charts the growing diversity of interests of a man who seems to have just discovered life outside work. Carnegie records his reactions to his trips, his establishment of a manor in Scotland, his marriage, his writing, and his new-found intellectual interests, but before he turns his attention away from business entirely, he includes a short defense of his actions during the Homestead strike of 1892.

Although Carnegie was in Scotland when the simultaneous lockout and strike occurred at the Carnegie Homestead plant, he followed events. On July 6 five strikers and three Pinkerton guards were killed in a gunbattle, and five days later the governor of Pennsylvania called out 8,000 members of the state militia to maintain order. Eventually the steel mill was reopened under military protection, and workers were permitted to return on an individual basis.

In the autobiography Carnegie avoids mentioning the details of the strike and its aftermath that destroyed his reputation as one of the fairest employers in American industry. He does, however, argue that both sides in the confrontation were misled and wonders whether the results would have been different if he had been in the country. In an almost apologetic conclusion to his musings on the strike Carnegie includes quotations of praise from workmen he had received when he ran his company personally.

The final sections of the *Autobiography of Andrew Carnegie* complete the transformation from a narrative of success to a narrative of virtue as Carnegie chronicles his philanthropies. Carnegie had previously published his attitude toward great wealth in "The Gospel of Wealth," and in a private memorandum he had noted, "Man must have an idol—the amassing of wealth is one of the worst species of idolatry—no idol more debasing than the worship of money" (*The Gospel of Wealth*, xvi). "The Gospel of Wealth" appeared under the title "Wealth" in the *North American Review* in 1889, and at that time Carnegie recognized that his belief that a man's fortune should be distributed for the good of the community during his lifetime might be considered merely a platitude, so he began to follow his own advice. In his autobiography he remembers that after "The Gospel of Wealth" was published he resolved to stop his accumulation of wealth and begin the more difficult task of wise distribution. Using the title of his most famous work and adding a collection of other essays written between 1881 and 1899, Carnegie published "The Gospel of Wealth" in 1900. In 1901 he sold his interest in the Carnegie Steel Company to a consortium headed by J. P. Morgan for $225 million. One result of the sale was the establishment of the United States Steel Corporation; another was the launching of the career of a full-time philanthropist.

Carnegie recounts his benefactions with the same self-assured tone he used to list his business accomplishments. He considers both to be essential parts of his life, and as he outlines his gifts to pension funds, libraries, museums, hero funds, educational institutions, churches, and peace movements, readers can see that he took "wise distribution" as seriously as "accumulating."

Carnegie ends his narrative with a series of comments on politics, religion, and philosophy. After telling how he earned his wealth and then gave it away, Carnegie reveals his own beliefs, writing that enlightened self-interest and education will lead mankind away from superstition, war, and ignorance to a more perfect existence. He includes an example of his own enlightenment. After he had discovered Darwin and Spencer,

I remember that light came as a flood and all was clear. Not only had I got rid of all theology and the supernatural, but I had found the truth of evolution. "All is well since all grows better," became my motto, my true source of comfort. Man was not created with an instinct for his own degradation, but from the lower he had risen to the higher forms. Nor is there any conceivable end to his march to perfection. His face is turned to the light; he stands in the sun and looks upward. (327)

Carnegie's main concern during the final years of his life was world peace. He spoke out against the Spanish-American War and decried the American occupation of the Philippines. In 1907 he built the Peace Palace at The Hague in the Netherlands, hoping to establish an international tribunal that would make war obsolete. In his autobiography he does not mention the final five years of his life when he watched, in a deep depression, the slaughter during World War I.

CRITICISM

Andrew Carnegie is one of the most fascinating figures in American history, and the *Autobiography of Andrew Carnegie* is one of the seminal works of American culture. Irvin Wyllie, in *The Self-Made Man in America*, asserts that Carnegie became a symbol for several generations of Americans, the actual embodiment of the myth of a rise from rags to riches. Carnegie's name became associated with enterprise, wealth, and finally charity.

Criticism about Carnegie covers a wide spectrum. Early critics and biographers such as Bernard Alderson (*Andrew Carnegie: The Man and His Work*) and John Winkler (*Incredible Carnegie*) saw Carnegie as a personification of the success myth. More recent scholarship places Carnegie more firmly within the social and political context of his times, seeing him less as a wonder and more as a representative figure. Louis Hacker (*The World of Andrew Carnegie*) and Peter Temin (*Iron and Steel in Nineteenth-Century America*) provide productive studies of the man and his times. Two full and objective biographies of Carnegie are Burton Hendrick's *Life of Andrew Carnegie* and Joseph Wall's *Andrew Carnegie*.

While most of the criticism of Carnegie celebrates the man and his works, other views exist. Irvin Wyllie (*The Self-Made Man in America*) examines the ideology behind the myth and draws attention to the propagandistic elements in Carnegie's writing. Cecyle Neidle ("The Foreign-Born View America") sees the greatest value of Carnegie's autobiography in its recreation of the period of mercantile capitalism.

Like other autobiographies of successful immigrants, the *Autobiography of Andrew Carnegie* provided inspiration for other newcomers. A surprising number of ethnic autobiographers cite it as a source of encouragement. In addition, Carnegie's narrative provides readers with both an outline of the development of industrial America and a critique of the mere accumulation of wealth. The *Autobiography of Andrew Carnegie* is one of those works that defines the ideology of the nation.

BIBLIOGRAPHY

Carnegie, Andrew. *An American Four-in-Hand*. New York, 1882.

————. *Triumphant Democracy*. London, 1886.

————. "Wealth." *North American Review* 148 (June 1889): 653–64; 149 (December 1889): 682–98.

————. "How I Served My Apprenticeship." *The Youth's Companion* 23 (April 1896): 217.

————. *The Gospel of Wealth and Other Timely Essays*. 1900. Boston: Belknap Press of Harvard University Press, 1962.

————. *The Empire of Business*. Garden City, N.Y.: Doubleday, 1902.

————. *Autobiography of Andrew Carnegie*. Boston: Houghton Mifflin, 1920.

————. *Round the World*. Garden City, N.Y.: Doubleday, 1933.

Alderson, Bernard. *Andrew Carnegie: The Man and His Works*. London: Doubleday Page, 1902.

Bobinski, G. S. "Andrew Carnegie's Role in American Public Library Development." Ph.D. diss., University of Michigan, 1966.

Bridge, James H. *The Inside History of the Carnegie Steel Company*. New York: Aldine, 1903.

Hacker, Louis M. *The World of Andrew Carnegie, 1865–1901*. Philadelphia: Lippincott, 1968.

Harlow, Alvin S. *Andrew Carnegie*. New York: Messner, 1953.

Hendrick, Burton J. *The Life of Andrew Carnegie*. Garden City, N.Y.: Doubleday, 1932.

————. *The Benefactions of Andrew Carnegie*. New York: Carnegie Corp., 1935.

Neidle, Cecyle. "The Foreign-Born View America: A Study of Autobiographies Written by Immigrants to the United States." Ph.D. diss., New York University, 1962.

Shippen, Katherine B. *Andrew Carnegie*. New York: Random House, 1958.

Temin, Peter. *Iron and Steel in Nineteenth-Century America*. Cambridge: M.I.T. Press, 1964.

Wall, Joseph. *Andrew Carnegie*. New York: Oxford Press, 1970.

Winkler, John F. *Incredible Carnegie*. New York: Vanguard, 1931.

Wyllie, Irvin G. *The Self-Made Man in America: The Myth of Rags to Riches*. New York: Free Press, 1966.

EDWARD CORSI
(1897–1965)

In the Shadow of Liberty

BIOGRAPHY

Edward Corsi was born in the Abruzzi region of Italy in 1897, the son of Filippo Corsi, who was a disciple of Giuseppe Mazzini and editor of the radical paper, *La Democrazia*. Forced into exile in Switzerland for his criticism of King Umberto of Italy, Filippo Corsi relocated his family until he was elected to the Italian parliament. Soon after the family's return, however, Filippo Corsi died, leaving his widow and children without financial support. The Corsi family, faced with poverty at home, sailed for America in 1907, the same year that brought a record 1,285,349 aliens to the United States.

Corsi, like many other young immigrants, quickly adapted to American life. He was admitted to Home Garden, a settlement house, and later studied at Fordham University, receiving a law degree. In 1930 he was appointed to supervise the federal census in Manhattan, and in 1931 he was selected as immigration commissioner at Ellis Island by President Hoover. In 1934 Corsi left that position to become the director of relief for New York City.

Corsi continued his public service throughout his life. From 1943 to 1954 he was New York State's industrial commissioner. In 1938 he ran for the U.S. Senate and in 1950 for mayor of New York City. He lost both elections. In 1954 President Eisenhower appointed Corsi special assistant for refugee relief to Secretary of State John Foster Dulles, but after three months Corsi was dismissed for charging that under Dulles the management of the Refugee Act had become a national scandal. Corsi returned to New York and served in a variety of government positions until his death on December 13, 1965.

THE AUTOBIOGRAPHY

Corsi's autobiography, *In the Shadow of Liberty*, records the ideas of an immigrant-turned–public servant writing at the height of the Depression.

Published in 1935, *In the Shadow of Liberty* is both a narrative of personal experience and a statement of social concern. While Corsi begins his autobiography by recounting his own experiences, he focuses most of his attention on his work as commissioner of immigration. In doing so, Corsi provides an overview of American immigration policy and an illustrated history of immigration itself. As a result, his autobiography is more of a public statement than a personal narrative. Corsi, perhaps more than any other immigrant autobiographer, writes with a representative voice; as one of the millions who came, struggled, and prospered, he records not only his own arrival, but the arrival of countless others.

Like many other immigrant autobiographers, Corsi opens his narrative with a description of his life in the old country. The ideal of political service dominates even this section of the narrative. Corsi praises his father as a man who struggled against royal tyranny by attempting to establish a republican government in Italy. His father's exile and triumphant return as a member of parliament are the high points of the first section of Corsi's work. Equally important, however, are Corsi's descriptions of his countrymen's economic suffering and the stories of America that were filtering back to Italy. He recalls seeing many Italians who had left for America returning to their homes wearing gold watch chains and boasting of the ease with which fortunes could be made in the New World. He recounts the arrival of a distant cousin who returned from working in New York and announced to the assembled family: "How stupid all Italy is—not to go! Look at me. Here I was nothing. There I made more money than I could spend. It is easy!" (20). Although the cousin undoubtedly exaggerated the ease with which he gathered his fortune in America, his report and the news of other successes that were flowing across Italy convinced his relatives to emigrate. In 1907 the Corsi family joined the tide of immigrants coming to American shores.

Corsi's mother had remarried, and the newlyweds brought four children with them. The voyage, as most immigrants record, was rough. Corsi vividly recalls his arrival and initial adjustment to the new and strange culture. His first view of New York City presented him with marvels. First he saw the Statue of Liberty, and then, directly in front of his ship, what he believed to be large stone mountains. He thought that his stepfather was joking when he told him that they were not mountains but buildings, the tallest buildings in the world.

Corsi continues to record his astonishment at the strange sights of New York—elevated trains, Chinese and black faces, and the lack of beards on American men; in his confusion, Corsi thought that they were women. He immediately liked the noise and confusion, enjoying walking through the crowds in the streets. Not everything was good, however. The family's first home, a four-room tenement on the Upper East Side, was a disappointment to all, especially Corsi's mother.

She loved quiet, and hated noise and confusion. Here she never left the house unless she had to. She spent her days, and the waking hours of the nights, sitting at the one outside window staring at the little patch of sky above the tenements. She was never happy here, and, though she tried, she could not adjust herself to the poverty and despair in which we had to live. (23)

Many of the young immigrants prospered in the new atmosphere of America, but many of the old did not. Corsi's mother became ill and returned to Italy, where she soon died.

As in the autobiographies of other newcomers, Corsi's description of the city serves as a commentary upon the position of the newly arrived immigrant. Corsi states that his family's experience "on the East Side was typical of the lives of thousands upon thousands of immigrant families. It was a continuous struggle" (24). He provides one vivid example to illustrate the intensity of that struggle. The families living in his tenement had to provide their own heat, so he and his brother Giuseppe often raided the New York Central freight yards to gather the lumps of coal that had fallen from the cars. He recalls that on one cold winter day his brother lost an arm gathering coal, and that after he helped his brother home to the family apartment he watched his stepfather leave to borrow money to pay for the doctor who came to sew up the arm and the lawyer he hired to sue the railroad. Corsi's depiction of this incident clearly illustrates the precarious position of the newly arrived immigrant. Without any money, the victim of landlords, lawyers, railroad companies, and other commercial and industrial forces, the newcomer was forced to make do in the face of a growing corporate world that he did not understand.

One of the settlement houses established to help the children of immigrants provided Corsi with the opportunity he needed to begin his journey from the margin to the mainstream. Home Garden provided Corsi with the encouragement he required. Describing the settlement as "a decisive advance in my career," he writes:

It was as if a wide door to America had been opened to me. I caught the spirit of the settlement, entered into its program of leadership and service in the neighborhood, and thread by thread wove my life into it until it became an instrument of my own ideals and purposes and shaped my ambition. (26)

Corsi later obtained a law degree from Fordham University, served in the army, and became a reporter, describing conditions in Mexico for *Outlook* and life in Italy under fascism in the *New York World*. He became an authority on the foreign-born, and this led to his selection as supervisor of the census and commissioner of immigration.

Corsi provides these details of his life briefly; his is not a narrative of personal success. He sees his life as but one example of the stories of the thirty-seven

million made by aliens who came to America. As a result, when he begins
to describe his work at Ellis Island, he writes of immigration in general rather
than his own accomplishments.

The nature of immigration had changed dramatically since Corsi arrived
in 1907. Congress had tightened immigration laws, providing strict quotas in
response to several decades of anti-immigration agitation. Corsi recognized
this, and refers to himself as the "Guardian of the Gate." He announces that
when he accepted the position,

I foresaw that a large portion of my duties would relate to deportation—that is, the
weeding out of the ugly and sick elements in our national life, and consequently, the
vitalization of that life in general. I would be sort of a physician to the whole country,
delegated to cut out cancers and amputate the infected limbs. (36)

Earlier immigrant writers, while they recognized the hardships involved
in coming to the United States, almost universally praised the United States
for providing the opportunity for millions to come here. They asserted that
immigration was good for both the immigrants and America. By 1931, however, that attitude had changed, at least on the part of most Americans. Corsi
is aware of this, and in his history of American immigration he sees that
opposition to foreigners has been a consistent facet of American history,
citing Cotton Mather's attempt to exclude Quakers as but the first in a long
series of native responses to newer arrivals.

Sensitive to the feelings of immigrants but responsible for enforcing government policy, Corsi became a compassionate commissioner, and the overview of immigration he provides in *In the Shadow of Liberty* is a defense
of the immigrants and their children. His account is balanced, however; he
writes of both successes and failures, giving examples of both the "mighty
parade" of "gorgeous costumes, uplifted chins, and eager determined eyes"
and the "retreat of the maimed, wounded, and dying" (281).

The nature of immigration had changed with the American attitude toward
it. In 1932, for the first time in more than a hundred years, more people left
the United States than those who sought to enter it, and in 1933 the number
of arrivals was less than one-fifth of those who returned to Europe. Corsi is
well aware of the significant change that has taken place, and his history of
American immigration is a story of an event that had, for all practical purposes,
ended.

Corsi begins his overview with histories of New York's Castle Garden and
Ellis Island, which served as the main entryways for European immigrants.
Corsi provides a history of the buildings and operations of the U.S. Immi-
gration Service and then moves to an analysis of the people who arrived.

Corsi seldom resorts to mere statistics; he illustrates his narrative with
portraits of individual people. One of the most moving sections of his narrative
is his description of his interview with an inspector who handled Italian

immigrants in 1907, the year he and his family arrived. The inspector, of course, cannot remember him, and Corsi admits that he may have passed under the watchful eyes of a different official, but the conversation between the immigrant commissioner and the old inspector illustrates Corsi's observation about the success of immigration well.

Not all of Corsi's illustrations are so warmhearted. Corsi describes the battery of tests that immigrants faced, recalling cases where some members of a family were admitted and others rejected. In addition, he documents both the deportations and capture of illegal aliens, both jobs of the Immigration Service. In one chapter, for example, Corsi chronicles the deportation of radicals following the enactment of tighter immigration laws after World War I. He provides Emma Goldman as the example of the most interesting radical to pass outward from Ellis Island. Corsi is in no way a red-baiter, and although he enforced the deportation of radicals during his tenure as commissioner, his tone is remarkably mild. He calls the entire matter of the exclusion of foreign radicals "a long and troubling history, which every American should read and reflect upon" (183). Citing the freedom of belief guaranteed in the Constitution, Corsi calls most of the anarchist, socialist, and Communist deportations mistakes. Discrimination because of politics, he argues, has no place in America.

Corsi concludes his autobiography with some observations on American immigration. Again he strives for objectivity:

Many mistakes blot the record of Ellis Island and great have been the hardships, the humiliations and the exploitation suffered by the immigrant. Yet, I am sure, there have also been instances of exaggeration in which the vitriol of the public and the press has been unwarrantedly directed at a Service which, in a last analysis, has been more sinned against than sinning. (296)

He argues that the immigrant must be looked upon not as a potential source of labor in America, but as a potential citizen of the United States, someone with whom to share the best of American laws and customs. In concluding his autobiography, Corsi calls for Americans to treat immigrants, from the moment of their arrival, as fellow citizens, for most of them will become Americans too.

CRITICISM

Although Edward Corsi is best known for his years of public service, several writers have focused on his autobiographical writing. Olga Peragallo, writing in *Italian-American Authors and Their Contributions to American Literature*, notes that *In the Shadow of Liberty* is "a valuable document of the immigration evolution in this country," and she points out that contemporary reviewers praised Corsi for both the subject of his narrative and his effective storytelling (56).

In the Shadow of Liberty is not a traditional immigrant narrative. It does, however, complement most immigrant stories. Corsi's autobiography provides a frame of reference within which individual life histories take on added significance. In writing his narrative of Ellis Island, Edward Corsi revealed as much about himself as he did when he described his own arrival in the first sections of his book.

BIBLIOGRAPHY

Corsi, Edward. "The Voice of the Immigrant." *Outlook*, September 21, 1927, 88–90.
————. *In the Shadow of Liberty*. New York: Macmillan, 1935.
————. *Pathways to the New World*. N.p., 1940.
Cordasco, Francesco, ed. *Studies in Italian American Social History: Essays in Honor of Leonard Covello*. Totowa, N.J.: Rowman and Littlefield, 1975.
————, ed. *Italian Americans: A Guide to the Information Sources*. Detroit: Gale, 1978.
Miller, Wayne Charles, ed. *A Gathering of Ghetto Writers*. New York: New York University Press, 1972.
Neidle, Cecyle. "The Foreign-Born View America: A Study of Autobiographies Written by Immigrants to the United States." Ph.D. diss., New York University, 1962.
Peragallo, Olga. *Italian-American Authors and Their Contributions to American Literature*. New York: S. F. Vanni, 1949.

LEONARD COVELLO
(1887–1982)

The Heart Is the Teacher

BIOGRAPHY

Leonard Covello was born in 1887 in Avigliano, Italy. In 1895 he was brought to the United States by his parents, who settled in the Italian community of East Harlem. Covello attended the New York City public schools (P.S. no. 83 and Morris High School) and Columbia University, where he received his B.S. degree in 1911. He began teaching French and Spanish at De Witt Clinton High School and served as chairman of the Department of Italian there from 1926 to 1934. Covello was the principal of Benjamin Franklin High School from 1934 to 1956 and taught as an adjunct professor at New York University from 1929 to 1942. In 1944 he received his Ph.D. in educational sociology from New York University, and his thesis, *The Social Background of the Italo-American School Child*, which was published in 1967, proved to be a pioneering study of immigrant children in America.

Throughout his life Covello was active in the affairs of the Italian-American community. He was an influential member of the Italian League for Social Service and the Young Men's Italian Educational League, and he was instrumental in persuading the New York City Board of Education to approve of the teaching of Italian in the city's schools. Covello was active in the work of Casa Italiana of Columbia University and helped in the foundation of the American Italian Historical Association. In 1972 Covello moved to Sicily and became a consultant to the Dolci Center for Study and Action. He died on August 19, 1982.

THE AUTOBIOGRAPHY

Leonard Covello's *The Heart Is the Teacher* employs the experimental structure of many immigrant autobiographies: background, exodus, arrival, and adjustment. But like all successful writers, Covello adapts this universal pattern to a particular purpose. Covello's autobiography is dominated by the author's training and interest in education and sociology. The dominant theme is the experience of confronting America, but that experience is filtered through a specific, personal frame of reference.

The Heart Is the Teacher is dedicated to "those who believe that a struggle for a better world will be won or lost in our schools." It is the success story of an immigrant who discovers that education is the most efficacious way of coming to terms with American culture. Covello's presentation of his early life in Italy stresses the poverty that he and his family faced and the representativeness of their situation. The first image of Italy he presents in the narrative is one of himself as a child looking out from a window onto a dying town:

The town of Avigliano faced west, and it was westward that my father had gone, one more of the thousands upon thousands of Southern Italians traveling to America in search of bread for his family. I was the oldest of three children, and already the idea of family and the sense of responsibility was taking hold of me. (3)

These images establish the themes for the Italian sections of Covello's narrative; poverty, futility, and the inevitability of migration dominate the early chapters of his autobiography. Covello also provides his readers with memories of his childhood: his uncle's huge dining room in which the extended family gathered, local legends and ghost stories, his grandmother's knotted grey hair, the stations of the cross in his village church, and the taste of burnt coffee and sugar. All of these memories evoke a sense of place and community, associations that will soon be broken. He recalls other things as well, and these serve to prefigure future events in his life. He remembers waiting for his father's letters and writing return letters for his mother. Already he is the family scribe. He also recalls a prophecy of his grandmother, "The gold you will find in America will not be in the streets, as they say, it will be in the dreams you will realize—the golden dreams of the future" (18). While fond memories of the homeland are typical of immigrant narratives, Covello recalls those that stress education rather than wealth, or rather education as a way to success, which is the major theme of this autobiography.

In 1896 Covello's father sent for his family, and they made the journey to New York. Although the passage was harsh, Covello did not suffer much because "a child adapts to everything." His mother, however, was greatly affected. Covello describes the voyage briefly but effectively in terms that the many others who came to New York by ship at the turn of the century could appreciate. He writes that the voyage was rough and the arrival was confusing; he describes storms at sea and wandering through the streets of New York. He concentrates, however, on his mother's strength at keeping the family together and her inability to adapt to the strange new land. The newness and strangeness of America made Covello's mother turn backward; she dreamt of Italy as long as she lived, but Covello adapted, and to the young and the adaptable America offered a future.

Covello's father saw the possibility of progress in the future and advised his son, "In me you see a dog's life. Go to school. Even if it kills you. With a pen and with books you have a chance to live like a man and not like a beast of burden" (41). Covello took his father's advice; he liked school, seeing it not only as a path to a better future but also as an escape from the drudgery of work that wore out both his mind and body. He became an excellent student, and upon graduation from high school he received a scholarship to Columbia University.

Covello is careful never to idealize or sentimentalize his childhood as he narrates his early life in New York City. His ambition, hard work, and success are grounded in the factual descriptions of his East Harlem neighborhood. While he sees school as a way out of poverty, he never glorifies it. Covello vividly re-creates the turn-of-the-century classroom—rote lessons, corporal punishment, and the enthusiastic teaching of "Americanism." Shortly before he entered Columbia, his mother died, and Covello realizes the irony. His mother, who always was more at home with her memories of Italy than with the reality of America, died just as he received his symbolic acceptance into American culture. He recognized finally the real gap between himself and his parents, and between all those who came to America young and their parents. The gap was, he thought, inevitable. The old would remain immigrants; the young could become Americans.

At Columbia, Covello directly confronted the newness and strangeness; although the grade school and the mixed school were American experiences, Columbia was a totally Anglo environment. He discovered that his Italian background and experiences as an immigrant, while very important to himself, were a complete mystery to others. He set out to establish his own intellectual and emotional identity as an Italian-American. He joined the university soccer team to show his classmates that he had "the stuff." He began to appreciate the bulky sandwiches of crusty Italian bread heaped with salami, cheese, or Italian sausage that he had kept hidden or eaten before school so that his friends of the "white bread and ham" upbringing would not laugh at him. At Columbia, Covello's friends were curious about him and wanted to know about Italian-American communities and the reason for the reported crime in these depressed areas. They told him, 'We can talk to you; you're not like the others" (71). He attempted to tell them about his life and the lives of other Italians he had known in his East Harlem community. Just as he does in his autobiography, Covello attempted to destroy stereotypes. His time at Columbia coincided with the peak years of Italian immigration, and Covello describes reading everything he could find on the subject of immigration in order to understand and explain the phenomenon. When he was asked, "Why do they keep flocking over here by the thousands? I've seen how these people live here. How are they any better off than where they come from?" he answered that many wished they had remained in Italy:

But it seems that the idea of improving one's condition can't be killed. For the hundreds who live in poverty, there is one who becomes a success. He is the one that counts. In Italy there is no chance of success, only hopelessness. That's why they come. That's why they'll keep right on coming, because if the success does not come to them, it will come to their children. (71)

The dual ideas of America as the land of opportunity and the chance to rise in the world come through clearly in Covello's reply. Although Covello does support the idea of the American Dream, he refuses to accept the more stringent demands of "Americanism," the divestment of all native habits and customs.

Covello's interest in immigration and the Italian-American community in New York City led him to volunteer as an English teacher in YMCA-sponsored classes for immigrants. He was instructed not to speak Italian in class and to make his students forget Italian completely. His students failed to respond to his instruction, finding it difficult to pronounce or understand words that had no meaning for them. Finally, in desperation, Covello let out a long tirade in Italian. His students were shocked and delighted; one whispered to another, "Il professore e italiano!" Covello, who overhead the remark, replied, "Why with a name like Covello what did you think I was—an Egyptian?" (76). He soon learned that he could be a more successful teacher by having his students draw on their knowledge of Italian. He found that assimilation does not necessarily imply a rejection of Italian heritage, but rather that it fosters an adaptation of that heritage to a new set of environmental circumstances. Covello quickly became an effective and popular teacher within the Italian-American community.

Covello majored in languages at Columbia, and upon graduation he became a foreign-language teacher at De Witt Clinton High School. His service was interrupted by World War I, during which Covello served as a special information and intelligence officer on the French-Spanish border. When he returned to De Witt Clinton after the war, he received permission to begin an Italian language class. His belief "that the students from the Low or Upper East Side had a right to the spiritual lift that comes from knowing the achievements of one's own people" and his action to get Italian language into the curriculum were part of the movement to break from the strictures of pure "Americanization" and incorporate elements of cultural pluralism in education.

Because of his success, Covello was invited to teach languages at New York University, and there also he introduced a course in Italian. While at New York University he began working on his doctorate, convinced that only when

Italian-Americans assumed leadership roles within the public school system would fundamental changes be made that would assist the thousands of Italian-American children in the city's schools. He began a comprehensive study of the social background of the southern Italian immigrant and discovered that

in the mind of the average Southern Italian immigrant a constant tug-of-war takes place. On the one hand he wants his son to have the advantages of an education never possible for himself, and on the other, centuries of tradition tell him that a boy must work, have responsibility, and contribute to the family. These are not easy to reconcile—school and work. In the average family it leads to a great deal of friction. (165–66)

He also discovered that "the source of cultural strength for any immigrant must be the country of his birth. Until the immigrant can be assimilated to the point where he begins to draw from American sources, he must look backward into the past" (167).

Covello recognized the problems of assimilation, the conflicts facing the first- and second-generation immigrant families, and the necessity of developing a sense of ethnic history and pride. Thus, despite his espousal of education as a necessary means to cultural adjustment, he also advocated cultural pluralism. This dualism is the crucial part of his autobiography. He argues from personal experience that he and his people can, and perhaps should, be both American and Italian. Yet Covello's faith in education never wavered.

In 1933 Covello was appointed principal of the new, experimental Benjamin Franklin High School that was to serve the East Harlem immigrant community. In accord with Covello's educational theories, Benjamin Franklin was to be an experimental school that would relax the rigid structures of most city schools and develop methodologies appropriate for the education of immigrants and their children. The final chapter of *The Heart Is the Teacher* chronicles Covello's success at Benjamin Franklin. Covello even quotes Franklin's own adage, "If a man empties his purse into his head, no one can take it from him. An investment in knowledge always pays the best interest," as a model for his own life and his philosophy as a school principal.

CRITICISM

Leonard Covello was a pioneering member of the Italian-American educational community whose service to his colleagues and students earned him wide respect. Writing in *Studies in Italian American Social History*, Francesco Cordasco observes:

It was Leonard Covello who more than anyone else understood the need for the study of the Italian experience in the United States; and it was he who strove for decades to direct the energies of the Italian community to critical assessments of its needs and prospects in an American society essentially indifferent and hostile to Italian immigrant aspirations....Leonard Covello is a protean figure whose long life and multiplicity of identities with the changing fortunes of the Italian-American community make him both a witness to, and a surrogate for, the Italian-America past. (ix)

During his long and productive life Covello was a teacher, a scholar, and a social activist. *The Heart Is the Teacher* is the autobiography of an immigrant who came to study and encourage study of the immigrant experience. In his narrative Covello addresses two audiences, immigrants and academics, and he provides lessons for both. He teaches the teachers that there is value in the cultures that immigrants bring with them to the United States, and he provides a valuable model for the immigrants and their children. *The Heart Is the Teacher* reaches out from the personal experiences of one man to address universal concerns, and in doing so it has become a popular American autobiography.

BIBLIOGRAPHY

Covello, Leonard. "A High School and Its Immigrant Community." *Journal of Educational Sociology*, February 1936, 333–46.
———. "The School as the Center of Community Life." In *The Community School*, edited by Samuel Everett. New York: Appleton, 1937.
———. "A Community Centered School and the Problems of Housing." *Educational Forum*, January 1943, 133–43.
———. "The Community School in a Great Metropolis." In *Education for Better Living: The Role of the School in Community Improvement*. Washington, D.C.: Government Printing Office, 1957.
———. *The Heart Is the Teacher*. New York: McGraw-Hill, 1958.
———. *The Social Background of the Italo-American School Child: A Study of Southern Italian Family Mores and Their Effect on the School Situation in Italy and America*. Totowa, N.J.: Rowman and Littlefield, 1972.
———, and Francesco Cordasco. *Educational Sociology: A Subject Index of Doctoral Dissertations Completed at American Universities, 1941–1963*. New York: Scarecrow, 1965.
Cordasco, Francesco, and Salvatore La Gumina. *Italians in the United States: A Bibliography of Reports, Texts, Critical Studies, and Related Materials*. New York: Oriole, 1972.
———, ed. *Studies in Italian American Social History: Essays in Honor of Leonard Covello*. Totowa, N.J.: Rowman and Littlefield, 1975.
Holte, James. "Private Lives and Public Faces: Ethnic American Autobiography." *Ethnic Groups* 4, 1–2 (1982): 61–83.
Neidle, Cecyle. *The New Americans*. New York: Twayne, 1967.
Peebles, Robert. "Leonard Covello: An Immigrant's Contribution to New York City." Ph.D. diss., New York University, 1967.

NICKY CRUZ
(1938–   )

Run, Baby, Run

BIOGRAPHY

Nicky Cruz was born in Puerto Rico in 1938. In 1955 his parents sent him to New York City to live with his older brother. On the island Cruz had been brought up by spiritualist parents who practiced a form of witchcraft, and in New York he quickly found school and work boring. He joined a street gang, the Mau Maus, and by 1956 he had become a gang leader. In 1958 Cruz met evangelist David Wilkerson, who was working with ghetto children in New York, and became a Christian. In the early 1960s Cruz attended Bible school in California, and by 1965 he had begun preaching and working with Outreach for Youth. Cruz remains a popular Christian evangelist. His autobiography, *Run, Baby, Run*, has sold over two million copies since 1968, and the fictionalized story of his conversion, *The Cross and the Switchblade*, is a popular novel and a popular film.

THE AUTOBIOGRAPHY

Run, Baby, Run is a religious narrative. Cruz and coauthor Jamie Buckingham use a specific model to organize the material in the text. Cruz sees his experiences as religious and structures them around his conversion in much the same way as Augustine did with his *Confessions* and John Bunyan did in *Grace Abounding to the Chief of Sinners*. These and other conversion narratives are built around the dramatic conversion experience and emphasize the qualitative difference in the life of the autobiographer before and after that conversion. Cruz's intent is didactic; he is less interested in revealing himself as an individual than in presenting his life as an example. Ultimately the center of the narrative is less Nicky Cruz and more the "power of the Holy Spirit" that infuses and transforms him. Daniel Shea, writing in *Spiritual Autobiography in Early America*, points out that "since Paul and Augustine, indeed since Pentecost, Christians have been evangelizing in the first person" (88). In using a conversion experience to evangelize, a writer forms an argument in which he presents evidence from his personal experience in a pattern that details the conversion process and gives witness to a life changed by that conversion. In *Run, Baby, Run* Cruz is not primarily interested in the conversion process itself; rather, he presents himself in his autobiography as a witness to the power of Jesus Christ and the effect of that power on his life.

Run, Baby, Run is also part of another tradition, a tradition begun in colonial New England and carried throughout the development of American literature. Like William Bradford's *History of Plymouth Plantation*, John Winthrop's *History of New England*, and even Cotton Mather's *Magnalia Christi Americana*, Cruz's narrative can be seen as a personal history celebrating God's workings in the new land, workings full of mystery, purpose, and power. Like these writers, Cruz sees God working actively upon individuals to lead a chosen people to salvation, and he presents his own life as but one more example of God's remarkable providences.

Cruz constructs his narrative of dramatic conversion around certain obvious contrasts: his character before his conversion and his character after, the grim setting of the early part of the narrative and the religiously infused setting after, and his criminal activities prior to his conversion and his Christian action after. Also, since Cruz intends to make his conversion as dramatic as possible, the narrative is tightly structured; dramatic incident follows dramatic incident, and action is more important than motivation, at least until the moment of conversion. To heighten the contrast further between the old Cruz and the spiritually reborn Cruz, the autobiography emphasizes the worst aspects of Cruz's life prior to his conversion and the best after. Cruz develops the two-part structure of the narrative by placing the conversion itself at the center of his work. Thus part one presents Cruz's swift descent into the world of crime and sin, while part two chronicles his struggle to make use of his gift and live the life of a born-again Christian.

Since *Run, Baby, Run* is essentially a religious narrative, Cruz is less concerned with the specific problems caused by his being Puerto Rican in New York than he is with the more universal and representative aspects of his life. His crimes, drug experiences, gang leadership, and sexual exploits could have been those of any urban street tough, and his description of his behavior after his conversion serves as an example of how a born-again Christian should act in a contemporary urban environment. Although his concerns are not primarily Puerto Rican, it would be a mistake to assume that the narrative of his life throws no light upon the Puerto Rican experience in America. He is very successful in his re-creation of the prejudice faced by Puerto Ricans in the new land, of the street culture of New York City, of the problems caused by the inability to speak English, of the effects of poverty, and of the shock of the movement from rural Puerto Rico to the streets of New York. Also, Cruz's narrative does demonstrate that some Puerto Ricans do survive and prosper in this country, and that evangelical Christianity, an old and powerful force in America history, has reached America's most recent newcomers.

Cruz opens his narrative with his first American experience. As with many Puerto Ricans and earlier immigrants, the introduction is harsh. The first words that Cruz hears from an American are "pig" and "filthy spic." Cruz then uses the weather to develop a contrast between New York City and Puerto Rico. He first describes the cold streets filled with dirty melting snow and then shifts to a memory of his warm home on the island. The contrast is effective.

While Cruz is careful to build a striking contrast between the island and the city in order to emphasize the shock of the arrival, he does not sentimentalize the island; he calls it a "land of witchcraft and voodoo, of religious superstition and great ignorance" (1). His father, in fact, was a leading spiritualist on the island who sent his son away to New York because he could not control him. As in many ethnic-American autobiographies, the impact of the city upon the newcomer is totally unsettling. Since he speaks no English, Cruz cannot get around the city and is a victim of unfair treatment without even being aware of it. A restaurant owner charges him ten dollars for two hamburgers, leaving him penniless. Cruz then describes how he wanders around the city for a week eating what he can steal and sleeping in doorways and in abandoned buildings until he meets a kindly old man who speaks Spanish and helps him to get in contact with Cruz's older brother, who lives in the city. In the opening chapter of his autobiography Cruz skillfully recreates the first impressions of a stranger in New York: the cold, rudeness, hunger, confusion, and constant sense of motion. Cruz sets the loneliness and the helplessness of the newcomer against the massiveness and indifference of the urban landscape.

Much has been written about the fate of Puerto Rican children in the New York City public schools, and Cruz's depiction of his school experiences is illustrative of much of that material. Cruz describes his black and Puerto Rican school as more like a jail than a school. He chronicles fights and intimidations, drawing a picture of an institution in which the teachers and administrators spend their time in a futile attempt to impose discipline and students spend theirs trying to win or stay out of fights. Cruz decides that school is useless and that his brother is trying to be a father to him, so he leaves both for a life on the streets. There he quickly begins to learn more about urban life. Like other immigrant autobiographers, Cruz comments on the contrast between his expectations and the reality he discovers in New York. The promise of America, which attracts millions, is set against the actual circumstances that the immigrants find on their arrival. In this passage Cruz is both personal and representative:

After two months I still wasn't accustomed to life in New York. Back in Puerto Rico I had seen pictures of the Statue of Liberty and the United Nations Building. But here, in the ghetto, as far as the eye could see there was nothing but apartments, filled with human flesh. Each window symbolized a family, eking out a miserable existence. I thought of the zoo in San Juan with the pacing bears and the chattering monkeys behind bars. They wallow in their own filth. They eat stale meat or wilted lettuce. They fight among themselves and the only time they get together is when they are attacking an intruder. Animals aren't meant to live this way, with only a painted jungle scene on the rear of a cage to remind them of what they are supposed to be. And neither are people. But here, in the ghetto, they do. (30)

Cruz uses this same analogy through the first half of his narrative, effectively creating a sense of the city as a "concrete jungle." In this jungle, survival is the only real priority, and in order to survive on the street Cruz turns to robbery in order to get money for his rent and food. Finally, he joins a street gang, the Mau Maus, in order to have protection and to be part of an effective social unit.

The depictions of his gang activity are the most graphic part of the auto-biography and, from the standpoint of the conversion motif, the most important section of the first part of the narrative, for they show the depths of the degradation into which he sinks prior to his conversion. The gang quickly becomes Cruz's family, his reason for living, and the only social structure for which he has any respect—the one social unit fit to exist and survive in the urban jungle. It provides protection, community, sex, money, drugs, and an escape from the ugly reality of the ghetto for its members. Cruz presents New York as a city of warring gangs, each controlling an area of the city, defending its territory against all outsiders, whether the outsiders are members of rival gangs or the police. Without membership in a gang, an individual cannot survive, and Cruz provides several examples of what happens to people who do not belong. The luckiest get off with a severe beating; the unlucky ones are killed or maimed. Although the gang structure provides much for its members, it also demands much: absolute courage, absolute loyalty, and the ability to undergo a vicious initiation. The depiction of the initiation is of central importance to the narrative because it concretizes the violence that infuses the first part of the autobiography and demonstrates the lengths to which Cruz was willing to go in search of a way to deal with his position as an outsider. Cruz describes the initiation of the new members by Carlos, the leader of the Mau Maus:

"I'm gonna turn and walk twenty steps to the other wall," he said, "you stand right where you are. You say you're a tough kid. Well, we're gonna find out just how tough. When I get to twenty, I'm gonna turn and throw this knife. If you flinch or duck you're chicken. If you don't, even if the knife sticks in you, you're a tough kid and can join the Mau Maus. Got it?" (45)

Cruz effectively combines language and action to create the ever-present threat of violence. When the initiate falters, he is stabbed in both armpits and thrown out into the streets. Rather than being repelled by this violence, Cruz is fascinated by the blood; when it is his turn, he chooses a second method of initiation, fighting five gang members at once. He loses, of course, but he proves himself. When regains consciousness, he is given a pistol and welcomed into the family.

Once he is a member of the family, Cruz quickly rises within it; in less than one year he becomes president of the gang and is its most violent and proficient fighter. Under his leadership the gang engages in mass street wars, numerous robberies, attacks on neighborhood churches, and a suicidal open war against the police. After this reign of terror, he is finally arrested for attacking a policeman, and when taken to the police station he is told:

The only way to handle these S.O.B.'s is to beat the hell out of them. They're all a bunch of filthy, stinking pigs. We got a jail full of niggers, wops, and spics. You're just like all the rest, and if you get out of line, we'll make you wish you were dead. (89)

Cruz responds to this threat with a threat of his own: "Go ahead and hit me, but one day I'm gonna come to your house and kill your wife and your children" (90). Cruz includes this response to indicate how far his alienation had gone; he has declared total war upon society and does not care about the consequences of his actions. At the age of eighteen he has a record of twenty-one arrests, ranging from robbery to assault with intent to kill. This section of the narrative depicts how life in the jungle has taken its toll; when he is brought before the juvenile judge, he is told that he "lives like an animal and acts like an animal." Instead of sending him to prison, however, the judge recommends psychiatric care. It fails, and Cruz returns to the streets.

Cruz places his arrest and the failure of psychiatric care directly before the conversion in his narrative. His comments to the police and his psychiatrist's despair at his behavior mark the limits of his descent. At this point in the narrative he describes himself as barely human, cut off from all people and activities outside of the gang. It appears that the only options for him are prison or death on the streets.

The transformation of Cruz's life is presented in the following chapter, entitled "The Encounter." Here Cruz dramatically describes his confrontation with the Reverend David Wilkerson, love, and the power of God. Wilkerson is a Pentecostal minister specializing in teen crusades in East Coast cities. He has canvassed the Puerto Rican community, advertising a youth crusade directed at Puerto Rican gang members. The Mau Maus are challenged by Wilkerson to attend, and they go, planning to disrupt the meeting. However, in the middle of Wilkerson's sermon on repentance and the power of prayer Cruz is strangely moved. He describes looking into himself for the first time in years and being repulsed by what he sees. For the first time since he was a child, Cruz cries, and under Wilkerson's direction he pours himself out to God. Cruz's comments on his conversion are quite simple:

I opened my mouth, but the words that came out were not mine. "O God, if You love me, come into my life. I'm tired of running. Come in my life and change me. Please change me."

That's all it was. But I felt myself being picked up and swept heavenward.

While some readers might find such a sudden and complete conversion too dramatic or too startling to be realistic, it must be remembered that Cruz is describing a religious and emotional experience, not an intellectual one, and he is describing it within an accepted religious context. In addition, writers of conversion narratives have often employed the convention of a moment of illumination and transformation to describe their conversion experiences. Paul's confrontation on the road to Damascus is the best-known example, of course, and Cruz's conversion is part of that tradition. His narrative is an illustration of just this point: He presents himself prior to his conversion as the product of years of neglect, dissipation, and the influence of the ghetto, yet in one dramatic instant he is changed by the power of God. Cruz does not explain his conversion; he presents it to his audience to take as a matter of faith.

A dramatic change in tone and pace takes place at this point in the narrative. The new direction is established in a conversation that Cruz has with Wilkerson shortly after the conversion. Wilkerson tells Cruz that he will be filled with power and the gifts of the Holy Spirit, and when Cruz asks about the gifts Wilkerson responds with a catechismal definition of Pentecostalism. Cruz, like a good student, asks questions, and Wilkerson provides the correct doctrinal answers. In this passage Wilkerson tells Cruz that he must tarry until he receives his gifts.

The second half of the narrative recounts this tarrying and baptism. Less dramatic and less expressive of elements of the Puerto Rican experience in the United States, it presents Cruz's preparation, baptism, and work for the Lord as a kind of initiation, but in this case the initiation is not into the culture at large, but into a special part of American subculture—Pentecostal Christianity. These events help to strengthen the contrast between the first and second parts of the narrative and place Cruz's actions within the pattern established by earlier ethnic writers by moving him out of the city, providing him with an education, and enabling him to return to the city with a new perspective. Wilkerson sends Cruz to the Bible Institute at La Puente, California, where he studies English and the Bible, practices self-discipline, and finally, while assisting at a Pentecostal mission in Los Angeles, is filled with the Holy Spirit and baptized. With his heart and mind transformed, Cruz returns to New York to establish a ministry within the ghetto from which he came. Like a number of conversion narratives, *Run, Baby, Run* ends pointing toward the future, with Cruz leaving New York with his ministry established, about to perform the Lord's work across the nation.

CRITICISM

Writing in *The Nuyorican Experience: Literature of the Puerto Rican Minority*, Eugene Mohr remarks that Cruz's autobiography has enjoyed a long popularity because, aside from its church sponsorship, "there is an additional appeal in the book's being a double success story: Nicky escapes both a life of sin and life in El Bárrio. And one life is an objective correlative of the other" (68). Almost every commentary about Cruz's work places it within a religious context. Billy Graham, for example, calls the book remarkable because "it has all the elements of a tragedy, violence and intrigue—plus the greatest of all ingredients: the power of the gospel of Jesus Christ" (*Run, Baby, Run*, vii).

Run, Baby, Run is also a work for nonevangelicals. Cruz's autobiography, while an excellent example of the traditional conversion story, provides a stark instance of the impact of New York City and, by extension, urban American culture on a newcomer. It documents the poverty, hostility, and racism that many Spanish-speaking Americans confront. In addition, Cruz shows how a traditional narrative form can be used effectively by a contemporary writer.

BIBLIOGRAPHY

Cruz, Nicky, with Jamie Buckingham. *Run, Baby, Run*. 1968. New York: Jove, 1978.

Cordasco, Francesco, Eugene Bucchioni; and Diego Castellanos. *Puerto Ricans on the United States Mainland: A Bibliography of Reports, Texts, Critical Studies, and Related Materials*. Totowa, N.J.: Rowman and Littlefield, 1972.

Mohr, Eugene. *The Nuyorican Experience: Literature of the Puerto Rican Minority*. Westport, Conn.: Greenwood Press, 1982.

Shea, Daniel. *Spiritual Autobiography in Early America*. Princeton, N.J.: Princeton University Press, 1968.

Wakefield, Dan. *Island in the City: The World of Spanish Harlem*. Boston: Houghton Mifflin, 1959.

JAMES MICHAEL CURLEY
(1874–1958)

I'd Do It Again

BIOGRAPHY

James Michael Curley, four-term mayor of the city of Boston, twice U.S. congressman, and one-term governor of Massachusetts, was one of the major Irish political bosses in American history. Like Richard Daley of Chicago and Christopher Buckley of San Francisco, Curley rose from ward-level offices to control a powerful urban political machine. For over fifty years Curley was a major force in Massachusetts politics.

Curley was born on November 20, 1874, in Boston. His parents, Michael Curley and Sarah Clancy, were immigrants who fled the poverty and starvation of Ireland following the famine of the middle decades of the nineteenth century. After working at a variety of odd jobs and attending Boston Evening High School, Curley entered politics. From 1900 to 1910 he served on the Boston Common Council, in the state legislature, as an alderman, and on the city council. In 1910 he was elected to Congress. He returned to Boston as mayor in 1914, and he was elected to that office three other times: 1922, 1930, and 1947. In addition, Curley was elected governor of Massachusetts in 1935 and returned to Congress in 1943.

Curley's career was by no means a universal success, however. Six times he was defeated when he ran for the office of mayor of Boston, and three times the voters rejected his bid to become governor of Massachusetts. Curley also served two terms in prison. Early in his career he spent sixty days in the Suffolk County Prison for taking a civil service examination for a friend, and in 1947 he served almost half a year in Danbury Prison for mail fraud. In 1949, after his release from prison, he ran for a fifth term as Boston's mayor in a campaign that became the source for Edwin O'Conner's acclaimed novel and John Ford's film *The Last Hurrah*. Curley died in Boston in 1958.

THE AUTOBIOGRAPHY

James Michael Curley's autobiography, *I'd Do It Again: A Record of All My Uproarious Years*, is much more than just the memoirs of a successful politician. Curley's political career began at the turn of the century, when ethnic ward leaders controlled urban neighborhoods with their patronage and often their fists. It ended as television began to change the way political campaigns were conducted. Curley was well acquainted with most of the major Democratic politicians from William Jennings Bryan to John F. Kennedy, and his comments on these and other national leaders make for fascinating reading. More importantly, *I'd Do It Again* provides a record of the transformation of ethnic-American politics with James Michael Curley as the focus. When Curley first ran for public office, the Irish and other ethnic-Americans in eastern and midwestern cities had yet to enter the mainstream of American political life. Curley's rise to power within the Democratic party of Massachusetts parallels the rise of ethnic political power within the United States, culminating with the coalition Franklin Delano Roosevelt put together during the 1930s.

I'd Do It Again is, in addition, a repository of a way of life. In his autobiography Curley records his beliefs, prejudices, and passions. Throughout his narrative Curley continually affirms his faith in the Catholic church, the Democratic party, and the ethnic neighborhood. For Curley, these structures provide support for the average man and stand in opposition to the forces of privilege: Republicans, bankers, Protestants in general, wealthy Boston Protestants in particular, and anything British or connected with Harvard. The way of life that Curley championed changed as Irish-Americans and other ethnics moved into the middle class and out into the suburbs. From there many moved into the mainstream of American culture, and a large number of the white ethnics moved into the Republican party and voted for Richard Nixon in 1968 and 1972 and Ronald Reagan in 1980 and 1984. Curley might not have been surprised by this defection from the Democrats, for although he was a partisan politician and a fanatical Democrat, many of the issues he championed—home, family, religion, anticommunism—have become Republican issues. Curley's successive mayoral defeats in 1949, 1951, and 1955 and the rise of John F. Kennedy, a new-style Irish Democratic candidate who appealed to a much wider audience than Curley, marked the end of an era in American politics. *I'd Do It Again* chronicles the transformation.

James Michael Curley begins his autobiography by defining the autobiographical character he is about to create:

It is as the friend and the defender of the poor, the alien and the persecuted that I hope to be remembered—as the "Mayor of the Poor." (7)

For most of his political life, that meant mayor of the Irish, because when Curley entered politics Boston was perhaps the most class-bound city in the

United States, controlled by a Republican government and swarming with Irish immigrants and their children.

Between 1847 and 1899, the year Curley was first elected to public office, the Irish population of Boston grew, primarily as a result of the famines in Ireland of 1847 and 1867, from 5,000 to over 225,000. In the opening chapters of his autobiography Curley describes the anti-Irish attitude prevalent at that time:

There were signs in office windows telling all the world that "No Irish Need Apply"; and in one instance at least, a bulletin board informed prospective employees: "No Irish or Negroes Wanted." Mayor Fredrick Prince was defeated for re-election in 1877 because he appointed a number of Irishmen to the police force. . . .

Advertisements for maidservants in the staid *Boston Evening Transcript* read, even after the turn of the century: "Maid wanted. Only Protestants need apply." (10–11)

Curley's parents arrived from Ireland in 1864, joining the thousands of other Irish refugees who were about to transform the city of Boston.

Politics was the vehicle for the rise of Curley and the Irish, and the driving force in Boston politics was the ward boss, whom Curley describes as

a community advisor, a combination of padrone, father confessor, employer's agent, foster parent, juvenile court judge, and social service worker. He was a person who worked 365 days a year for the little man, a person who made it unnecessary for the down-and-outer to subject himself to the inquisitional terrors of organized charity. (17)

The ward boss is the central figure in Curley's narrative because Curley's success as a politician was a direct result of his mastery of ward politics and his extending those skills to citywide levels.

Curley's descriptions of ward politics are the most engaging and insightful parts of his autobiography. Other writers have provided accounts of Irish immigration and Irish-American assimilation (Andrew Greeley's *That Most Distressful Nation* and Oscar Handlin's *Immigration as a Factor in American History* are two excellent sources), but no other writer makes the business of neighborhood politics as dramatic as does Curley. He gives his readers a lesson in urban political organization. He and other members of the Boston Democratic party modeled their organization on the famous (and infamous) Tammany Club of New York City. Wards were divided into districts; districts were led by captains who divided their areas into smaller units run by lieutenants. The lieutenants canvassed their territories to get out the vote. The more proficient lieutenants received more patronage from the ward bosses.

Curley describes planning outdoor rallies, parades, and speeches, often relying on organized rooters and ex-boxers to create enthusiasm and silence opponents. These political machines were effective. Prior to an election, a well-run organization usually knew the probable vote total within 10 percent, and the political machine was responsible for keeping registration rolls; if extra votes were needed, they could usually be found.

I'd Do It Again demonstrates how effective a political machine could be, and Curley proves that urban politics was as much a passion as it was a profession. It is clear that Curley loved his work. Curley is also careful to demonstrate the political machine's virtues. The machine was effective, he argues, because it served the people of Boston. Curley sees his political machine and his candidacy for public office as early forms of Franklin Roosevelt's New Deal. Curley cheerfully admits that he has critics, but he answers their complaints by pointing to his results. During his administrations he raised the salaries of public employees, built public hospitals, tore down tenements, and created parks. For Curley, as for Chicago mayor Richard Daley, the political machine was effective because it addressed the needs of the poor and the working class, the majority of the population.

The structure of *I'd Do It Again* changes after Curley describes his organization and rise to political power. The autobiography becomes a more traditional memoir in which Curley records the major events of his life—elections, campaigns, meeting with the pope—and his reactions to those events and the famous people with whom he came in contact. Curley fought with both presidents Roosevelt and Truman, believing that they failed to recognize his proper place in the national Democratic party. Curley responded much more warmly, however, to Father Charles Coughlin, the famous right-wing commentator, and Senator Joseph McCarthy, finding their anti-Communist, Irish Catholic politics a reflection of his own concerns.

Curley concludes his autobiography by looking back over his long life and career and admitting his satisfaction at what he has accomplished. He claims he was just another Boston Irishman who worked his way to the top. He also knows that he was a lot more.

CRITICISM

Two populist themes run throughout *I'd Do It Again*. The first is anti-intellectualism. As Richard Hofstader demonstrated in *Anti-Intellectualism in American Life*, attacks on the educated have always been a part of American culture and politics. Curley, himself primarily self-educated, continually links the forces of reaction and privilege with "over-educated Harvard graduates."

A second populist theme running through Curley's autobiography is the linkage of politics and morality. Curley depicts the home and the church as the twin sources of virtue, and any political system or movement was to be measured by its support of these two foundations of society. According to Curley, government erred when it moved away from the teachings of the Catholic church or when it imposed itself on the concerns of the family.

Curley himself is most widely known as the character upon whom Edwin O'Conner based his famous novel *The Last Hurrah*. In that work the Curley character emerges as a kind, paternal politician whose ethnic roots and concerns no longer attract Boston's voters. The novel and John Ford's equally popular film adaptation turn Curley into a grandfather figure, something his political opponents would have never believed.

James Michael Curley of Boston was a type, a kind of political figure familiar to millions of Americans. His autobiography, while providing a record of his personal accomplishments, is also a history of a significant kind of American electoral politics.

BIBLIOGRAPHY

Curley, James Michael. *I'd Do It Again: A Record of All My Uproarious Years*. Englewood Cliffs, N.J.: Prentice-Hall, 1957.

Angoff, Charles. "Curley and the Boston Irish." *American Mercury* 69 (November 1949): 619–27.

Dineen, Joseph Francis. *Purple Shamrock: The Hon. James Michael Curley of Boston*. New York: Norton, 1949.

Donnelly, Edward Lawrence, ed. *That Man Curley: Being an Interesting and Instructive Journey around, with, and about Doctor James Michael Curley, the Enigmatic Political Figure of Massachusetts*. Boston: Donnelly, 1947.

Greeley, Andrew. *That Most Distressful Nation: The Taming of the American Irish*. Chicago: Quadrangle, 1972.

Handlin, Oscar. *Boston's Immigrants*. Cambridge: Harvard University Press, 1941.

———. *Immigration as a Factor in American History*. Englewood Cliffs, N.J.: Prentice-Hall, 1959.

Hofstader, Richard. *Anti-Intellectualism in American Life*. New York: Knopf, 1963.

O'Connor, Edwin. *The Last Hurrah*. Boston: Little, Brown, 1956.

Thernstrom, Stephan. *The Other Bostonians*. Cambridge: Harvard University Press, 1973.

EMMA GOLDMAN
(1869–1940)

Living My Life

BIOGRAPHY

Emma Goldman was one of the most notorious women in American history. An avowed anarchist, Goldman was accused of attempting to overthrow the government of the United States, assassinate President McKinley, destroy the American family, subvert the sexual morals of the nation, and undermine faith in God. Throughout her life she was a controversial figure, considered a menace by many and a working-class hero by others.

Goldman was born in Kaunas, Lithuania, in 1869. Growing up in czarist Russia, Goldman received the beginnings of a good education and became acquainted with the radical literature that circulated widely throughout the country. After the failure of her father's several business ventures, Goldman emigrated to the United States in 1886, where she settled in Rochester, New York, and married Jacob Kersner. In 1889 she left her husband and moved to New York City to devote herself to the anarchist movement. Four years later she was arrested for inciting a riot and was sentenced to a year in prison. Upon her release she went to Vienna to study nursing and midwifery. In 1901 she returned to the United States and again began to lecture on anarchism, women's rights, and birth control. From 1906 to 1917 Goldman edited *Mother Earth*, the influential radical journal. After the outbreak of World War I, Goldman was arrested and convicted of inducing persons not to register for the draft. After serving two years in federal prison at Jefferson, Missouri, Goldman was deported to the Soviet Union, along with 248 other "dangerous radicals."

In the Soviet Union Goldman discovered that the Bolsheviks were as hostile to anarchism as were the capitalists in the United States. She left the Soviet Union in 1921, living and lecturing in Europe for the next decade. She wrote her autobiography, *Living My Life*, in France in 1931. She returned to the United States in 1934 to conduct a ninety-day lecture tour, and in 1936 she went to republican Spain to help support the government and its anarchist allies in their war with Franco. She died in Toronto, Canada, in 1940, and at her request she was buried in Waldheim Cemetery in Chicago, near the gravesite and monument for the victims of the Haymarket Riot of 1886.

THE AUTOBIOGRAPHY

Emma Goldman, like Benjamin Franklin before her, wrote her autobiography when she discovered that she had unexpected leisure time in Europe. Both Franklin and Goldman wrote at the suggestion of friends, and both Franklin and Goldman created autobiographical works that reveal as much about America as they do about the autobiographers. *The Autobiography of Benjamin Franklin* describes the rise of capitalism in America and the transformation of a child of the Puritans into the father of the work ethic. *Living My Life* chronicles the excesses of American capitalism in the Gilded Age and the development of an articulate political voice. Both autobiographies present America in transition and provide readers with valuable insights into the economic and political history of the United States.

Living My Life presents readers with an eyewitness account of some of the most turbulent events in American history. Between the Civil War and World War I, populist, socialist, and anarchist movements influenced millions of Americans, many of them immigrants or children of immigrants. In her autobiography Goldman captures the social and political ferment of the times and leaves a detailed account of the issues, causes, battles, and personalities that marked the political landscape of America around the turn of the century. In addition, Goldman recreates a narrative voice that demonstrates why she was one of the most effective public speakers of her time.

Goldman begins her narrative with a description of her arrival in New York City after her years in Rochester. This, she asserts, rather than the traditional arrival from Europe, is the real beginning of her life in the United States. She had abandoned her husband and her job in a clothing factory to join the anarchist movement. Prior to this decision, Goldman's experiences in America were typical of those of a recently arrived immigrant. She came to the United States at the age of seventeen, joined her older sister in Rochester, and began working to support herself. In November 1887, however, five of the radical leaders were executed for conspiracy in the assassination of the police officers who had died in the explosion at the mass meeting in Chicago's Haymarket Square the year before. Although the actual bomber was never discovered, eight anarchist leaders of the rally were arrested, and the Chicago district attorney announced in open court that anarchy itself was on trial. Many foreign-language newspapers covered the incident closely, and one in particular, Johann Most's *Die Freiheit*, carried on a crusade defending the accused and calling the trial a frame-up. Goldman writes that she followed the events closely in *Die Freiheit*, and when she read of the execution of the

Haymarket speakers she became convinced that she must leave her husband and job to join the anarchist movement to fight for social justice.

Under the guidance of Most, Goldman quickly became an effective speaker and organizer, addressing audiences in New York and Rochester. She writes that she organized demonstrations on the anniversary of the Haymarket Riot and that she helped set up the first May Day celebrations in the United States.

Although a leader in the anarchist movement for several years, Goldman did not become a national figure until 1892. In May of that year a bitter strike broke out in the Homestead Steel Mills near Pittsburgh between the Carnegie Steel Company and the Amalgamated Association of Iron and Steel Workers. Henry Clay Frick, chairman of the Carnegie Company, closed the steel mills, refused to recognize the union, and evicted the families of the workers from company housing. Goldman and her lover Alexander Berkman made plans to go to Pittsburgh to help the strikers, but before they left New York, word reached them that a number of the strikers had been killed by Pinkerton agents escorting strikebreakers to the mills. Berkman and Goldman changed their plans; they now intended to assassinate Frick.

Goldman provides a dramatic account of their plans, Berkman's shooting of Frick, and the following trial in *Living My Life*, and her depictions read like passages from an adventure novel. Goldman never apologizes for assisting Berkman, asserting that if they had had enough money for two train tickets to Pittsburgh, she would have accompanied him and shared in the actual attempted assassination. Frick survived the shooting, and in the sensational trial that followed Goldman became known as "Red Emma," Berkman's associate. Goldman writes that she was too busy raising funds for Berkman's defense to be flattered by her new notoriety.

After Berkman's conviction and imprisonment, mere belief in anarchy was considered criminal, and Goldman notes that she became a target for special attention. She continued to give speeches on anarchism, and in 1893 she spoke at New York's Union Square and was arrested for urging "revolution, violence, and bloodshed." She was convicted and sentenced to spend a year in prison at Blackwell's Island. Goldman notes in her autobiography that this and her later arrests were without foundation, because although she was an anarchist, she never advocated violence in her speeches. All the prosecution testimony, she asserts, was manufactured.

Like many other political prisoners, Goldman discovered that prison offered her an opportunity to read and learn. Writing of her year at Blackwell's Island, Goldman says:

It was the prison that had proved the best school. A more painful, but a more vital school. Here I had been brought close to the depths and complexities of the human soul; here I found ugliness and beauty, meanness and generosity.... The prison had been the crucible that had tested my faith.... The State of New York could have rendered me no greater service than by sending me to Blackwell's Island Penitentiary. (148)

In prison Goldman discovered another cause. She became an assistant to Dr. White, the prison physician, and after her release she was persuaded by her friends to go to Vienna to study medicine. She learned nursing and obstetrical techniques, and for a time considered entering medical school. She remained in Europe until 1901, when she returned to New York with combined interests in women's rights and anarchism.

Shortly after her return, Leon Czolgosz, a young Polish-American with an interest in anarchism, assassinated President McKinley, and Goldman, as America's most famous anarchist, was implicated. Shortly after the president's death she was confronted by detectives who were shocked at her lack of sympathy for the president. She includes her famous reply to their questions in her autobiography:

"Is it possible," I asked, "that in the entire United States only the President passed away this day? Surely many others have also died at the same time, perhaps in poverty and destitution leaving helpless dependents behind. Why do you expect me to feel more regret for the death of McKinley than of the rest?" (308)

In 1906 Alexander Berkman was released from federal prison and joined Goldman in publishing the radical journal *Mother Earth*. Goldman argues that *Mother Earth* was not a purely anarchist journal, but rather a vehicle for all kinds of radical thought: "It pleaded for freedom and abundance in life as the basis for art. . . . It treated anarchism less as a dogma than as a liberating ideal" (395). Lecturing on women's rights and editing *Mother Earth*, Goldman remained an irritation to conservative America until 1917, when she was arrested and sentenced to prison for obstructing the draft.

In describing her activities prior to the American entrance into World War I, Goldman emphasizes two issues. She writes that during this part of her career she focused her energies on birth control and opposition to conscription. She argues that her belief that women should have control over their own bodies compelled her to undertake lecture tours around the nation providing women with information about birth control. Many cities and states had laws prohibiting the dissemination of such information, and Goldman describes the many times she was attacked by the press or arrested by local police for her advocacy of "immorality."

Of equal importance in the years preceding World War I was Goldman's effort to resist the war. She opposed American entry into the struggle, seeing it as a battle among capitalistic nations in which workers would inevitably be the losers. She organized a no-conscription campaign and fought to keep the United States neutral. After the United States entered the war, Goldman was arrested, convicted, and sentenced to two years in federal prison at Jefferson, Missouri.

Goldman remembers her time in prison as both a period of anticipation and a time of hard work. A network of friends and supporters kept her informed of world events, and she writes that the news of the revolution in Russia filled her with joy. She believed, she says, that the time when the workers of the world would finally unite was at hand. Goldman tempers her optimism with a description of the tedium of prison work. Inmates supported the institution by working in the prison clothing factory, which Goldman describes as one large sweatshop. Shortly after the end of the war and her release from prison, Goldman, along with many other foreign-born radicals, had her citizenship rescinded and was sent to the Soviet Union.

Perhaps because of its harsh criticism of the Soviet Union and the controversy it caused in the American Left, Goldman's account of her experiences in revolutionary Russia is the most famous part of her autobiography. She remembers leaving the United States on the *Buford*, a freighter known as the "Red Ark," thrilled with the opportunity to witness the dawn of what she considered to be the new and benign world order, but she was crushed by what she discovered in the Soviet Union. She expected a land of bread and roses, and she writes that she found a land with the secret police in control and all opposition to the government suppressed. Her anger is clear as she writes:

People raided, imprisoned and shot for their *ideas*! The old and the young held as hostages, every protest gagged, iniquity and favoritism rampant, the best human values betrayed, the very spirit of the revolution daily crucified. . . . I felt chilled to the marrow of my bones. (757)

Goldman describes sadly her discovery that anarchism was as unacceptable to the leaders of the Soviet Union as it was to the leaders of the United States. Neither communism nor capitalism, she argues, could accept a political philosophy that demanded the absolution of all government control and even the dissolution of the state itself. Goldman remembers that John Reed, the American writer whose *Ten Days That Shook the World* proclaimed the birth of the Soviet Union to Western readers, attempted to warn her about what she would discover. Goldman at first refused to take the warning seriously, but after watching dissent being stifled everywhere in Russia, Goldman, disillusioned and angry, left.

In the final sections of her narrative Goldman presents an extended comparison between the United States and the Soviet Union. She proclaims that she loves American people and the ideals that the United States stands for, but that to become a great nation America must match democratic rhetoric with democratic action. America, even when Goldman was in exile, was important to her:

There is still a large place in my heart for my erstwhile country. Regardless of her shabby treatment, my love for all that is ideal, creative and humane in her would not die. But I would rather never see America again if I could do so only by compromising my ideas. (988)

While the failure of American reality to match American ideals disappointed Goldman, the failure of Soviet reality to match Soviet ideals outraged her:

What a comedy on the Communist state outdoing "Uncle Sam." The poor boob went only as far as deporting his foreign-born opponents. Lenin and Company, themselves political refugees from their native land only a short time ago, were now ordering the deportation of Russia's native sons. (913)

CRITICISM

Goldman wrote *Living My Life* while living in Saint-Tropez, France. When it was published in 1931, it caused a major controversy. Opponents of the Soviet Union saw Goldman's denunciation of Lenin and the Bolsheviks as an opportunity for celebration, while supporters of the Soviet Union viewed Goldman's comments as the worst kind of heresy. *Time* magazine and the *New York Times*, for example, praised the autobiography, while the *New Republic* and the *Nation* criticized it. This split of opinion over her autobiography was a reflection of attitudes toward Goldman herself when she lived in the United States. People had strong feelings about her. Radicals and many liberals saw her as a fighter for freedom, while such establishment figures as Theodore Roosevelt and J. Edgar Hoover saw her as a dangerous variation of a common criminal.

Even within the considerable criticism of Goldman and her writing a dualism emerges. Most of the criticism prior to 1970 focuses on Goldman's political activities and writings, while the more recent criticism, in response to the rise in feminism and feminist criticism, focuses on Goldman's activities and writings dealing with women's rights. Two examples of this diversity of criticism are Richard Drinnon's *Rebel in Paradise*, a pioneering biography that places Goldman in the political and social context of the period, and Candace Falk's *Love, Anarchy, and Emma Goldman*, which is a more personal biography of Emma Goldman, the woman.

Living My Life is, ultimately, the autobiography of an activist, and critics have been more interested in Goldman's actions than in her reflections. Nevertheless, *Living My Life* is a significant work. In describing her life and her beliefs, Emma Goldman demonstrates why radical movements were so appealing to large numbers of Americans, foreign-born and native, around the turn of the century. In addition, Goldman writes eloquently of a belief in political and social equality shared by many Americans. Finally, as Edward Corsi, commissioner of immigration at Ellis Island and himself an immigrant, observed, Goldman was one of the most interesting persons to pass through American immigration, and her story and observations are well worth reading.

BIBLIOGRAPHY

Goldman, Emma. *Anarchism and Other Essays*. New York: Mother Earth Publishing, 1910.

———. *The Social Significance of the Modern Drama*. Boston: Richard G. Badger, 1914.

———. *Anarchism on Trial: Speeches of Alexander Berkman and Emma Goldman before the United States District Court in the City of New York, July 1917*. New York: Mother Earth Publishing, 1917.

———. *My Disillusionment in Russia*. London: Daniel, 1925.

———. *Living My Life*, 1931. New York: Da Capo Press, 1970.

———. *Voltairine de Cleyre*. Berkeley Heights, N.J.: Oriole Press, 1932.

———. *Red Emma Speaks: Selected Writings and Speeches of Emma Goldman*. Edited by Alix Kates Shulman. New York: Random House, 1972.

Cook, Blanche Wiesen. "Female Support Networks and Political Activism: Lillian Wald, Crystal Eastman, Emma Goldman." In *A Heritage of Her Own: Toward a New Social History of Women*, edited by Nancy F. Cott and Elizabeth H. Pleck. New York: Simon and Schuster, 1979.

Drinnon, Richard. "Emma Goldman: A Study in American Radicalism." Ph.D. diss., University of Minnesota, 1957.

———. *Rebel in Paradise*. Chicago: University of Chicago Press, 1961.

Falk, Candace. *Love, Anarchy, and Emma Goldman*. New York: Holt, 1984.

Frazer, Winifred L. *E.G. and E.G.O.: Emma Goldman and The Iceman Cometh*. Gainesville: University of Florida Press, 1974.

Ganguli, B. N. *Emma Goldman: Portrait of a Rebel Woman*. Bombay: Allied, 1979.

Harris, Frank, "Emma Goldman, the Famous Anarchist." In *Contemporary Portraits, Fourth Series*. London: Grant Richards, 1924.

Meltzer, Milton. *Bread—and Roses: The Struggle of American Labor, 1865–1915*. New York: Knopf, 1971.

Rosenberg, Karen. "An Autumnal Love of Emma Goldman." *Dissent* 30, Summer 1983, 380–83.

Shulman, Alix Kates. *To the Barricades: The Anarchist Life of Emma Goldman*. New York: Crowell, 1971.

Wexler, Alice. *Emma Goldman: An Intimate Life*. New York: Pantheon, 1984.

ZORA NEALE HURSTON
(1901–1960)

Dust Tracks on a Road

BIOGRAPHY

Zora Neale Hurston, one of the major black writers of the first part of the twentieth century and a dominant figure in the Harlem Renaissance, died penniless and forgotten in Fort Pierce, Florida, in 1960. Since her death, her works have been reissued, and her reputation as a novelist, folklorist, and anthropologist now appears secure. Her life was as dramatic as that of any of her fictive characters. She was born in 1901 in Eatonville, Florida, the first incorporated black town in the United States. After her mother died and her father remarried, she left Eatonville. She was a student at Howard University from 1919 to 1923, and there she began to write. She moved to New York on the advice of Alain Locke, editor of *The New Negro*. There she continued to write and enrolled at Barnard College, where she studied with noted anthropologist Franz Boas.

Her most important work appeared in the 1930s. Hurston organized musicals in Harlem, conducted studies of folklore and anthropology in Florida, Louisiana, and Haiti, and saw the publication of her major works of fiction and folklore: *Jonah's Gourd Vine, Mules and Men, Their Eyes Were Watching God, Tell My Horse*, and *Moses, Man of the Mountain*. In 1942 her autobiography, *Dust Tracks on a Road*, appeared, and in 1948 *Seraph on the Suwanee* was published.

In 1948 Hurston was charged with committing an indecent act with a minor and was arrested. Although the charge was dropped, her career was destroyed. She wrote a series of newspaper articles during the 1950s, but she died in poverty and obscurity in Fort Pierce in 1960.

THE AUTOBIOGRAPHY

Dust Tracks on a Road is an unusual autobiography. Unlike many of the most famous black autobiographers, Hurston does not write as a representative member of an oppressed social group, nor does she depict her life as a struggle against stereotype and oppression. Hurston's narrative is essentially personal; it is the record of a maturing, articulate voice. Unfortunately, it ends in 1942, before her experiences of poverty and discrimination. One wonders how her autobiography would differ if she had published it later in her life.

In the early chapters of *Dust Tracks on a Road* Hurston records a memory of a time and a place; she presents a vision of Eatonville, first as a historian might and then as seen through the eyes of an intelligent child. The historical portrait is straightforward. Eatonville was incorporated in 1886 as the first black town in the United States. Hurston recounts how three ex-Union officers, after returning from an attempt to make fortunes in Brazil after the Civil War, established the town of Maitland, five miles from Orlando. They then decided to begin an experiment in self-government and established Eatonville, just west of Maitland, as a black community.

When Hurston begins describing her own family's life in Eatonville, she shifts tone. The distance disappears, and a folk narrative emerges. Her father, John Hurston, was the Baptist minister in Eatonville and also served several terms as the town's mayor. John Hurston and Zora Neale Hurston battled continually. Her mother advised her to "jump at de sun," to attempt anything. Her father was more conservative and careful, however. He told her that too much spirit was a dangerous thing for a black girl.

Hurston develops her family's struggles within the context of the communal life of Eatonville. She combines the objectivity she learned as an anthropologist at Barnard College with her love of the Eatonville community when she describes her early life. The town, as much as the family, provided Hurston with her sense of self, and it is not surprising that the town, an extended family, becomes the real focus of the early chapters of the autobiography.

When writing about her childhood, Hurston always places herself in relation to other members of her Eatonville family. Even when she describes her birth, she sets it against a ritual of communal activity:

People were digging sweet potatoes, and then it was hogkilling time. Not at our house, but it was going on in general all over the country like, being January and a bit cool. Most people were either butchering for themselves, or off helping other folks do their butchering, which was almost just as good. It is a gay time. A big pot of hasslits cooking with plenty of seasonings, lean slabs of fresh-killed pork frying for the helpers to refresh themselves after the work is done. Over and above being neighborly and giving aid, there is the food, the drinks and the fun of getting together. (36)

Hurston uses the rituals of Eatonville to mark her growth. The center of the town's life was Joe Clarke's store porch, where people gathered to talk, and the center of Hurston's narrative is the porch as well. From that vantage point she recounts stories about her family, friends, and neighbors, moving from the voice of a professional anthropologist to the individual voices of her townspeople.

The opening chapters of *Dust Tracks on a Road* contain the most personal writing in the autobiography. Hurston recreates her childhood with both the clarity of distance and the intimacy of fond remembrance. Eatonville, the source for so many of her other works, becomes the emotional center from which she measures the distances she travels.

Hurston's world changed with the death of her mother. She had always been closer to her mother than to her father, and when she died and Hurston was unable to convince her father to carry out her mother's wishes—not to cover the bedroom clock and to leave the deathbed pillow on the bed— Hurston realized a major change that had taken place:

It seemed as she died that the sun went down on purpose to flee away from me. That hour began my wanderings. Not so much in geography, but in time. Then not so much in time as in spirit.

Mama died at sundown and changed a world. (97)

John Hurston remarried soon and sent his daughter to Jacksonville, Florida, to school. Her wanderings, a prolonged exile from the warmth of Eatonville, had begun.

The central chapters of *Dust Tracks on a Road* chronicle Hurston's physical and intellectual journey from a childhood in a small, black, southern town to maturity in New York at the height of the Harlem Renaissance. As for many other ethnic-Americans, education provided Hurston with the opportunity to move into the mainstream of the culture, and like many ethnic authors, she celebrates American education in her autobiography.

Hurston's love of education began early; she received awards in her Eatonville grade school and developed a passion for reading. In Jacksonville, school helped Hurston survive the transition away from her family and Eatonville. Her teachers and her classes provided her with some continuity in her changing world. She writes that she missed the landscape she knew, however, and even such treats as gingersnaps, cheese, and sour pickles could not replace her home. Hurston depicts school as the focus of her life. Although she held a variety of jobs, including working as a maid for an actress in a traveling show, Hurston's coming of age is marked by her progress in school. First in Jacksonville and then in night classes in Baltimore, Howard University, and finally Barnard, Hurston demonstrated a love of language and a talent for writing.

Hurston's description of her education shows her appreciation of the opportunities provided and her ability to adapt to a variety of environments. She succeeded academically and was at home socially at both traditionally black Howard University and predominantly white Barnard College, and she writes with pride of her education at both. Her life changed as a result of her education. She writes that shortly before graduation "Dr. Boas sent for me and told me that he had arranged a fellowship for me. I was to go south and collect Negro folklore" (179).

Hurston describes her search for black folklore in a chapter entitled "Research." She outlines her initial failure, caused by approaching her subjects and asking, "in careful Barnardese, 'Pardon me, but do you know any folk-tales or folk-songs?' " (183). She then provides examples of some of her "adventures," living in sawmill towns in Polk County, Florida, studying with voodoo priests in Louisiana, and searching for cures in Haiti. In recounting the Polk County songs and stories in particular, Hurston's narrative approaches the immediacy of the early sections; she is at home again in small, black, southern towns, listening and remembering.

This listening and the memories of Eatonville were to become the subject matter of her most successful fiction and folklore collections, *Jonah's Gourd Vine*, *Mules and Men*, and *Their Eyes Were Watching God*, which use autobiographical material to portray a coming of age in a small, black, southern town at the beginning of the twentieth century.

In the final sections of her autobiography, Hurston's tone shifts again. She writes of love, religion, and race. These sections are essentially topical essays, and although Hurston provides some personal information in them, they are curiously detached, as if Hurston were backing away from revealing too much about herself. One passage, however, is illuminating in that it shows Hurston's attitude toward the question of race, which is a buried subtext for most of the narrative:

So I sensed early, that the Negro race was not one band of heavenly love. There was stress and strain inside as well as out. Being black was not enough. It took more than a community of skin color to make your love come down on you. That was the beginning of my peace.

Light came to me when I realized that I did not have to consider any racial group as a whole. God made them duck by duck and that was the only way I could see them. I learned that skins were no measure of what was inside people. So none of the race clichés meant anything anymore. (242–43)

CRITICISM

Zora Neale Hurston's work has been rediscovered, and to the delight of a new generation of readers her major fiction is available. In his excellent literary biography of Hurston, Robert Hemenway recognizes that a serious examination of Hurston's fiction and folklore of black America is just beginning. C. W. E. Bigsby, in *The Black American Writer*, cites Hurston for her artful handling of black folk material, and Darwin Turner, in *In a Minor Chord*, notes that Hurston was both a major black folklorist and the most published black American woman writer of her time. Hurston's work, like that of other ethnic-American writers, is just now beginning to find a place in the changing literary canon of the United States.

Dust Tracks on a Road is a difficult autobiography to classify. At times Hurston's prose is immediate, sensual, and playful, but at other times it is reserved and formal. In addition, despite Hurston's assertions that race was not an issue in her life, the Eatonville and folklore sections of her narrative indicate that it was, not only as the source for her best material but also as a dramatic influence on Hurston herself. *Dust Tracks on a Road* presents a contradiction. Perhaps because Hurston addresses both black and white audiences, or perhaps because the autobiography reflects the contradiction of a culture that endorsed with equal fervor notions of racial segregation and individual opportunity, the autobiography does not resolve itself. Perhaps its author never resolved herself either.

BIBLIOGRAPHY

Hurston, Zora Neale. *Jonah's Gourd Vine*. Philadelphia: Lippincott, 1934. Reprint. Philadelphia: Lippincott, 1971.

———. *Mules and Men*. Philadelphia: Lippincott, 1935. Reprint. New York: Negro Universities Press, 1969. Reprint. New York: Harper and Row, 1970.

———. *Their Eyes Were Watching God*. Philadelphia: Lippincott, 1937. Rerprint. Greenwich, Conn.: Fawcett, 1965. Reprint. New York: Negro Universities Press, 1969. Reprint. Urbana: University of Illinois Press, 1978.

———. *Tell My Horse*. Philadelphia: Lippincott, 1938.

———. *Moses, Man of the Mountain*. Philadelphia: Lippincott, 1939. Reprint. New York: Arno Press, 1969. Reprint. Philadelphia: Lippincott, 1971.

———. *Dust Tracks on a Road*. Philadelphia: Lippincott, 1942. Reprint. New York: Arno Press, 1969. Reprint. Philadelphia: Lippincott, 1971.

———. *Seraph on the Suwanee*. New York: Scribner's, 1948. Reprint. New York: AMS Press, 1974.

Bigsby, C. W. E., ed. *The Black American Writer*. 1969. Baltimore: Penguin, 1971.

Butterfield, Stephen. *Black Autobiography in America*. Amherst: University of Massachusetts Press, 1974.

Hemenway, Robert. *Zora Neale Hurston: A Literary Biography*. Urbana: University of Illinois Press, 1977.

Neal, Larry. "A Profile: Zora Neale Hurston." *Southern Exposure* 1 (1974).

Rayson, Ann. "*Dust Tracks on a Road*: Zora Neale Hurston and the Form of Black Autobiography." *Negro American Literature Forum* 7 (1973).

Turner, Darwin. *In a Minor Chord*. Carbondale: Southern Illinois University Press, 1971.

LEE IACOCCA
(1924–   )

Iacocca

BIOGRAPHY

Lido Anthony Iacocca was born on October 15, 1924, the son of Italian immigrants. His father, Nicola Iacocca, was a successful businessman until the Depression took its toll on the family finances. Iacocca graduated from Allentown High School in 1942 and went to Lehigh University to study engineering. He graduated in 1945 and then attended Princeton, where he earned a masters degree in mechanical engineering.

Iacocca always wanted to be an automobile executive, and upon graduation he began to work for the Ford Motor Company. He soon left engineering for sales, and operating from Chester, Pennsylvania, he launched a number of successful sales campaigns. He quickly rose within the company and was transferred to Ford's headquarters in Dearborn, Michigan. There Iacocca became a protégé of Ford president Robert McNamara and was named company vice president and general manager of the Ford division in 1960.

Iacocca's major success of the 1960s was the design and promotion of the Ford Mustang, which proved to be the company's largest seller since World War II. In 1970 Henry Ford II named Iacocca Ford president.

Despite Iacocca's success at Ford, he and company chairman Henry Ford were never comfortable, and in 1978 Ford fired Iacocca, who immediately joined the Chrysler Corporation. As the new head of Chrysler, Iacocca faced problems of funding, staffing, and automobile quality. He first began reorganizing the company and then led the fight to have the federal government provide over one billion dollars in loan guarantees to keep Chrysler solvent. After considerable debate, the government agreed, and Iacocca was able to transform Chrysler into a profitable company and repay the loans ahead of schedule.

In the 1980s Iacocca remains a visible figure. Several best-selling books have been written about him, and President Reagan named him chairman of

the Statue of Liberty–Ellis Island Centennial Commission. He was later relieved of that office but remained the head of the fundraising commission.
Despite denials of interest, Iacocca has attracted attention as a presidential
candidate.

THE AUTOBIOGRAPHY

When *Iacocca: An Autobiography* appeared in 1984, it quickly became a
best-seller. The success of the autobiography was not a surprise; Iacocca had
been for a number of years the most public of American corporate heads.
His battles with Henry Ford and with a reluctant Congress as well as his
personal advertising for Chrysler had made Iacocca a cultural hero. In addition, he was the son of immigrants and had risen to the highest ranks of
American business. Readers expected a narrative of success that extolled the
American Dream, and Iacocca provided it for them. *Iacocca* is a success
narrative, a form of the autobiography popular in the late nineteenth century
and one adopted by such well-known ethnic autobiographers as Andrew
Carnegie and Edward Bok. The traditional American narrative of success
chronicles the autobiographer's rise from poverty and obscurity to a position
of wealth and celebrity in the culture, and in so doing it celebrates both the
virtues of the writer and the opportunities provided by America. Lee Iacocca
is well aware of the form he is using. In his prologue he writes that his story
will be a narrative of success, but one with a twist. He will write of a rise
and a fall followed by an even greater rise. Drawing on the tradition of
Carnegie, Franklin, and Alger, Iacocca provides his readers with an edifying
narrative of struggle and success. He appropriately calls his first section "Made
in America."

Like many other ethnic autobiographers, Iacocca begins his narrative with
a description of life in the old country and the voyage and arrival of the
family in the new land. Iacocca writes that his father, Nicola, had come to
America from San Marco, a town twenty-five miles from Naples. He was,
Iacocca observes, like so many immigrants, full of ambition and hope, and
when he arrived in 1902, one of the millions who came to Ellis Island that
year, he was poor and alone but had the Statue of Liberty to inspire him.
Iacocca's use of the Statue of Liberty at the beginning of his autobiography
is deliberate; he will use it as a symbol for what America offers throughout
his narrative, and when he describes his own role as chairman of the Statue
of Liberty–Ellis Island Commission at the end of his autobiography, Iacocca
emphasizes not only his own success but also the potential for success for
all immigrants and their children.

In describing his family Iacocca stresses traditional values and virtues—
his father worked hard to support the family and his mother ran the household
efficiently. His father was a success; he owned several movie houses in Allentown, Pennsylvania, owned and operated a restaurant there, and made

money in real estate. Iacocca remembers that for a few years the family was wealthy, but then the Depression hit.

Iacocca's father lost his theaters and real estate holdings, and Iacocca remembers that the hard times made his mother an even more important figure in the family. He describes her efforts to keep the family well fed despite having almost no money and her willingness to look for work outside the home to make ends meet.

Iacocca's depiction of the family's economic difficulties and his parents' hard work establishes the point from which his own rise will begin. Iacocca, like many other ethnic-American writers, credits education with providing a way into the mainstream of American culture, and the second part of the autobiography describes his own education.

Iacocca begins charting his journey by describing his own alienation:

I was eleven before I learned we were Italian. Until then, I knew we came from a real country but I didn't know what it was called—or even where it was. I remember actually looking on a map of Europe for places called Dago and Wop. (13)

Even though ethnic slurs continued throughout Iacocca's education, he recalls that "school was a very happy place for me" (15). He also admits that he was a good student, graduating from high school near the top of his class.

Iacocca graduated from high school in 1942, and while most of his classmates were called up into the military, Iacocca, who had had rheumatic fever as a child, received a medical deferment and decided to study engineering in college. He chose Lehigh because of its reputation in engineering and because it was only half an hour away from his family's home.

At Lehigh, and later at Princeton, Iacocca was lucky. As more and more students were drafted, his classes became smaller, and as a result he had the opportunity to take seminars with the best engineering faculty on both campuses. Because of his education and the dedication to hard work inspired by his father, Iacocca was ready for his job with Ford.

Iacocca's account of his rise from student engineer to company president provides the central narrative movement for the autobiography, and as Iacocca charts his climb up the corporate ladder he provides a commentary on both his own personal success and the role of the automobile industry in American society. The second issue, the relationship of American industry to American culture, will become Iacocca's main concern in the later sections of his narrative as he details his work as the head of Chrysler, but in the early sections it is an important frame of reference for Iacocca's chronicle of his rise to wealth.

Iacocca's apprenticeship at Ford began with a loop training course, which provided new engineers with experience in all phases of automobile manufacturing from mining coal and lime to working on the assembly line. Iacocca remembers that "it was the best place in the world to learn how cars were really made and how the industrial process worked" (29). After nine months, however, he realized that he wanted to work in marketing rather than engineering because he "liked working with people more than machines" (31).

This move to marketing proved to be a wise one for Iacocca. In the years immediately following World War II, demand for cars was strong since there had been no automobile production during the war. Iacocca's timing was perfect. By 1949 he was a zone manager in Wilkes-Barre, Pennsylvania, working with eighteen Ford dealers, and it was there that he learned the crucial lesson of the automobile business: The dealers were at the heart of the American automobile industry because they represented the company to the consumers, and they were the people who were actually selling and servicing cars. Iacocca kept the dealers in mind, especially in 1956 when his promotional campaign "56 for 56," which encouraged dealers to sell cars for 20 percent down and monthly payments of just $56, helped Ford sell an additional 75,000 cars. Iacocca's marketing skills were recognized in Detroit, and late in 1956 Ford president Robert McNamara brought Iacocca to company headquarters as national truck-marketing manager. By 1960 he was head of the Ford division,

"the general manager of the biggest division in the world's second largest company. Half the people at Ford didn't know who I was. The other half couldn't pronounce my name. (46)

In the following sections of the autobiography Iacocca describes his continued success at Ford, highlighted by his development and marketing of the Mustang. By 1974 Iacocca was president of the Ford Motor Company, second only to Henry Ford himself, and as Iacocca records his work as head of Ford during the turbulent decade of the 1970s, the autobiography becomes an exposé.

Iacocca's fall from grace at Ford was as swift as his rise, and his account of his confrontation with Henry Ford is the most dramatic part of the autobiography. Iacocca describes Ford as a rich, spoiled playboy who runs the company for his own ends. Looking back, Iacocca says that he should have been aware of the confrontation much earlier, but at the time Ford's increasing hostility took him by surprise. When he was let go in 1978, Iacocca was relieved.

Had Iacocca ended his narrative here, it would have been a conventional tragedy, the rise and fall of a man who, through no fault of his own, is confronted by circumstances that overwhelm him. Iacocca was not, however, overwhelmed. After leaving Ford, he joined Chrysler and brought that failing company back to health, with, of course, a good deal of help from the federal government.

The Chrysler section of Iacocca's autobiography details the best-known phase of Iacocca's life. Chrysler's economic troubles, its struggles to get government-backed financing, and Iacocca's eventual success have all been fully documented elsewhere. In addition, Iacocca himself appears as a public spokesman for Chrysler products on television, so there is little new information in this part of the autobiography. There is, however, a revealing look at Iacocca himself and his views.

Iacocca, after describing his move to Chrysler, concentrates on his campaign to secure loans for his new company. He begins by summarizing the views of those opposed to aid to Chrysler:

For most of them, federal help for Chrysler constituted a sacrilege, a heresy, a repudiation of the religion of corporate America. The aphorisms started flowing like water and the old clichés got dusted off. Ours is a profit and loss system. Liquidation and closedowns are the healthy catharsis of an efficient market. A loan guarantee violates the spirit of free enterprise. It rewards failure. It weakens the discipline of the marketplace. Water seeks its own level. Survival of the fittest. Don't change the rules in the middle of the game. A society without risk is a society without reward. Failure is to capitalism what hell is to Christianity. Laissez-faire forever. And other assorted bullshit! (202)

Against this chorus of disapproval, Iacocca mounted a successful campaign to save Chrysler, arguing that the loss of jobs caused by Chrysler's bankruptcy would devastate the economy. In describing himself at Chrysler, first as representative to an unwilling government and then as spokesman for Chrysler products, Iacocca emerges not only as a corporate success but also as a man capable of changing his ideas to conform with the world around him. Corporation heads do not ask the government for money or peddle their products themselves. Iacocca did, and in the process became the best-known corporate executive in the United States.

In the final sections of the autobiography Iacocca turns from his own life story to an analysis of contemporary America. He writes, for example, of his awe at the power of television to sell products and ideas. He argues that in order to survive as an industrial nation the United States must have a coordinated industrial policy, and looking back at his own history he writes:

As someone who comes from a family of hardworking immigrants, I'm a strong believer in the dignity of labor. As far as I'm concerned, working people should be well paid for their time and effort. I'm certainly not a socialist, but I am in favor of sharing the wealth—as long as the company is making money. (303).

Like many other ethnic autobiographers, Iacocca ends his narrative on a celebratory note. His final chapter, "The Great Lady," is a hymn to ethnic America with the Statue of Liberty serving as the unifying image. Iacocca, seeing himself as a representative of ethnic-American success, summarizes his view of American life:

Hard work, the dignity of labor, the fight for what's right—these are the things the Statue of Liberty and Ellis Island stand for. (340)

He then urges his readers, as Horatio Alger would, to work hard and be grateful for living in such a free society.

CRITICISM

Response to the publication of *Iacocca: An Autobiography* was immediate and positive. Robert Townsend, in the *New York Times*, wrote, "Lee Iacocca is as American as the Statue of Liberty—both have their origins in Europe. Every mother who has sons or daughters headed for a business career will want to give them *Iacocca* for Christmas." Bernard Weisberger, in the *Washington Post*, called the autobiography "strong, illuminating, and a rousing read." And Robert Lekachman, writing in the *Nation*, noted the *Iacocca* is an unusually candid book by a rare adult who is capable of changing his mind.

Most reviewers observed that the confrontation between Iacocca and Ford was the most dramatic element in the narrative, but they also stressed the didactic nature of the autobiography—the success narrative of an ethnic-American would attract readers. Perhaps one of the most insightful commentaries was provided by Barry Gewen in the *New Leader*. Gewen noted that there were three reasons for the immediate popularity of *Iacocca*: scandal, business advice, and commentary on the relationship between politics and business. He dismisses the first two as "bad reasons," and focuses on the more serious elements of the autobiography that call into question platitudes about free enterprise and a marketplace economy.

A successful autobiography does more than provide the details of the life of a man or a woman; it creates a picture of a particular time and place and emphasizes certain fundamental ideas that shape the narrative. *Iacocca* is a success for these reasons; it goes beyond fame and the mere celebration of success to restate some of the basic values of American culture: belief in hard work, family, and ethnic identity. In some ways *Iacocca* is a very old-fashioned autobiography, and that is part of its appeal.

BIBLIOGRAPHY

Iacocca, Lee, with William Novak. *Iacocca: An Autobiography*. New York: Bantam, 1984.

Abodaher, David. *Iacocca*. New York: Macmillan, 1982.

Adams, Cindy. "Lee Iacocca in High Gear!" *Ladies' Home Journal* 103 (March 1986): 32–37.

Anderson, K. "A Spunky Tycoon Turned Superstar." *Time* 125 (April 1, 1985): 37–46.

Gewen, Barry. "The Education of Lee Iacocca." *New Leader* 67 (December 10, 1984): 3–4.

Glassman, J. K. "The Iacocca Mystique." *New Republic* 191 (July 16–23, 1984): 20–23.
Gordon, Maynard. *The Iacocca Management Technique*. New York: Dodd, Mead, 1985.
Hall, Stephen. "Italian-Americans Coming into Their Own." *New York Times Magazine*
    132 (May 15, 1983): 28+.
Lekachman, Robert. "Executive Sweets." *Nation* 239 (November 17, 1984): 523–25.
Moritz, Michael, and Barrett Seaman. *Going for Broke: Lee Iacocca's Battle to Save
    Chrysler*. Garden City, N.Y.: Doubleday, 1984.
Review of *Iacocca*. *Commentary* 79 (May 1985): 74–77.
Review of *Iacocca*. *New Republic* 192 (May 15, 1985): 23–28.
Review of *Iacocca*. *New York Review of Books* 33 (April 10, 1986): 11+.
Review of *Iacocca*. *New York Times Book Review* 89 (November 11, 1984): 30.
Spitz, Bob. "Mr. America." *Life* 9 (June 1986): 34–42.
Townsend, Robert. "Chrysler's Hard Charger." *New York Times*, December 23, 1984,
    30.
Weisberger, Bernard A. "The Man Who Saved Chrysler." *Washington Post*, October
    28, 1984, 5–6.

MAXINE HONG KINGSTON
(1940–   )

The Woman Warrior

BIOGRAPHY

Maxine Hong Kingston was born in Stockton, California, on October 27, 1940. Her father, Thomas Hong, ran a laundry with his wife, Ying Lan, who also practiced midwifery. After attending public schools in Stockton, Kingston enrolled at the University of California, Berkeley, where she graduated in 1962. In the same year she married actor Earl Kingston.

She began teaching English and mathematics at Sunset High School in Hayward, California, in 1965. In 1967 she moved to Hawaii, where she taught English and language arts for ten years at various local schools. In 1977 Kingston was appointed visiting associate professor of English at the University of Hawaii, Honolulu.

Kingston's autobiography, *The Woman Warrior: Memoirs of a Girlhood among Ghosts*, a moving narrative of coming of age as a Chinese-American woman, appeared in 1976 to popular and critical acclaim. It received the general nonfiction award from the National Book Critics Circle in 1976, and in 1979 *Time* called it one of the ten best nonfiction works of the decade. In 1980 Kingston completed a second book about Chinese-American life, *China Men*, which became a Book-of-the-Month Club selection.

In 1980 Kingston was named a "Living Treasure of Hawaii" and a National Education Association writing fellow. She continues to live in Hawaii and is working on a novel.

THE AUTOBIOGRAPHY

The Woman Warrior is a complex autobiography, combining legend, myth, history, and personal experience. In her examination of what it means to be a Chinese-American woman in the middle decades of the twentieth century, Kingston employs a variety of narrative techniques, combining fact and fiction to re-create the consciousness of a sensitive and imaginative young woman caught between two cultures. Kingston's narrative voice, that of a young woman searching out truth in the stories her mother tells her about China and her own observations about America, leads readers through a recollection of a childhood dominated by alienation and ambiguity.

Kingston divides her autobiography into five sections, and each is a reflection of one of the influences that shaped her life. The first section is called "No Name Woman," and Kingston begins her narrative with a provocative and ironic warning:

"You must not tell anyone," my mother said, "what I am about to tell you. In China your father had a sister who killed herself. She jumped into the family well. We say that your father has all brothers because it is as if she had never been born." (3)

The Woman Warrior, like many autobiographies, is a narrative constructed around the development of an identity, and in "No Name Woman" Kingston provides her readers with one of the models for her own developing identity.

The No Name Woman, or her "Father's-drowned-in-the-well-sister," provides a warning for Kingston. Her mother tells her the story as an example of the fate of women in China before the revolution and as a lesson in virtue for the women in the family. Kingston, however, retells the story in a different way.

In her mother's version, No Name Women is a victim of male oppression. After her husband left the home village in China, Kingston's aunt became pregnant. She told no one the name of the father, and on the night her child was born the villagers stormed into the family house, breaking furniture, killing livestock, and scattering the family's food in order to drive away the evil spirits brought down on the village by Kingston's aunt's crime. Later that night the aunt threw herself and her new-born child into the village well.

Kingston's mother follows the story with her admonition:

"Don't let your father know that I told you. He denies her. Now that you have started to menstruate, what happened to her could happen to you. Don't humiliate us. You wouldn't like to be forgotten as if you had never been born. The villages are watchful." (5)

Kingston herself draws a different lesson. She wonders if her anonymous aunt had been raped or seduced and if she loved the father of her child. She eventually comes to see the suicide as an act of defiance and her aunt as a hero.

Kingston recounts that "night after night my mother would talkstory until we fell asleep" (24). The stories provided models, and Kingston writes that Chinese girls learned from adult stories that they failed if they grew up to be wives and slaves. The could grow up to be heroes.

Kingston continues to re-create the complexities she faced as she recalls the story of Fa Mu Lan, the legendary young girl who took her father's place in battle and became the famous woman warrior who avenged the wrongs of her people. In the second section of the autobiography, "White Tigers," Kingston retells the tale her mother often told from the first person; Kingston becomes Fa Mu Lan, and the autobiography becomes legend. In Kingston's version of the Fa Mu Lan story, elements of Chinese legend, American culture, and myth combine to create a character who becomes the ideal model for Kingston.

Like other legendary heroes, Fa Mu Lan is taken from her family and initiated into the ways of power and wisdom. After years of trial and education she returns to her native village and her family. She takes her father's place in the army, and with the knowledge and power she has acquired she first becomes general of the army and then overcomes the warlords and landlords who have been terrorizing the ordinary Chinese people. Finally Fa Mu Lan returns to the home of her husband and submits herself to her in-laws:

Wearing my black embroidered wedding coat, I knelt at my parents-in-law's feet, as I would have done as a bride. "Now my public duties are finished," I said. "I will stay with you, doing farmwork and housework, and giving you more sons." (53–54)

Fa Mu Lan is a projection of the narrator's desires. She is both powerful avenger and obedient daughter and wife. In legend Kingston finds an answer to the questions of identity that face her.

The problems of identity continue in the third section of the narrative, "Shaman," as Kingston details the history of Brave Orchid, her mother. Brave Orchid's story is also one of identity and dislocation. Prior to coming to the United States in 1940 to join her husband, Brave Orchid had studied for two years at the To Keung School of Midwifery, where she had demonstrated "through oral and written examination, her Proficiency in Midwifery, Pediatrics, Gynecology, 'Medicine,' 'Surgery,' Therapeutics, Ophthalmology, Bacteriology, Dermatology, Nursing, and Bandage" (68). Returning from school, "she wore a silk robe and western shoes with big heels, and she rode home carried in a sedan chair. She had gone away ordinary and come back miraculous" (90). When she left for America she reversed the process: She left miraculous and arrived ordinary. Instead of a doctor she was a wife and a mother, someone who worked in the family laundry and cooked the family's food.

Despite her apparent loss of status, Brave Orchid remains a strong figure in the narrative. She provides her daughter with advice, an example, and, most importantly, the stories that inspire her. Professionally Brave Orchid may have fallen far in coming to America, but personally she has not. Just as Fa Mu Lan's heroism is a balance to No Name Woman's suicide, Brave Orchid's courage in facing an alien culture is balanced by the fear felt by her sister, Moon Orchid.

For thirty years, Moon Orchid has received money from her husband in America, a successful physician living in Los Angeles with his second wife. When Brave Orchid forces her to confront her husband, she is dismissed. Her husband, who never wrote to tell her he wasn't going to return and wasn't going to send for her, explains: "It's as if I had turned into a different person. The new life around me was so complete; it pulled me away. You became people in a book I had read a long time ago" (179). Unlike her sister, Moon Orchid is not able to survive the challenges of the strange new land, and she spends the rest of her life in a California asylum.

In the final section of the narrative Kingston pulls together all of the influences on her life. "A Song for a Barbarian Reed Pipe," which at first appears to be a memoir of the narrator's young education, is actually the center of the autobiography, for in it Kingston demonstrates how No Name Woman, Moon Orchid, Fa Mu Lan, Brave Orchid, American reality, and Chinese heritage affected her.

Throughout this section, as throughout the entire autobiography, there is a consistent doubling. Elaine Kim observes in *Asian American Literature*:

The narrator of *The Woman Warrior* "sees double" almost all the time: she has two vantage points, and the images are blurred. Continually confronted with dualities, contradictions, and paradoxes, she struggles to discern "what is real" from what is illusory by asking questions, trying to name the unnamed, and "speaking the unspeakable." (199)

Kingston's two vantage points are, of course, Chinese heritage and American cultural and personal reality. As she chronicles her painful movement into American culture, a movement encouraged and made more traumatic by the public school system, she discovers that Chinese and American cultures are sending her contradictory messages.

Growing up Chinese-American creates a series of questions that Kingston must confront. First, of course, is the question of Chinese-American identity. School, the official agency of the culture, provides her with one set of standards: She should speak loudly, be aggressive, and mix socially with her classmates. Her immigrant parents, on the other hand, have quite different standards: She should be formal, obedient, and well behaved. In perhaps the most moving scene in her autobiography, Kingston describes her encounter with another young Chinese-American girl who refused to speak at school. Her anger at her fellow student is clearly displaced self-hatred, and Kingston's description of the confrontation between the two girls is a metaphor for the conflicts within a Chinese-American child.

Even within the culture inherited from China, Kingston receives ambiguous advice. On one hand, Chinese tradition asserts that women are of little value. Kingston's great-grandfather, when he watches his great-granddaughters eating, cries, "Maggots! Where are my grandsons? I want grandsons." And throughout the autobiography Kingston quotes familiar Chinese sayings that assert that girls are useless, such as "Feeding girls is like feeding cowbirds," and "Better to raise geese than girls."

Finally, then, Kingston writes about a double displacement: being Chinese in America and being a woman in a male culture. Because of these distances, Kingston feels isolated, neither Chinese nor American, neither an outcast nor a hero. The autobiography becomes, then, a journal of discovery in which the narrator records her search for a viable identity.

CRITICISM

Reviewers responded immediately and positively to the publication of *The Woman Warrior* in 1976. Major reviews appeared in such important sources as the *New York Times*, the *Washington Post*, *Time*, the *New York Review of Books*, and the *New Yorker*. Most of the reviewers praised Kingston for her depiction of her struggle for identity as an ethnic-American woman and for her imaginative blending of literary forms. Later critical responses have agreed with these early assessments.

Like the initial reviews, the criticism of *The Woman Warrior* has been almost universally positive. In *Asian American Literature: An Introduction to the Writings and Their Social Context*, Elaine Kim notes that Chinese-American writers Frank Chin and Jeffery Paul Chan accuse Kingston of attempting to "cash in on a feminist fad" and that the Chinese-American writer and psychologist Ben Tong classifies Kingston's work as "white-pleasing autobiography passing for pop cultural anthropology" and accuses her of "selling out her own people" (198). Kim's own comment, however, reflects the attitude of most critics:

A comprehensive look at *The Woman Warrior* and at *China Men* (1980) reveals that Kingston is never anti-male. Moreover, it can be said that she shares the fundamental concerns expressed in literature by Asian American men: *The Women Warrior* is an attempt to sort out what being a Chinese American means, and *China Men* lays claim to America for Chinese Americans, thereby permanently reconciling the immigrant and American-born Chinese. (199)

Cheng Lok Chua agrees. In "Golden Mountain: Chinese Versions of the American Dream in Lin Yutang, Louis Chu, and Maxine Hong Kingston," Chua observes that Kingston's books show how the Chinese-American immigrant's dream of acquiring wealth

has given place to a concern that is much more in the mainstream of contemporary American intellectual life—the quest for identity. Kingston emphasizes three aspects of this quest: the quest for identity as a woman, as a writer, and as an American. (46)

The Woman Warrior is a major work and has been recognized as such. Like many other contemporary American writers, Kingston is concerned with the problem of identity, the role of sex, race, and class in American culture, and the discovery of a form with which to tell her story. Like Norman Mailer and Truman Capote, Kingston combines elements of fact and fiction in her narrative, and like them she succeeds dramatically.

BIBLIOGRAPHY

Kingston, Maxine Hong. *The Woman Warrior: Memoirs of A Girlhood among Ghosts.* New York: Knopf, 1976; Vintage, 1977.

———. *China Men.* New York: Knopf, 1980.

Blackburn, Sara. "Notes of a Chinese Daughter." *Ms.*, January 1977, 39–40.

Chua, Cheng Lok. "Golden Mountain: Chinese Versions of the American Dream in Lin Yutang, Louis Chu, and Maxine Hong Kingston." *Ethnic Groups* 4 (1982): 39–40.

Didion, Joan. Review of *The Woman Warrior. Booklist* 73, 5 (1976): 385.

———. Review of *The Woman Warrior. Kirkus Review* 44, 14 (1976): 826.

Fong, Kathryn M. "Woman's Review of 'Woman Warrior.' " *San Francisco Journal*, January 25, 1978, 6.

Gray, Paul. "Book of Changes." *Time* 108 (December 23, 1976): 91.

Kim, Eliane H. *Asian American Literature: An Introduction to the Writings and Their Social Context.* Philadelphia: Temple University Press, 1982.

Levy, Audrey. Review of *The Woman Warrior. Books West* 1 (April 1977): 27.

McPherson, William. "Ghosts from the Middle Kingdom." *Washington Post Book World*, October 10, 1976, E1.

Malloy, Michael. " 'The Woman Warrior': On Growing Up Chinese, Female, and Bitter." *National Observer*, October 9, 1976, 25.

Methewson, Ruth. "Ghost Stories." *New Leader* 60 (1977): 14–15.

Robertson, Nan. " 'Ghosts' of Girlhood Lift Obscure Book to Peak of Acclaim." *New York Times*, February 12, 1977, 26.

Tong, Benjamin R. "On the 'Recovery' of Chinese American Culture." *San Francisco Journal* 4, 45 (1980): 5–7.

Wakeman, Frederick. "Chinese Ghost Story."*New York Review of Books* 27, 13 (1976): 42–44.

Wong, Sharon. Review of *The Woman Warrior. Library Journal* 101 (1976): 1849.

———. "Woman Warrior: Real Oppressions But No Answers." *Equality* 1, 3 (1978): 1.

MALCOLM X
(1925–1965)

The Autobiography of Malcolm X

BIOGRAPHY

Malcolm X was born on May 29, 1925, in Omaha, Nebraska. His father, the Reverend Earl Little, was a Baptist minister and an organizer for Marcus Garvey's Universal Negro Improvement Association. Little moved his family to Lansing, Michigan, shortly after Malcolm was born. In 1931 Malcolm's father died, and after struggling to keep the family together, Malcolm's mother was committed to the Michigan State Mental Hospital in Kalamazoo. The Little children were sent to live in foster homes, and in 1941 Malcolm moved to Boston at the invitation of his aunt.

In Boston Malcolm discovered both the black bourgeoisie and black street life. He was immediately attracted to the latter, and in Boston and later in New York Malcolm alternated ordinary jobs with a career as a street hustler. In 1946 he was arrested for robbery, and after his conviction he was sentenced to serve ten years.

While serving his sentence, Malcolm became aware of the teachings of Elijah Muhammed, and through the influence of his brother he became a member of the Nation of Islam. In addition, he used his time in prison to educate himself, reading widely in philosophy and history. Upon his release he became a spokesman for the Nation of Islam, and he quickly rose to the position of an influential and powerful leader within the Black Muslim community.

Malcolm began his organizational work in Harlem in 1954, and by the early 1960s he had become one of the best-known black spokesmen in the United States. He eventually disassociated himself from Muhammed's Nation of Islam and was in the process of establishing a new organization, the Organization of Afro-American Unity, when he was assassinated at the Audubon Ballroom in Harlem on February 21, 1965.

THE AUTOBIOGRAPHY

The Autobiography of Malcolm X is a complex narrative and a major American autobiography. The first complexity of the narrative concerns authorship. Malcolm worked with Alex Haley on the manuscript, and, as in any collaboration, there is a question of how much of the narrative is Malcolm's and how much is Haley's. Haley himself, however, acknowledges that Malcolm provided all of the information and initialed every page of the manuscript, and he insists that the work is Malcolm's own autobiography, not a biography written by Alex Haley.

A second complexity is the issue at the center of the autobiography, the question of what is an American. Like the Quaker and Puritan autobiographers who provided the foundations for the genre in America, Malcolm X created a narrative in which the first half shows him to be a member of a persecuted minority while the second half emphasizes the autobiographer's role as a member of and spokesman for a religious and political community that literally offers him a new life. Again, like Puritan autobiographers, Malcolm X saw his conversion as the crucial event in his life and saw history as a teleological adventure. The conversion experience led him to a belief in the brotherhood of man, and although there are great differences between the ideologue of progress and the black nationalist prophet, Malcolm's narrative, like Benjamin Franklin's *Autobiography*, is a version of a success story that draws a parallel between the development of a sense of self and the liberation of a colonized people. Although the setting and material seem far removed from Puritan conversion narratives and colonial success stories, its structure is classically American. Malcolm's narrative opens with an account of his family and early life, which leads to a moment of crisis and illumination. A dramatic conversion follows, and that conversion leads to study, preparation, and then the assumption of the role of the prophet and spokesman for the entire community of believers.

The Autobiography of Malcolm X is, however, more than a simple conversion narrative. The autobiography shows both a conversion and an analysis of that conversion. It is both a black narrative and a tale of a universal experience. The book was begun in 1963 when Malcolm was still a member of the Nation of Islam, the original dedication was to Elijah Muhammed, an all of the proceeds from the sale of the autobiography were intended to go to the Black Muslims. At this early stage in the project Malcolm saw himself as a propagandist rather than an autobiographer, and his narrative was to be completely orthodox. As coauthor Alex Haley later said of the notebook that Malcolm kept, "It contained nothing but Black Muslim philosophy, praise of Mr. Muhammed, and the evils of the 'white devil.' He would bristle when I tried to urge him that the proposed book was *his* life" (388). Haley's arguments with Malcolm about the didactic nature of the autobiography, along with Malcolm's own unhappiness with the movement and his eventual excommunication from the Nation of Islam, compelled him to reexamine his life, and the product of that reexamination is *The Autobiography of Malcolm X*, a book that uses the conventional forms of the conversion narrative but goes beyond the usual limitations of that mode.

The conventions of the conversion narrative demand a contrast built around the conversion experience, and in describing his transformation from street hustler and shoe-shine boy to minister and spokesman for a large segment of the black community in the United States, Malcolm X juxtaposes black and white in American society. He begins in the first chapter of his narrative, "Nightmare," where he presents both Ku Klux Klan riders and members of Marcus Garvey's United Negro Improvement Association. The effects of racism in America dominate the early sections of the narrative. Malcolm provides his readers with examples of violence, poverty, and the destruction of his family in the first twenty pages of his book. Four of his uncles were killed, and he suspects that his father was as well. After his father's death, the Little family was forced to subsist on homegrown food and welfare until Malcolm's mother finally broke under the strain and was committed to an institution. Malcolm and his brothers and sisters were then sent to different homes. This life of poverty and limitations changed, however, when Malcolm visited the city for the first time.

Malcolm describes his first impressions of urban life effectively:

I couldn't have feigned indifference if I had tried to. People talked casually about Chicago, Detroit, New York. I didn't know the world contained as many Negroes as I saw thronging downtown Roxbury at night, especially on Saturdays. Neon lights, nightclubs, poolhalls, bars, the cars they drove! Restaurants made the streets smell— rich, greasy, down-home black cooking! Jukeboxes blared Erskine Hawkins, Duke Ellington, Cootie Williams, dozens of others. (35)

The nightlife provided Malcolm with one alternative, and his aunt Ella provided him a second, life as a member of the black bourgeoisie, who, according to Malcolm, prided themselves on being more cultured and cultivated than their neighbors in the ghetto; "Under the pitiful misapprehension that it would make them 'better,' these Hill Negroes were breaking their backs trying to imitate white people" (40).

Malcolm's descriptions indicate that the fast life of the street was obviously more attractive to him. He documents how he learned about the "cats" and adopted their way of life. He soon found work as a shoe-shine boy in a dance hall and made extra money selling drugs, alcohol, and girls. The homeboy had come to town in a big way.

As he describes the life of a black hustler in Harlem during the 1940s, Malcolm creates a new persona in his autobiography. No longer is he Malcolm Little, homeboy from Michigan; instead he is Detroit Red, streetwise and tough. In the hustler sections of *The Autobiography of Malcolm X*, Malcolm demonstrates his ability to survive in a hostile environment, a central part of black autobiographical writing. These chapters also show Malcolm's initiation into a subculture set apart from the white mainstream in America. In addition, they serve to set up the major transition in the narrative, Malcolm's religious conversion.

After his arrest and conviction for robbery, Malcolm was sentenced to ten years in prison, where he was converted to the Nation of Islam. Malcolm describes the experience quickly and effectively. In 1948, after he had been transferred to Concord Prison, he received a letter from his brother Philbert urging him to join the Nation of Islam. In another letter from his family, this one from his brother Reginald, he was advised not to eat pork or smoke cigarettes.

Malcolm was, of course, interested. Conversion is a process of casting off and taking on, and Malcolm uses this convention of breaking habits, a device employed by other writers of conversion narratives, in the description of his own conversion:

Quitting cigarettes wasn't going to be difficult. I had been conditioned by days in solitary without cigarettes. Whatever this chance was, I wasn't going to fluff it. After I had read that letter, I finished the pack I then had open. I haven't smoked another cigarette to this day, since 1948.

It was about three or four days later when pork was served for the noon meal. I wasn't even thinking about pork when I took my seat at the long table. Sit-grab-gobble-stand–file out; that was the Emily Post in prison eating. When the meat platter was passed to me, I didn't even know what the meat was; you usually couldn't tell anyway—but it was suddenly as though don't eat any more pork flashed on a screen before me. . . .

Later I would learn, when I had read and studied Islam a good deal, that, unconsciously, my first pre-Islamic submission had been manifested. I had experienced, for the first time, the Muslim teaching, "If you will take one step toward Allah—Allah will take two steps toward you." (156)

Malcolm then describes the years he spent in prison, but he emphasizes his growth in faith rather than the difficulties of confinement. All of the standard conventions of the conversion experience are present in the narrative: the descent into the depths of sin, confusion, despair, and prison; the direct illumination of the sinner, much like Jonathan Edwards' sweet infusion of saving grace; and an outer transformation to match the inner conversion. The use of external changes to mirror internal conversion continues in the narrative as Malcolm describes in detail his purchase of new clothes, new glasses, and a new watch as he leaves prison. He has also taken on a new name to match his new awareness of himself. Malcolm Little is no more; Malcolm X has been born.

What follows is also part of the traditional conversion narrative. Malcolm presents himself as the convert who becomes a spokesman for the community, defending the faithful from attack and supporting them and the faith. Again, like many earlier conversion narratives, *The Autobiography of Malcolm X* depicts the oppressed community's conflicts with the larger, unconverted part of society. After the conversion, it is time for the acts.

Malcolm's depiction of his work as a minister of the Nation of Islam chronicles a dramatic rise from the depths of prison to the heights of power and fame. Malcolm is not, however, interested in recounting his achievements for their own sake; instead, the narrative of his work for the Nation of Islam emphasizes the position of blacks in a hostile white culture and the impact that faith can have on the lives of those who accept it.

In the second half of his autobiography Malcolm X changes the tone of his writing, adapting his language to his message. In the first half of his story he employed the language of the street and the rhythms of jazz as he recounted events of his early life. Later, as he describes building his faith and converting people to the Nation of Islam, he employs the language of a preacher and teacher. He is aware of his double audience—while recalling the way he spoke in storefronts to black audiences in Harlem, he now addresses the black and white audience reading his autobiography. His life story becomes, then, another opportunity to convince and convert.

Malcolm's success was remarkable. Beginning as an assistant minister in Detroit in 1953, he became, by 1959, the editor of *Muhammed Speaks* and one of the best-known spokesmen for the black community in the United States. He was at the height of his power in November of 1963 when, after the assassination of President Kennedy, he gave a speech linking the assassination to white violence against blacks called "God's Judgment on White America" with the theme "as you sow, so shall you reap" (301).

Malcolm X had been speaking about the violent nature of American society for over a decade, but the reaction to his comments was so strong that Elijah Muhammed silenced him for ninety days and ordered him to submit to the total authority of the Nation of Islam. Later Malcolm discovered that he was being driven from the Nation of Islam because some of its leaders perceived him as a threat. He was eventually excommunicated.

The final sections of *The Autobiography of Malcolm X* treat Malcolm's life after his split with the Nation of Islam. In this part of the narrative Malcolm reexamines the conversion he has undergone. Again Malcolm is in a state of confusion and crisis: "I felt as though something in nature had failed, like the sun or the stars" (304). His expulsion had denied him the support of the community he had served for over a decade, and while he never abandoned his conversion to Islam, he began to see it in a new light, especially after his pilgrimage to Mecca. Like his earlier conversion in prison, a second, or an affirmation of the first, takes place in Mecca. And again the result is a renewed sense of self and a rededication to the struggle for racial equality.

Malcolm's pilgrimage to Mecca dominates the final sections of his autobiography. He spends over fifty pages describing the experience and the lessons he learned. Malcolm details how he discovered the errors in the teaching of Elijah Muhammed, especially his teachings on the nature of the "white devil." On the way to Mecca Malcolm had discovered the international brotherhood of Islam, what he later calls "the color blindness in the Muslim world" (338).

Malcolm returned from his pilgrimage convinced that a more orthodox Islam would provide the framework for a solution to the racial problems in the United States. In the final months of his life Malcolm X began to build a new movement, the Organization of Afro-American Unity, which he hoped would eventually represent all the blacks in the United States. he was assassinated on February 21, 1965, before he could put his plans into action.

CRITICISM

The Autobiography of Malcolm X is a conversion narrative transformed by changing events. The simple, single-minded vision of conversion to the Nation of Islam is replaced by a more complex self-examination. Conversion, as Malcolm ultimately came to see it, was an ongoing, creative process, not a single static experience, and his narrative demonstrates this complexity. The final sections show the autobiographer in a continued state of transformation, a state of becoming, moving away from a separatist view of American society to a more complex one that refused to hold, for example, that all whites were "devils."

Literary critics have recognized the importance of this autobiography. G. Thomas Causer, in *American Autobiography: The Prophetic Mode*, places the autobiography within the mainstream of American letters by comparing it to the major American autobiographies written by Puritans and Quakers. C. W. E. Bigsby, in *The Second Black Renaissance*, calls it a crucial document in black literature and a classic example of a survival story. Stephen Butterfield, in *Black Autobiography in America*, calls the work a masterfully crafted political and rhetorical document.

The Autobiography of Malcolm X is an important work of American literature for a number of reasons. First, it is a dramatic narrative of one's man's struggle to come to terms with himself and his society. Because the man was black and articulate, the coming to terms with a white society is even more dramatic. Second, Malcolm X's narrative does document survival and speaks for all outcasts in society. Finally, *The Autobiography of Malcolm X* addresses the question of identity, of what it means to be an American and a black American. Malcolm X provides a variety of answers, suggesting that the real answer may well be a process rather than a product.

BIBLIOGRAPHY

Malcolm X, with Alex Haley. *The Autobiography of Malcolm X*. New York: Grove Press, 1965.

Malcolm X. *Malcolm X Speaks*. Edited by George Breitman. New York: Grove Press, 1965.

————. *The Speeches of Malcolm X at Harvard*. Edited by Archie Epps. New York: Apollo Editions, 1969.

————. *Malcolm X on Afro-American History*. New York: Pathfinder, 1970.

————. *The End of White World Supremacy*. Edited by Benjamin Goodman. New York: Monthly Review Press, 1971.

Adoff, Arnold. *Malcolm X*. New York: T. Y. Crowell, 1970.

Bigsby, C. W. E. *The Second Black Renaissance: Essays in Black Literature*. Westport, Conn.: Greenwood Press, 1980.

Breitman, George, ed. *Malcolm X, the Man and His Ideas*, New York: Pathfinder, 1965.

————. *The Last Year of Malcolm X*. New York: Schocken, 1968.

————, Herman Porter, and Baxter Smith, eds. *The Assassination of Malcolm X*. New York: Pathfinder, 1976.

Bradley, David. "My Hero, Malcolm X." *Esquire* 100 (December 1983): 488 +

Butterfield, Stephen. *Black Autobiography in America*. Amherst: University of Massachusetts Press, 1974.

Causer, G. Thomas. *American Autobiography: The Prophetic Mode*. Amherst: University of Massachusetts Press, 1979.

Clarke, John Henrik, ed. *Malcolm X*. New York: Macmillan, 1969.

Curtis, R. *The Life of Malcolm X*. Philadelphia: MacRae Smith, 1971.

Davis, Lenwood, and Marsha Moore. *Malcolm X: A Selected Bibliography*. Westport, Conn.: Greenwood Press, 1984.

Goldman, Peter Lewis. *The Death and Life of Malcolm X*. New York: Harper and Row, 1973.

Holte, James. "The Representative Voice: Autobiography and the Ethnic Experience." *MELUS* 9, 2 (1983): 25–46.

Ohmann, Carol. "*The Autobiography of Malcolm X*: A Revolutionary Use of the Franklin Tradition." *American Quarterly* 22 (1979): 131–49.

Wolfenstein, Eugene Victor. *The Victims of Democracy: Malcolm X and the Black Revolution*. Berkeley: University of California Press, 1981.

JERRE MANGIONE
(1909–   )

An Ethnic at Large

BIOGRAPHY

Jerre Mangione was born on March 20, 1909, in Rochester, New York. The
son of Sicilian immigrant parents, Mangione grew up in a multiethnic neighborhood in Rochester. After graduation from public school, Mangione attended Syracuse University, receiving his B.A. in 1931. Like many other
aspiring writers, Mangione moved to New York City, where he became a staff
writer for *Time* magazine. Later he worked as a book editor for Robert M.
McBride, and from 1937 to 1947 he served as a writer, editor, information
specialist, and public relations officer for a variety of government agencies.
From 1948 to 1961 Mangione worked for the Columbia Broadcasting System,
and then he became a professor of English at the University of Pennsylvania.

In 1943 Mangione published *Mount Allegro*, a highly praised novel based
on his visit to Sicily in 1936. He followed that book with a number of others,
including *The Ship and the Flame* (1948), *Night Search* (1965), *America Is
Also Italian* (1969), *Mussolini's March on Rome* (1975), and *An Ethnic at
Large: A Memoir of America in the Thirties and Forties* (1978).

THE AUTOBIOGRAPHY

Jerre Mangione is, in some ways, representative of an entire generation of
immigrants' children. He has assimilated; he is a success. The son of working-
class immigrants, he has become a respected professional. *An Ethnic at Large*
is, however, more than another narrative of success. Mangione was at the
center of American cultural life during the 1930s and 1940s, and his narrative
is as much about America during those two decades as it is about the life of
one Italian-American. *An Ethnic at Large* is one man's account of the contrast
of the possibilities provided by the United States in the twentieth century
with the limitations inherent in an immigrant upbringing.

Mangione begins his autobiography with a description of growing up Sicilian in America in the early part of the century. His depiction of his early years in Rochester provides a moving illustration of the cultural conflicts faced by many first-generation Americans. At home English was a forbidden language so that the entire family could communicate in Italian, but beyond the family fence children of Polish, German, and Russian immigrants spoke English. Mangione lived in two mutually exclusive worlds. He recalls:

As I tried to bridge the wide gap between my Sicilian and American lives, I became increasingly resentful of my relatives for being more foreign than anyone else. It irked me that I had not been born of English speaking parents, and I cringed with embarrassment whenever my mother would scream at me from an upstairs window, threatening to kill me if I didn't come home that minute. If I rushed to obey her, it was not because I was frightened by her threat (there was nothing violent about her except the sound of her anger), but because I did not want my playmates to hear her Sicilian scream a second time. (14)

Mangione became aware of the differences between Sicilian and American cultures early. His father refused to permit him to become a Boy Scout when he learned that Scouts carried knives, the weapons Americans associated with Italian criminals. His father also distrusted the police and the schools. The police, he believed, failed to respect Italian immigrants; it was better to go to the local mafioso for help when necessary. He, at least, knew the meaning of respect and honor. He thought that the schools were even worse. They encouraged a host of vile, shocking customs that led to immorality, disrupted family life, and undermined his position as the head of the household. Mangione's father knew for a fact that American schools permitted boys and girls to date without chaperons and encouraged young people to marry without their parents' permission. Mangione's mother, however, believed in education; she wanted to send one of her sons to college, an impossible dream in the old country. She selected Jerre, her oldest son, and began urging him to be a doctor or lawyer, the two most noble professions for the children of immigrants.

Looking back at his boyhood, Mangione observes that more than custom or language kept his Sicilian and American worlds apart. He discovered a basic difference in philosophy:

Ingrained in the Sicilian by centuries of poverty and oppression were strong elements of fatalism which my relatives called *Destino*. In their minds *Destino*, the willingness to resign oneself to misfortune, was the key to survival; to refuse to believe that an almighty force predetermined the fate of all people was to court disaster. (32)

American culture, on the other hand, offered Mangione freedom: free will, free enterprise, and the belief that any individual could change and improve his situation in life. Like many other bright, eager children of immigrant parents, Mangione opted for Americanism.

As it had for millions of other new Americans, education provided Mangione with the avenue to mainstream America. He was an excellent student in high school, and in 1928 he arrived at Syracuse University. Mangione was planning to become a poet and a philosopher, and he was impressed by the university, which seemed to him to be "a noble kingdom directed by sages who, in their wisdom, had seen fit to admit me" (35).

Mangione continued to be an enthusiastic student. He remembers studying the work of Crane, Stein, and Joyce, becoming, for a time, sympathetic with the art-for-art's-sake school of criticism. Eventually he came around to the position that emphasized a writer's social responsibility. He writes that "the shock of the Sacco and Vanzetti executions, along with Mussolini's increasing stranglehold on Italy, made me feel no writer worth his salt could turn his back on social justice" (49).

With the rest of the class of 1931 Mangione discovered that the experiences of four years in college had little meaning in an America caught in a deep depression. At first, Mangion felt secure. Because of his work on the Syracuse student newspaper, he had obtained a position on the editorial staff of *Time*. He was initially assigned to the business and finance staff, but after a few months he was transferred to the milestones section, where he made the serious blunder of referring to a prominent Jew as a "socialite." He was immediately reprimanded. "No Jew is ever a socialite," he was told, "certainly not in the pages of *Time*" (61).

Despite the continuing Depression, Mangione quit his job. His descriptions of life in the 1930s in New York echo the depictions of urban life found in much of the proletarian fiction of the period. Mangione supported himself as a part-time reviewer for the *New Republic*, librarian at Cooper Union, and book editor at Robert McBride. Despite the hunger, poverty, and uncertainty that he faced, Mangione remained optimistic. He discovered the artistic community of Greenwich Village, the antifascist movement among some members of the Italian-American community, and the intellectual, political Left.

One of the strengths of *An Ethnic at Large* is Mangione's re-creation and analysis of the popularity and excitement of the Left among American intellectuals. Mangione, who describes his own position as that of a "fellow traveler," traces the popularity of Marxism in the 1930s to the rise of Hitler and Mussolini and the collapse of the American economy. He recalls the spirit of the times effectively:

In September 1932, two months before the presidential election, fifty-three American writers and artists (among them Edmund Wilson, John Dos Passos, Malcolm Cowley, Sidney Hook, and Waldo Frank) signed their names to a pamphlet which denounced the Democratic and Republican parties as hopelessly corrupt, rejected the Socialist party as a "do nothing group," and declared their support of the Communist party on the grounds that it alone presented a viable program for fighting fascism and eliminating poverty. (120)

Mangione began attending meetings of the John Reed Club and writing for such leftist periodicals as the *Partisan Review* and *New Masses*. Although Mangione eventually broke with the hard-line radicals, as did many of the progressives of the 1930s, he never rejected the antifascism that was one of the major elements of the movement.

Mangione recalls that after living in New York for five years he found his bonds to his family growing stronger. He began to become obsessed with the "Sicilian Way," despite the faith in the Horatio Alger myth he had been taught in public school. He began to wonder how he could reconcile the American concept of the melting pot with Sicilian history, and out of these wonderings came a desire to explore his own ethnic identity. To do that he planned to travel to Sicily.

Mangione's description of his trip to Sicily and Italy is the pivotal section of the autobiography. Prior to his journey Mangione was searching for his identity; when he returned to America he had discovered it. Traveling to Italy convinced Mangione that he was neither Italian nor American; instead he was something new, an Italian-American, that curious hybrid aware of ethnicity that emerged in a variety of forms in the 1930s and 1940s as the children of immigrants grew to maturity and began confronting their own concerns about identity.

Mangione remembers his pilgrimage to Palermo and Agrigento as a time full of both joy and fear. He was welcomed in Sicily by a host of relatives who showered him with hospitality and affection. At the same time he was aware that he was an antifascist writer traveling in Mussolini's Italy. He was afraid, because of his parents' Italian birth, that he would be drafted by the Italians and sent to fight in Ethiopia. Instead, however, he traveled throughout Italy arguing with writers and intellectuals he met about the merits of such antifascist writers as Alberto Moravia, Ignazio Silone, and Luigi Pirandello. He returned to the United States without incident, despite the fact that the Italian government was at that time waging an anti-American campaign in response to U.S. criticism of the Italian war with Ethiopia. In addition, he had managed to collect much of the material that he would use in his first novel, *Mount Allegro*.

In 1936 Mangione became an information specialist for the Federal Re-settlement Administration. From there he moved on to the Federal Writers' Project, which he would later write about in *The Dream and the Deal: The Federal Writers' Project, 1936–1943*. In addition, he held positions in the Census Bureau, the Department of Justice, and the Immigration and Naturalization Service.

Mangione devotes several chapters of his autobiography to the depiction of his work as a writer for the government under the Roosevelt administration.

His description of government service as the nation moved from the depths of the Depression to preparations for war make interesting reading, but his account of his work as a special assistant to the commissioner of the Immigration and Naturalization Service during the internment of enemy aliens is one of the most important sections of his narrative.

In February 1942 the U.S. government interned over 110,000 Japanese on the West Coast. With over 300,000 German nationals and 600,000 Italian nationals in the United States at the outbreak of World War II, mass internments would have created a host of problems, and Mangione reports that plans were being developed to arrest and intern all enemy aliens. The Justice Department, however, adopted a policy of selective internment, and during the course of the war only 10,000 people were interned (aside from the Japanese on the West Coast). Mangione toured the major camps as part of his job, and his recollections make for provocative reading.

Mangione concludes with the end of the war and the rise of McCarthyism. From a trusted government official he became a suspected collaborator and was investigated. One of his neighbors told him that she had been questioned about his sexual habits, his reading, and his taste in music. Mangione was indignant, and records that she said that she answered only one question affirmatively. When asked if she had ever seen any "foreign-looking persons" visiting Mangione, she answered yes, his father and mother.

CRITICISM

Mangione has received many awards and honors for his work. He has been awarded seven Yaddo creative writing fellowships, eight MacDowell Colony creative writing fellowships, a Fulbright research fellowship, and a Rockefeller Foundation research grant. In addition, he was given a Commendatore decoration by the Italian government in 1971, and his book *The Dream and the Deal* was nominated for the National Book Award.

Mangione's first book, *Mount Allegro*, remains his most popular, and both Olga Peragallo in *Italian-American Authors and Their Contributions to American Literature* and Rose Basile Green in *The Italian-American Novel* praise his work. *An Ethnic at Large* conveys the same sense of immediacy and social concern as much of Mangione's other work. It also demonstrates the distance traveled in one lifetime by the children of immigrants. Mangione, who sees himself as "ethnic" and thus representative of a specific class of Americans, moved from the margin of American society to the mainsteam. In addition to describing that journey, his autobiography provides firsthand information about American social and political life in two of the important decades of this century. It is a book well worth reading.

BIBLIOGRAPHY

Mangione, Jerre. *Mount Allegro*. Boston: Houghton Mifflin, 1943.
————. *The Ship and the Flame*. New York: Current Books, 1948.

————. *Reunion in Sicily*. Boston: Houghton Mifflin, 1950.

————. *Night Search*. New York: Crown, 1965.

————. *A Passion for Sicilians: The World Around Danilo Dolci*. New York: Morrow, 1968.

————. *America Is Also Italian*. New York: Putnam, 1969.

————. *The Dream and the Deal: The Federal Writers' Project, 1936–1943*. Boston: LIttle, Brown, 1972.

————. *Mussolini's March on Rome*. New York: F. Watts, 1975.

————. *An Ethnic at Large: A Memoir of America in the Thirties and Forties*. New York: Putnam, 1978.

Green, Rose Basile. *The Italian-American Novel*. Rutherford, N.J.: Fairleigh Dickinson University Press, 1974.

Peragallo, Olga. *Italian-American Authors and Their Contributions to American Literature*. New York: S. F. Vanni, 1949.

Pisani, Lawrence Frank. *The Italian in America*. New York: Exposition, 1957.

MICHAEL PUPIN
(1858–1935)

From Immigrant to Inventor

BIOGRAPHY

Michael Pupin was born in the frontier village of Idvor, Hungary, in 1858. Idvor was at that time part of the Austrian empire and a hotbed of Serbian nationalism. Like many other young Serbs growing up during the final decades of the Hapsburg rule, Pupin became a Serbian nationalist, and when the Austrian government began calling up students for military service, Pupin decided to emigrate to the United States in hope of finding political freedom and the opportunity for a college education. He arrived in New York in 1874.

From 1874 to 1879 Pupin worked in a variety of jobs while he began to learn English and attended lectures at Cooper Union, which provided free education to thousands of immigrants. In 1879 Pupin received a scholarship to Columbia College. After graduation he studied physics at Cambridge University and on the advice of Dr. John Tyndall, director of the Royal Institute in London, went to University of Berlin to study advanced physics. There he earned his doctorate and returned to Columbia as a faculty member in 1889.

Pupin served as professor of electro-magnetism at Columbia until 1931. In addition to teaching, he specialized in research, and the thirty-four patents he received made him rich and famous. He first became known to the public for his work with X-rays. Pupin developed a procedure that dramatically shortened the time needed to make an X-ray photograph, allowing its efficient use in medicine. Shortly after that breakthrough Pupin perfected the inductance coil, which enabled the American Telephone and Telegraph Company to establish reliable long-distance telephone service throughout the United States. Pupin's final major invention was the electrical resonator, which permitted clear transmission and reception of sound for both radio and television.

In addition to his scientific work, Pupin served his adopted country as a representative of the commission that studied national aspirations in Europe after World War I, and later he became a member of the National Advisory Committee for Aeronautics. He died, a wealthy and respected American citizen, in 1935.

THE AUTOBIOGRAPHY

Michael Pupin's autobiography, *From Immigrant to Inventor*, is a traditional success narrative. Pupin, like a number of other successful immigrants, writes of his youthful poverty in his homeland, a traumatic Atlantic crossing, a disorienting arrival in the new land, a struggle to find work, and an eventual rise to financial success and cultural celebrity in America. Pupin's narrative is a story of celebration. In describing his life Pupin extols the values taught by the apostles of success—hard work, self-denial, and education—as well as the nation that encourages the practice of these virtues. Pupin is aware of his unique perspective as a successful immigrant. He writes, for example, "A foreign-born citizen of the United States has many occasions to sing praises of the virtues of this country which the native-born citizen has not" (311).

Pupin calls the first chapter of his narrative "What I Brought to America," and he uses it to establish two major themes of his autobiography: the importance of education and the need for political and economic freedom. He recounts that he began learning those lessons in Idvor from his family and neighbors, and although he uses his description of his youth in Hungary to establish a contrast with what he discovers after his emigration to the United States, he suggests that such American virtues as self-determination and the desire to rise in the world are universal. Pupin traces his love of learning to his mother, who advised him:

My boy, if you wish to go out into the world about which you hear so much at the neighborhood gatherings, you must provide yourself with another pair of eyes; the eyes of reading and writing. There is so much wonderful knowledge and learning in the world which you cannot get unless you can read and write. Knowledge is the golden ladder over which we climb to heaven; knowledge is the light which illuminates our path through this life and leads to a future life of everlasting glory. (10)

Pupin took his mother's advice to heart. He quickly outgrew the one school in Idvor, and on the advice of his teacher he was sent to a higher school in Panchevo, a town fifteen miles away. It was there, Pupin recalls, that he first heard of America.

At Panchevo Pupin's world widened. In addition to learning about America he discovered natural science, a subject unknown in Idvor. When he returned to Idvor he told his parents and neighbors about Benjamin Franklin and his electrical experiments. Such ideas, he was told, were heresy, since everyone knew that thunder was caused by St. Elijah's cart rumbling across the heavens. Pupin preferred the scientific explanation.

In 1872 Pupin moved to Prague to continue his studies, and there he encountered ethnic prejudice and hostility. Political tension is a major theme in Pupin's autobiography, and he describes how he was caught up in the rising nationalism that marked the decline of the Austrian empire. He depicts himself as a Serbian nationalist and portrays the Austrian domination of the other ethnic groups within the empire as colonial exploitation. Pupin recalls that because of his accent and his dress he was considered a rude barbarian and a potential revolutionary. His only relief was discovering some traveling Americans who introduced him to stories about Benjamin Franklin and Abraham Lincoln; they also urged him to read *Uncle Tom's Cabin*. Pupin quickly adopted America as a political and economic ideal. Pupin imagined an America that was the opposite of the Austrian empire, and when he learned that his father had died and he was about to be called up to serve in the Austrian army, Pupin sold his possessions to pay for passage to the land of his hopes.

Pupin's account of his journey and arrival conforms to the accounts left by other immigrant writers: The journey was rough and the arrival was confusing. Pupin recalls hearing advice stories from fellow immigrants, each one telling the others how to get rich quickly in America. Arrival at New York's Castle Garden and examinations by immigration officials silenced all of the newcomers, however. Pupin remembers telling the immigration service officers that he only had five cents and had no relatives in America. He did mention, however, that he knew three Americans: Franklin, Lincoln, and Harriet Beecher Stowe. He writes that one of his examiners was pleased and told him, "You showed good taste when you picked your American acquaintances" (40).

The second chapter of Pupin's narrative is called "The Hardships of a Greenhorn," and in it Pupin recounts his adventures as he worked at a variety of jobs in and around New York. Inherent in the narrative of success is a rise from poverty to prosperity, and like other writers of success narratives, Pupin describes his struggles at temporary jobs and his determination to learn English and get an education. These depictions of poverty and hard work serve as a backdrop for his central theme, the struggle for an education.

Pupin's formal education began at Cooper Union, where he and thousands of other immigrants studied in the evenings after work. Pupin made the study of practical sciences his goal, and he includes a long passage describing a large painting called "Men of Progress" that hung in the Union's reading room. The figures of great inventors in the painting served as his inspiration, and while he studied he linked political ideas with material progress, writing that he realized that "the English made us write the Declaration of Independence, and they also gave us the steam engine with which we made our independence good" (78).

Pupin enrolled at Adelphi Academy in Brooklyn and studied English, Greek, and Latin to prepare for entrance examinations at Columbia. He passed, and enrolled in September 1879 on a full scholarship. Pupin calls his chapter on his college education "From Greenhorn to Citizenship and College Degree," and he recounts his four years at Columbia as a successful rite of passage. Pupin began college as an outsider, but he quickly became accepted by his fellow students and his teachers. In his autobiography he writes with equal enthusiasm of his scientific studies, athletic events, and college life in general. At Columbia Pupin became an American, and his fond descriptions of the process reveal how much he enjoyed it.

Pupin became an American citizen the day before he graduated. In addition, Columbia awarded him a fellowship to study physics at Cambridge University. At this point Pupin's narrative changes. Pupin describes his life prior to his graduation as a transformation from foreigner to citizen, and as a result he includes the variety of experiences that helped to shape him. Once he begins describing his transformation from student to physicist, however, he emphasizes science.

The late nineteenth century was a time of great excitement in physics. Both theoretical work and practical applications were occurring in the study of light, sound, and electricity. Pupin, first at Cambridge and later at the University of Berlin, had the opportunity to study mathematics and physics with the most outstanding scientists of his age. Pupin provides his readers with a detailed account of his work, frequently mentioning the work of Maxwell, Faraday, and Hertz. Pupin was fascinated by electricity and had begun to work on some practical applications using the new science when he received an invitation to return to Columbia as a faculty member of the Department of Electrical Engineering after he had completed his doctoral work at Berlin. He sailed into New York harbor in 1889 with little more money than he had on his first arrival, but with "some prospects which modesty prevents me from mentioning" (278).

Pupin's prospects included a faculty position and several ideas. Much like young Benjamin Franklin entering the city of Philadelphia with a loaf of bread under his arm and an eye toward the main chance, Pupin returned to New York ready to put his ideas into practice. Before beginning to write of his teaching at Columbia and his revolutionary inventions, however, Pupin digresses from his narrative to state his theme:

The main object of my narrative has been to describe the rise of idealism in American science, and particularly in physical sciences and the related industries. I witnessed this gradual development; everything I have written so far is an attempt to qualify as a witness whose testimony has competence and weight. (311)

Idealism in American science was, for Pupin and others, the engine that drove the train of democracy. American science was primarily technological, and the technology of the nineteenth century had provided Americans with such working ideas as the steam engine, the cotton gin, the telegraph, and a national rail system. All of these made democracy work; they created jobs, expanded the nation, and improved the quality of life. Pupin writes as an evangelist for science, believing science to be as important in American life as political and religious liberty. Pupin himself was far more than a witness, as the final sections of his autobiography demonstrate, but he wished to downplay his own role, remembering, perhaps, Franklin's advice on the virtue of humility.

In the final sections of *From Immigrant to Inventor* Pupin combines a narrative of his own work as a teacher and inventor with observations on the relationship of science and society. In describing his three most significant inventions—the inductance coil, which made long-distance telephone service practical, electrical resonators, which eliminated major problems in radio transmission, and X-ray photography, which enabled physicians to use X-rays effectively in medical treatment—Pupin depicts himself as the hardworking scientist following a moment of inspiration with months of experimentation. Pupin delights in recounting the beneficial outcome of his work—patients with broken bones saved from hours of agony and isolated people in flooded towns being kept in contact with their neighbors. From his days at Cooper Union Pupin recognized the importance of practical applications of ideas, and he stresses those applications in his autobiography.

At the same time, Pupin saw himself as a philosopher of science and an advocate of the integration of science and society, with the university serving as a creative matrix. Pupin called the American Telephone and Telegraph Company the "most perfect industrial organization in the world," and recommended it as a model for American society. He also called for the creation of an ideal democracy:

A state organism in which each human unit contributes its definite share to the physical and mental activities of the organism. The relation of the individual to the social body in an ideal democracy, as I conceive it, will be very similar to the relation of our cells to our body. Activities of individuals will be coordinated, just as the activities of our cells are, so that one composite mind will guide the resultant activities of the whole social body. (383–84)

Such a society would be efficient, and Pupin saw society as evolving toward a democracy based on coordination, order, and beauty. One wonders, however, whether such a society would be utopian or totalitarian.

CRITICISM

Michael Pupin's life provided an example for the advocates of open immigration; it demonstrated the success of the self-made man who came to the United States penniless and rose through his own efforts to a position of wealth and celebrity. Pupin's autobiography, *From Immigrant to Inventor*, went through eleven editions between 1923 and 1926, and Pupin received the Pulitzer Prize for his narrative in 1924. The book's popularity can be seen in its message: America is the land of opportunity, and those who come seeking freedom can give their adopted land as much as they take.

Despite the evolutionary, scientific utopianism of the final pages of Pupin's narrative, *From Immigrant to Inventor* is an accessible book. Structured around the familiar theme of a rise to wealth, Pupin's autobiography tells the familiar story of the poor young immigrant who finds political and economic freedom in America and in turn provides his new homeland with the fruits of his labors. In addition, Pupin provides readers with a firsthand account of the excitement generated during the height of the scientific revolution of the late nineteenth and early twentieth centuries, and readers living through another scientific revolution will recognize many of the hopes and fears Pupin describes.

BIBLIOGRAPHY

Pupin, Michael I. *From Immigrant to Inventor*. New York: Scribner's, 1923.
————. *Romance of the Machine*. New York: Scribner's, 1927.
Crowther, James. *Famous American Men of Science*. New York: Norton, 1937.
Fuller, Edwin. *Tinkers and Genius*. New York: Globe, 1956.
Langdon-Davies, John. *Radio: The Story of the Capture and Use of Radio Waves*. New York: Dodd, Mead, and Co., 1935.
Markey, Dorothy. *Explorer of Sound: Michael Pupin*. New York: Julian Messner, 1964.

JACOB A. RIIS
(1849–1914)

The Making of an American

BIOGRAPHY

Jacob Riis, one of the most influential reformers of the progressive movement, was born in Ribe, Denmark, in 1849. The son of a teacher in a local Latin school, Riis apprenticed himself to a carpenter instead of following his father's advice and pursuing a literary career. He emigrated to the United States in 1870. For four years Riis worked at a variety of demanding jobs, including shifts in the ironworks of western Pennsylvania and the shipyards of Buffalo, New York.

In 1873 Riis began working as a city editor for a weekly paper in Long Island City, in 1874 he became editor of the *South Brooklyn News*, and in 1878 he became the police reporter for the *New York Tribune*. From 1890 to 1899 Riis wrote for the *New York Evening Sun*.

Writing in the *Tribune* and later in the *Sun*, Riis examined life in New York City's Mulberry Street slums. His exposés of urban poverty won him an increasingly large audience, and in 1890 his famous text on slum conditions, *How the Other Half Lives*, was published by Scribner's. That book and its companion, *The Children of the Poor* (1892), by combining Riis's descriptions with photographs of the tenements, helped to create photojournalism and made Riis one of the most important reformers of his age.

From 1900 to 1914 Riis traveled, lectured, and wrote about the need for reform in American social life. In addition, he became a friend and advisor to Theodore Roosevelt. In 1904 he was stricken with a heart disease. He continued writing and lecturing, however, until he died at his home in Battle Creek, Michigan, in 1914.

THE AUTOBIOGRAPHY

The Making of an American, Jacob Riis's autobiography, was an immensely popular book, going through twelve editions in seven years. Riis, in telling the story of his life, captured the spirit of the progressive age as he describes how a poor immigrant boy suffered through poverty to eventually become rich, famous, and a spokesman for other immigrants and their children. While pointing out flaws in American society, Riis remained optimistic; he believed that Americans were capable of solving all problems—even poverty, disease, and ignorance—providing that the issues were brought to public attention.

The Making of an American is, in many ways, a traditional immigrant success narrative. Riis writes of his life in the old country, contrasts that life to his American experiences, and chronicles his adventures in the new land. The American adventures first expose Riis to poverty and discrimination, but they also teach him the value of determination and self-reliance. What makes Riis's autobiography something more than just another narrative of success is Riis's awareness of the impact of environmental circumstances on the lives of immigrants and his constant determination to convince his readers that society can and must change the social conditions that kept so many immigrant families in poverty.

Riis begins his narrative with a description of his birthplace, Ribe, Denmark. In his description, he emphasizes the age of the town and its backwardness, establishing a contrast for what he will eventually discover in the United States:

To say that Ribe was an old town hardly describes it to readers at this day. A town might be old and yet have kept step with the time. In my day Ribe had not. It had never changed its step or its ways since whale-oil lanterns first hung in iron chains across its cobblestone-paved streets to light them at night. There they hung yet, every rusty link squeaking dolefully in the wind that never ceased blowing from the sea. Coal-oil, just come from America, was regarded as a dangerous innovation. (12)

Riis's picture of his early life in Ribe and later Copenhagen emphasizes his desire to learn a useful trade, carpentry, and the need for him to leave his hometown. His father was a schoolmaster and raised a family of fifteen. Riis writes that he, like millions of other idealistic Europeans during the second half of the nineteenth century, decided to sail to America to "seek his fortune."

Riis's depiction of his arrival at Castle Garden in New York is similar to the descriptions by the countless other immigrants who left their impressions. Riis recalls his amazement at the "teeming hive" he discovered and his failure to find a job in the land of opportunity. He also expresses the immigrant's faith in both himself and his new land:

I had a pair of strong hands, and a stubbornness enough for two; also a strong belief that in a free country, free from the dominion of custom, of caste, as well as of men, things would somehow come to the right end, and a man get shaken into the corner where he belonged if he took a hand in the game. (35–36)

Riis then describes the "shaking" he encountered before he discovered his corner as a writer.

Riis began his exploration of America on the advice of a missionary he met at Castle Garden who was recruiting workers for the Brady's Bend Iron Works near Pittsburgh. Riis began as a carpenter, building houses for the ironworkers, and later tried his hand at coal mining, shipbuilding, railroad work, and bricklaying, even working as a fur trapper for a time as he wandered throughout the Northeast looking for steady employment. New York became his American home, however, and whenever he was out of work he returned to the city.

Riis's depiction of his search for work and his confrontation with poverty provides some of the most dramatic images of the autobiography, and those images establish the authenticity of his later work as an urban reporter and reformer. Riis describes his own descent into the depths of poverty effectively:

I was turned out in the street.... The city was full of idle men. My last hope, a promise of employment in a human-hair factory, failed, and, homeless and penniless, I joined the great army of tramps, wandering about the streets in the daytime with the one aim of stilling the hunger that gnawed at my vitals, and fighting at night with vagrant curs or outcasts as miserable as myself for the protection of some sheltering ashbin or doorway. I was too proud in all my misery to beg. I do not believe I ever did. But I remember well a basement window at the down-town Delmonico's, the silent appearance of my ravenous face at which, at a certain hour in the evening, always evoked a generous supply of meat bones and rolls from a white-capped cook who spoke French. (66)

Throughout his presentation of his struggles, Riis never complains about the economic system he was confronting in America. He expected to have to work hard, and he expected setbacks. In addition, he describes how he adopted the economic philosophies of such prominent Americans as Horace Greeley, Henry Ward Beecher, and Andrew Carnegie, all of whom advocated poverty as a virtue that fostered the development of the qualities necessary for success.

Another influence on Riis was Christianity. During the second half of the nineteenth century Christian missionaries, led by the Methodists and the Baptists, organized a series of revivals aimed at members of the rapidly growing urban immigrant communities. Riis recalls that he was converted by the Reverend Ichabod Simmons during a Methodist revival at the old Eighteenth Street Church in New York. He was struck with the desire to make a dramatic change in his life:

In fact, with the heat of the convert, I decided on the spot to throw up my editorial work and take to preaching. But Brother Simmons would not hear of it.

"No, no, Jacob," he said; "not that. We have preachers enough. What the world needs is consecrated pens."

Then and there I consecrated mine. (135)

Riss had by this time begun his journalistic work, and when he discovered that he could be employed and committed at the same time, his life changed.

There were other concerned journalists at work in America during the late nineteenth century. Objectivity was not the primary journalistic standard, and reporters and editors felt free to become advocates of social and political causes. In 1878, when Riss became a police reporter for the *New York Tribune*, he took advantage of the opportunity to combine his personal experience with poverty and slum life with his belief in the social gospel by becoming an outspoken advocate of urban reform.

As Riis describes in his autobiography, a policy reporter in the nineteenth century handled all the news that "means trouble to someone: the murders, fires, suicides, robberies, and all of that sort, before it gets into court" (203). The best police reporters, relying on their many sources and skills at asking embarrassing questions, became investigative journalists, following their stories far beyond the courthouses. Riis was one of the best, and while working for the *Sun* he became famous for uncovering pollution in New York City's water supply and averting a potential cholera epidemic.

Although Riis won fame for stories affecting the entire city, his heart remained in the East Side. For over twenty years his office was located on Mulberry Street, across from the police station in what Riis calls "the foul core of New York's slums." Riis writes that in walking Mulberry Bend at all hours of the night and day he discovered in tenement life and the dismal statistics of crime and poverty he recorded for his paper the subject for his "consecrated pen." Riis came to believe that if he could capture the destitution and squalor of Mulberry Bend for his readers, they would demand changes.

Riis's depiction of his work in the slums of the East Side provides the focal point for the entire autobiography. He recounts with vivid details his visits to overcrowded rooming houses and alleys full of waste and garbage. He remarks that his battle against profit-minded slum lords and an indifferent city government had little impact until he discovered a new weapon—the camera.

Photography provided Riis with the evidence he needed to convince his audience of the appalling conditions in the city tenements. He recounts writing a report to the New York Health Board of fifteen people sleeping on the bare floors of two rooms in a tenement and then getting no response until he added the evidence produced by his camera. Riis taught himself to make pictures, and both *How the Other Half Lives* and *The Making of an American* contain graphic examples of the power of Riis's photojournalism.

In *The Making of an American* Riis emphasizes the horrors he discovered in the tenements and downplays his own efforts to eliminate them; he is content to let his earlier work speak for itself. He describes almost matter-of-factly his career as a lecturer, which began on February 28, 1888, at the invitation of Dr. Joseph Strong, a prominent minister, and continued throughout the rest of his life. Riis, accompanied by his "magic lantern" and his slides of the tenements, spoke throughout New York, making urban renewal and civic improvement the focus of his life. The public lectures and photographs were the raw material of Riis's famous book, and in his autobiography he describes, again with reserve, how *How the Other Half Lives* came to be written:

One of the editors of *Scribner's Magazine* saw my pictures and heard their story in his church, and came to talk the matter over with me. As a result of that talk I wrote an article that appeared in the Christmas *Scribner's*, 1889, under the title "How the Other Half Lives," and made an instant impression. (300)

Riis assumes that most of his readers are familiar with his famous first book, and although he includes some material from it in his narrative, he emphasizes his own surprise at its popularity and expresses gratitude at its impact. Despite Riis's modesty, the description of the publication of *How the Other Half Lives* is the high point of *The Making of an American*. In fact, both works cover much of the same material—the former in a series of semiautobiographical descriptive accounts that focus on the tenements and their inhabitants, and the latter in a personal narrative that emphasizes the perceptions of the observer. Together the two books provide a complete vision of a part of the life of America's Gilded Age that is often ignored.

In the final sections of his autobiography Riis chronicles the successes of the reform movement, which he helped found, in New York City. Riis writes enthusiastically about the progressives' takeover of New York City government and the resulting passage of strict building codes and sanitation laws. He also includes a complimentary profile of his friend Theodore Roosevelt as the progressive president of the Police Board of the City of New York. Roosevelt and Riis were kindred spirits, and they worked together to eradicate the city's worst tenements. Roosevelt often accompanied Riis on his late-night visits to the slums of the East Side, and Riis writes of their friendship and adventures together with warmth and admiration.

Riis concludes his narrative where it began, in the town of Ribe, Denmark. He describes the return of a famous son, a man who was the friend of an American president and who had been knighted by King Christian of Denmark. The poor, young boy of the opening chapter has returned rich and famous. Riis, however, uses the comparison to emphasize his love of his adopted country. In the final scene of the narrative Riis describes himself lying sick in bed, feeling old and tired until he sees a ship sailing by flying an American flag:

I sat up in bed and shouted, laughed and cried by turns, waving my handkerchief to the flag out there. . . . I knew then that it was my flag; that my children's home was mine, indeed; that I had become an American in truth. And I thanked God, and, like unto the man sick of the palsy, arose from my bed and went home, healed. (443)

CRITICISM

Almost every history of American journalism recognizes Riis as a major influence on the development of both advocacy journalism and modern reporting. Similarly, historians of the progressive movement cite Riis as a major figure. Riis was fortunate in that the results of his work were dramatic and immediate; his writing caused tenements to be torn down and settlement houses and parks to be built. Riis's major biographers—Louis Ware, Alexander Alland, James B. Lane, and Edith Patterson Meyer—all emphasize Riis's impact on the urban landscape of the nineteenth century more than his rise to fame.

Louis Filler, on the other hand, sees Riis as an unprofound and unsophisticated reformer who "had no understanding of the nation as a whole and no conception of national policy." Even though Filler sees Riis's contribution as narrow, he admits that it was significant.

While not as famous as *How the Other Half Lives*, *The Making of an American* is an important American narrative. It conforms to the pattern of turn-of-the-century success narratives, but it provides much more than a recollection of a rise to celebrity and wealth. Jacob Riis was one of the most important men of his time, and his autobiography is a valuable source of information about his life and the lives of other American immigrants.

BIBLIOGRAPHY

Riis, Jacob. *How the Other Half Lives*. New York: Scribner's, 1890.
———. *The Children of the Poor*. New York: Scribner's, 1892.
———. *My Brother and I: Selected Papers on Social Topics*. New York: Hunt and Eaton; Cincinnati: Cranston and Curtis, 1895.
———. *Out of Mulberry Street*. New York: Century, 1898.
———. *The Making of an American*. New York: Macmillan, 1901.
———. *The Battle with the Slum*. New York: Macmillan, 1902.
———. *A Ten Years' War*. Boston: Houghton Mifflin, 1902.
———. *Children of the Tenements*. New York: Macmillan, 1903.
———. *The Peril and Preservation of the Home: Being the William L. Bull Lectures for the Year 1903*. Philadelphia: Jacobs, 1903.
———. *Is There a Santa Claus?* New York: Macmillan, 1904.
———. *Theodore Roosevelt, the Citizen*. New York: Macmillan, 1904.
———. *The Old Town*. New York: Macmillan, 1909.
———. *Hero Tales of the Far North*. New York: Macmillan, 1910.
———. *Christmas Stories*. New York: Macmillan, 1923.
Alland, Alexander. *Jacob A. Riis: Photographer and Citizen*. Millertown, N.Y.: Aperture, 1974.
Filler, Louis. *The Muckrakers*. University Park: Pennsylvania State University Press, 1968.
Fried, Lewis, and John Fierst. *Jacob A. Riis: A Reference Guide*. Boston: Hall, 1977.
Lane, James B. *Jacob A. Riis and the American City*. Port Washington, N.Y.: Kennikat Press, 1974.

Meyer, Edith Patterson. *Not Charity but Justice: The Story of Jacob A. Riis*. New York: Vanguard, 1974.

Ware, Louis. *Jacob A. Riis: Police Reporter, Reformer, Useful Citizen*. New York: Appleton-Century, 1938.

Ziff, Larzer. *The American 1890s*. New York: Viking, 1966.

RICHARD RODRIGUEZ
(1944-   )

Hunger of Memory

BIOGRAPHY

Richard Rodriguez was born in Sacramento, California, in 1944 to working-class, Mexican, immigrant parents. He spoke Spanish until he began attending Sacred Heart School, where the nuns made him learn and speak English. Rodriguez became an excellent student. He earned a B.A. in English at Stanford, a M.A. in philosophy at Columbia, and continued his graduate education at the Warburg Institute and the University of California at Berkeley.

When he began to apply for university teaching positions, Rodriguez was astonished by the large number of offers he received. He realized that many schools were interested in him for his ethnic status rather than his ability. He abandoned his search for a position and began writing about his experiences as a student within the affirmative-action educational system.

In 1982 his autobiography, *Hunger of Memory: The Education of Richard Rodriguez*, appeared to both critical acclaim and attack. Some readers saw Rodriguez' autobiography as a thoughtful analysis of American education, while others read it as an attack on all affirmative-action programs.

Rodriguez continues to write and lives in San Francisco.

THE AUTOBIOGRAPHY

Hunger of Memory: The Education of Richard Rodriguez is one of the latest in the long line of ethnic autobiographies emphasizing education. It is also one of the best written and most controversial. Throughout American history immigrants have discovered that education has offered a pathway to the mainstream, a way to assimilate into the culture, and as a result, many have written about their experiences in American schools. The best-known writers, Mary Antin and Booker T. Washington, for example, describe more than a successful life; they use their autobiographies to consider the function of education in American society. Rodriguez' autobiography is part of this tradition. *Hunger of Memory* is also an essay. Although Rodriguez' life provides the material for his narrative, his subject is as much the effect of education on minority students as his own personal experience. Like many ethnic autobiographers, Rodriquez becomes a spokesman for an entire class of people when he writes of his life.

Rodriguez begins his narrative with an observation of the distance he has traveled in his life: .

Once upon a time, I was a "socially disadvantaged" child. Mine was a childhood of intense family closeness. And extreme public alienation. Thirty years later I write this book as a middle-class American man. Assimilated. (3)

His autobiography charts a transformation induced by education. Unlike many ethnic autobiographies, *Hunger of Memory* is not a celebration. Rodriguez is aware of his success, but he is also aware of the cost of that success. The result is a narrative carefully balanced, a sober meditation on what is required if one is to become a middle-class American.

Rodriguez opens his first chapter, "Aria," with a memory of his entering his first classroom with only fifty stray English words. "Aria" is about language, the public language of school, English, and the private, familial language of home, Spanish. Each offers Rodriguez something important; Spanish is the language of security and warmth, while English is the language of achievement and reward. The result is a continual conflict between public words and private sounds, a conflict that Rodriguez sees as not only beneficial, but necessary. This struggle with language convinces Rodriguez that he has a public identity, that he is more than the son of his parents, and that this is the first lesson those who are being assimilated must learn.

Rodriguez is aware of the price paid for this public identity. As his proficiency in English increased, his ability to speak Spanish decreased, and as a result, he began to feel out of place at home. He feels the loss, but realizes, much later, that the loss implies a gain. He argues, generalizing from his own experience, that bilingual education is inherently unfair:

Today I hear bilingual educators say that children lose a degree of "individuality" by becoming assimilated into public society....But the bilingualists simplistically scorn the value and necessity of assimilation. They do not seem to realize that there are *two* ways a person is individualized. So they do not realize that while one suffers a diminished sense of *private* individuality by becoming assimilated into public society, such assimilation makes possible the achievement of *public* individuality. (26)

While language is the most important element in the process of assimilation, education is second, and Rodriguez' second chapter, "The Achievement of Desire," describes his life in the classroom from grade school through graduate school. Rodriguez organizes the chapter around his confession that his success in the classroom changed him and separated him from the life he enjoyed before he became a student. Change is the essential idea in this chapter. Rodriguez describes the transformations that take place in the boy who could barely speak English that enable him to conclude his studies in the quiet of the reading room of the British Museum.

It is at the British Museum that Rodriguez discovers Richard Hoggart's *The Uses of Literacy*, and in it a description of the scholarship boy, or, as he becomes aware, himself. For the first time Rodriguez discovers that there are others like himself, young students who must move between environments, the home and the classroom, that are cultural extremes. For Rodriguez and other scholarship boys, the process of education demands radical self-reformation, and "The Achievement of Desire" outlines the transformation of Richard Rodriguez from a private to a public person. The way is marked with books, assignments, and achievements, moments of initiation into the culture of letters. Education becomes a vehicle for a conversion that involves the transference of emotional identity from the private world of the family to the public world of the school.

In his third chapter, "Credo," Rodriguez declares that he is culturally a Catholic and uses the Catholic church as an example of one of the few places where his private life and his public life merged. Rodriguez describes the various facets of the church: The Church of the Sacred Heart in his neighborhood in Sacramento was the center of his universe as a child, his Catholic school provided him with the image of man the sinner, and his Catholic home stressed man the supplicant. He experienced no contradiction, because for Rodriguez the child, the Church was universal.

Rodriguez stresses the role of the church in his assimiliation. Although some view parochial education as a potentially divisive force, Rodriguez speaks for many who attended Catholic schools during the 1950s:

It is not enough to say that I grew up a ghetto Catholic. As a Catholic schoolboy, I was educated a middle-class American. Even while grammar school nuns reminded me of my spiritual separateness from non-Catholics, they provided excellent *public* schooling. A school day began with prayer—the Morning Offering. Then there was the Pledge of Allegiance to the American flag. Religion class followed immediately. But afterward, for the rest of the day, I was taught well those skills of numbers and words crucial to my Americanization. (79)

Rodriguez also described the church of his youth as a church of discipline and a church of ceremony. The ritual of the Mass and the ritual of feast days provided him with a community that was both personal and private. The church has changed, and in the final sections of the chapter Rodriguez muses on the modernization of American Catholicism. It has, he thinks, also become assimilated, and as a result, more public and less private. Just as he has been shaped by Americanization, his community of faith has as well.

The fourth chapter of *Hunger of Memory*, "Complexion," confronts the issue of race. Rodriguez establishes his theme with a recollection from his childhood. He remembers coming home in the summer, his face and arms tan against his white T-shirt. His mother would confront him:

"You look like a *negrito*," she'd say, angry, sorry to be angry, frustrated almost to laughing, scorn. "You know how important looks are in this country. With *los gringos* looks are all that they judge on. But you! Look at you! You're so careless!" (113)

For Rodriguez' mother, dark skin was the most important symbol of oppressive labor and poverty. It meant two things: long hours of work in the fields and the identification, by Anglos, with blacks. During his adolescence, Rodriguez saw himself as ugly because he was dark. Only later, while in college at Stanford and while working on a construction job during a summer vacation, does he come to the realization that his complexion makes no difference to the people he knows. Purposefully, he works without a shirt, growing darker and becoming one with the braceros, those men who work with their arms.

Rodriguez describes his color as contextual; in itself it means nothing. But when he registers at a hotel in London, the clerk assumes leisure in Switzerland. If he had entered the same hotel through the service entrance, it would mean something else. For Rodriguez, his long education created a public persona that overcame the stigma of color.

In "Profession," the fifth chapter of his autobiography, Rodriguez combines his public and private lives in an analysis of affirmative action in higher education and its effects on him. He begins with a definition:

Minority student—that was the label I bore in college at Stanford, then in graduate school at Columbia and Berkeley: a non-white reader of Spenser and Milton and Austin. (143)

He then outlines the impact of that definition. He sees himself as one of the "lucky ones," rewarded for his ethnicity and advanced for belonging to a specially designated group according to HEW guidelines. He describes being a token, looked upon by senior faculty members as "a future role model for other members of his race" or a "valued counselor to incoming minority students." Unfortunately, Rodriguez came to realize that he was only a statistical minority; he was no more disadvantaged than the white graduate students in his classes.

That realization leads Rodriguez to argue that the affirmative-action programs have been seriously misguided. First, he believes, by emphasizing race and ethnicity over class, affirmative-action programs have been unable to identify accurately those who would benefit most. Second, and equally significant, Rodriguez emphasizes that affirmative-action programs fail to recognize the real dilemma of disadvantaged students. While the programs push more and more nonwhite students into the universities, they fail to address the problem of good early schooling, which Rodriguez sees as the primary need of all children. By focusing attention on numerical quotas at the university level, affirmative-action programs diverted attention from the fundamental social changes necessary to address the problems of the poorly educated. The answer, Rodriguez argues, lies in the primary and secondary schools.

"Profession" also presents Rodriguez' refusal to play the game. He refuses to teach a minority literature course, questioning whether there is such a thing as minority literature. Finally, Rodriguez decides that he must protest what he saw as the inequalities caused by affirmative action. Although offered many teaching positions, he disqualifies himself from the profession. He rejects the offers.

Rodriguez recognizes the problems of confessional writing. Near the end of his autobiography he admits that he is writing about things his mother asked him not to tell. *Hunger of Memory* is both a private history and a public statement. Rodriguez writes as one who has made it in America, but his narrative is not a success story. The questions he raises about bilingual education and affirmative action challenge the conventional wisdom of many educational theorists. His autobiography provides an eloquent statement of the long struggle for change he has undergone. Rodriguez' autobiography, like the best writings in the American autobiographical tradition, is complex. It charts both the progress and the pain of becoming American.

CRITICISM

Hunger of Memory was both attacked and defended upon publication. The initial responses were political: Conservatives praised the book for its analysis of the failures of affirmative-action programs, and Chicanos and other ethnic-Americans attacked the implications of Rodriguez' criticisms. While many reviewers addressed the politics of *Hunger of Memory*, other readers saw the book as more of a story of individual maturation and education, a "meditation on education," in Rodriguez' own words. Those critics praised Rodriguez highly. Paul Zweig, whose commentary in the *New York Times Book Review* remains the major critical response to Rodriguez' work, called the autobiography a triumph and a superb autobiographical essay, and several critics saw the work as a tribute to the country and immigrant parents of children who do succeed in America.

Because of Rodriguez' criticisms of programs designed to assist minority children, his book remains controversial. Nevertheless, his narrative of the education of an outsider is part of the mainstream of ethnic-American writing and provides information for the continuing debate about the nature of minority cultures in a pluralistic society.

BIBLIOGRAPHY

Rodriguez, Richard. "Going Home Again: The New American Scholarship Boy." *American Scholar* 44 (Winter 1974–75): 15–28.

————. "On Becoming a Chicano." *Saturday Review* 2 (February 8, 1975): 46–148.

————. "Beyond the Minority Myth." *Change* 10 (1978): 28–34.

————. "The Achievement of Desire: Personal Reflections on Learning 'Basics.'" *College English* 40 (1978): 239–54.

————. *Hunger of Memory: The Education of Richard Rodriguez*. Boston: David R. Godine, 1982.

Adler, Susan S. "Ricardo/Richard." *Commentary* 74 (July 1982): 82–184.

Donohue, J. W. "Between Two Worlds." *America* 146 (May 22, 1982): 403–4.

Smith, Bruce M. "Review." *Phi Delta Kappan* 64 (December 1982): 289.

Strouse, Jean. "A Victim of Two Cultures." *Newsweek* 99 (March 15, 1982): 74.

"Taking Bilingualism to Task." *Time* 119 (April 19, 1982): 68.

Zweig, Paul. "The Children of Two Cultures." *New York Times Book Review* 87 (February 28, 1982):1 + .

CARL SCHURZ
(1829–1906)

The Autobiography of Carl Schurz

BIOGRAPHY

Carl Schurz was born in Liblar, Prussia, in 1829. Schurz's schoolmaster father insured that his son received a proper German education—village school, gymnasium, and finally university training. While at the University of Bonn, Schurz became active in politics; he was one of the publishers of a radical journal and took an active part in the national revolution of 1848. After the revolution was crushed by Prussian troops, Schurz, like thousands of other politically active Germans, fled his homeland. Many political refugees settled in the United States, and Schurz, after returning to Germany from England to assist his former teacher and fellow revolutionary Johann Gottfried Kinkel to escape from prison, emigrated to the United States in 1852.

Schurz settled in Madison, Wisconsin, where he quickly became involved in politics among the large German immigrant community there. He was an early supporter of the new Republican party, making anti-slavery speeches in German throughout the Midwest. In 1860 Schurz was named a delegate to the National Republican Convention, and after Abraham Lincoln's election Schurz was appointed American minister to Spain.

After the outbreak of the Civil War Schurz left Spain and returned to the United States to take a commission as a brigadier general in the Union army. He saw action in many of the major battles of the war, including Manassas, Chancellorsville, and Gettysburg.

After the Civil War Schurz continued to serve his adopted country. From 1869 to 1875 Schurz represented Missouri in the U.S. Senate, and in 1876 President Hayes appointed him secretary of the interior. In that position Schurz oversaw major civil service reform and strove to abolish the abuses within the Indian Bureau. After retiring from government service Schurz remained an influential advisor to American politicians until his death in New York City in 1906.

THE AUTOBIOGRAPHY

Schurz's autobiography, originally titled *The Reminiscences of Carl Schurz*, appeared in three volumes from 1906 to 1908. A one-volume abridgment appeared in 1961, making Schurz's life available to a wide audience for the first time. The autobiography is an unusual narrative, a combination of adventure, history, political testament, and essay. Schurz led a remarkable life, and his autobiography reflects his varied interests and experiences. It also is unlike most other immigrant narratives. *The Autobiography of Carl Schurz* is a heroic memoir. Few other immigrants had Schurz's opportunities or adventures. When Carl Schurz arrived in America, he was already a celebrated figure, admired throughout Europe for his activities in the German revolution. The discrimination and hostility that later immigrants confronted was negligible; Schurz and other German immigrants of the 1850s were seen as democratic refugees rather than competitors for jobs. Settling in large numbers throughout the Midwest, German immigrants kept their language and traditions within the larger English culture. This permitted them to assimilate more slowly, and perhaps more successfully, than members of other immigrant groups. In addition, Schurz arrived at a propitious time. Because of his political activity in Europe and the political and social instability in the United States, Schurz became an ideal mediator between the English-speaking mainstream and the growing German-American community.

Schurz's success in the United States was meteoric. Within ten years of his arrival, Schurz had been a political power broker in the Midwest, minister to Spain, and a general in the Union army. His adventures in America were as spectacular as his exploits in Europe, and his autobiography can be read as a series of heroic exploits. It is, however, far more than that. *The Autobiography of Carl Schurz* is a moving narrative of faith in the principles of democratic government and a testament of a man who fought for his ideals. It is also a record of a simpler America. Many of the hardships faced by American immigrants—prejudice, discrimination, economic deprivation—are absent from Schurz's book. The Midwest was open territory in the 1850s, and the Civil War provided the opportunity for many immigrants to prove themselves. Schurz's autobiography is not a representative story; it is an exhortatory one. It demonstrates what an immigrant can do for his adoptive country. This was a lesson Schurz intended for both natives and the newly arrived.

Although Schurz provides his readers with details of his childhood and education, his autobiography takes form with his description of the German revolution of 1848. Prior to that year, Schurz's life was ordinary; after 1848 nothing about it was ordinary. Like many others in Germany, Schurz was inflamed with revolutionary zeal. Inspired by the French overthrow of Louis Philippe and the proclamation of the Republic, German nationalists sought to establish a unified German nation based on republican principles. Schurz records the desires of the revolutionaries:

A convocation of a national parliament. Then the demands for civil rights and liberties, free speech, free press, the right of free assembly, equality before the law, freely elected representation of the people with legislative power, responsibility of ministers, self-government of the communes, the right of the people to carry arms, the formation of a civic guard with elective officers, and so on—in short, that which was called "a constitutional form of government on a broad democratic basis." (12)

Although he was only nineteen at the outbreak of the revolution, Schurz became actively involved with its organization. He led delegations to German states outside Prussia, helped to organize the local citizens' militia in Bonn, attended a pan-German student congress, and inspired a local tax revolt against the Prussian military. Schurz's description of Germany during the insurrection of 1848–1849 is a picture of a state drifting. Following the inspiration of the French, German nationalists proposed an alliance of democratic states and looked to Prussian King Frederick Wilhelm IV for leadership. The Prussian monarch refused to accept the German crown, and by 1849 German democrats were fighting royal Prussian troops. By the summer of 1849 Schurz and many other patriots had fled Germany and the victorious Prussian army.

Schurz provides more than a history of the revolution in his autobiography; he creates a dramatic adventure. He describes escaping from the encircling Prussians by hiding in the sewer system of Rastatt Fortress and then crossing open country disguised as a peasant. Throughout his narrative Schurz combines personal drama and historical background, and as a result, *The Autobiography of Carl Schurz* is an entertaining narrative. Perhaps the most dramatic section is Schurz's description of his freeing of Professor Kinkel from Spandau Prison.

Schurz presents his heroic gesture as a scene from a novel. He describes his life as a political exile and of hearing of his mentor's deterioration in jail. (Unlike Schurz, Kinkel was unable to flee from Germany and had been condemned to prison by a Prussian military court.) Schurz provides his readers with details of his plans and his actions. He explains how he was smuggled into Germany, found confederates in Spandau, bribed guards, and finally freed his old teacher and friend. Together they rode across Germany in disguise, finally sailing to England before moving on to Paris, home of many German exiles.

Schurz's heroism and daring made him a popular figure among European democrats. Schurz toured Europe, meeting such other revolutionary figures as Hungarian Louis Kossuth and Italian Giuseppe Mazzini. In 1852 Schurz realized that a rapid return to Germany would be impossible and that there was little hope for a successful return to democratic government. He believed that an exile's life was empty and began to look for a new homeland. He describes his options:

The fatherland was closed to me. England was to me a foreign country, and would always remain so. Where, then? "To America," I said to myself. "The ideals of which I have dreamed and for which I have fought I shall find there, if not fully realized, but hopefully struggling for full realization. In that struggle I shall perhaps be able to take some part. It is a new world, a free world, a world of great ideas and aims. In that world there is perhaps for me a new home." Ubi libertas ibi patria—I formed my resolution on the spot. (104)

Schurz's adaptation of the motto *ubi panis ibi patria* (where there is bread, there is the homeland) to *ubi libertas ibi patria* (where there is liberty, there is the homeland) both acknowledges the economic motivation for much of American immigration and establishes Schurz's quite different reasons. Nevertheless, Schurz's faith in the idea of America can be found echoed in the writings of countless others who came in search of a homeland.

Almost all immigrant autobiographies recount the struggles of adjusting to a new culture, and *The Autobiography of Carl Schurz* is no exception. Schurz writes of the problems of learning a new language and searching for a home. He had a number of advantages that other immigrants lacked. He was, upon his arrival in New York in 1852, an international political hero with money and letters of introduction to American writers and statesmen. Despite these advantages, however, Schurz was still an outsider and would remain one until he migrated to the Midwest in 1854 to settle in Wisconsin among the growing German-American community there.

By 1854 the midwestern cities of Pittsburgh, Cincinnati, Cleveland, Indianapolis, St. Louis, Chicago and Milwaukee had growing German-speaking communities, and Schurz describes leisurely touring them on his way to Watertown, Wisconsin, where one of his uncles had settled with his family. Schurz describes a vibrant ethnic community in the Midwest, complete with German-language schools, churches, and newspapers. The midwestern German community was rapidly becoming part of American culture, and it was soon caught up, like the rest of the nation, in the events leading to the Civil War.

The central chapters in *The Autobiography of Carl Schurz* chronicle the political animation of prewar America, the rise of Abraham Lincoln, and Carl Schurz's work for the new Republican party. Although most midwestern German-Americans were Democrats—the Democratic party presented itself as the protector of the political rights of the foreign-born—Schurz writes that "the Republican platform [of 1856] sounded to me like a bugle-call of liberty" (134). Because of his reputation as a freedom fighter, local Republican leaders asked him to be a Republican spokesman to the large German-speaking community. Arguing against slavery, Schurz spoke throughout Wisconsin during the 1856 campaign, and although Republican presidential candidate John C. Fremont lost the election, the Republican party and Carl Schurz were prepared for 1860.

Schurz lost the election for lieutenant governor of Wisconsin in 1857, but was elected delegate to the Republican convention of 1860 that nominated Abraham Lincoln. After the nomination he campaigned full-time for Lincoln, speaking before German-born voters in Wisconsin, Illinois, Indiana, Ohio, Pennsylvania, and New York. Schurz's campaigning provided him with an opportunity to meet thousands of German-Americans, and in his autobiography he writes that these meetings enabled him to discuss more than partisan politics:

It was a genuine delight to me thus to meet my countrymen who remembered the same old Fatherland that I remembered as the cradle of us all, and who had come from afar to find new homes for themselves and their children in this new land of freedom and betterment ... to talk to them ... about the pending questions to be decided and the duties we owed under existing circumstances to the great Republic that had received us so hospitably, and about the high value of the blessings we enjoyed and had to preserve, and how we could do no greater honor to our old Fatherland than by being conscientious and faithful citizens of the new. (164–65)

Schurz's efforts to elect Lincoln and to encourage his fellow German-Americans to become patriots of their adopted land were recognized by Abraham Lincoln, who appointed him to be American minister to Spain.

Schurz was not pleased with his appointment. As Southern states began to secede from the Union, he became convinced of the inevitability of war, and he proposed to contact ex-German officers and soldiers and establish a cavalry unit to defend Washington, D.C. The secretary of war, General Winfield Scott, believing that any war would be over in a matter of weeks, dismissed Schurz's plan, and prior to the outbreak of hostilities Schurz sailed for Europe.

Schurz did not remain long as minister to Spain. When it became apparent that the war would last some time, Schurz returned to the United States and was appointed a brigadier general. In his autobiography he recounts his military experiences in detail, writing to address both his readers and history. Schurz fought at many of the war's major battles, such as Manassas, Chancellorsville, Antietam, and Gettysburg, and his commentary is more professional and objective than his recollections of his revolutionary experiences in Germany.

After the war Schurz continued to serve in government. He was the senator from Missouri from 1869 to 1875 and secretary of the interior during the Hayes administration. Although he writes about both positions in his *Reminiscences*, *The Autobiography of Carl Schurz* concludes with the end of the Civil War.

CRITICISM

Carl Schurz is an important figure in American history and remains one of the nation's most famous and most successful immigrants. His life has been the study of several major works. In *The Americanization of Carl Schurz* Chester Verne Easum provides an excellent political and social background for Schurz's first ten years in the United States. Claude Moore Fuess, in *Carl Schurz, Reformer, 1829–1906*, provides an overview of Schurz's entire life with an emphasis on his role as the "incarnation of our national conscience." Cecyle Neidle, in her dissertation, "The Foreign-Born View America," cites Schurz as a distinguished patriot and moralist who served his adopted country in an extraordinary manner.

The Autobiography of Carl Schurz reinforces these opinions. In addition, Schurz's narrative provides firsthand insights about a number of significant aspects of American history: German immigration to the United States, the birth of the Republican party, ethnic politics in the Midwest, and the reform movement in the late nineteenth century. Schurz's comments about his experiences in the German-American community also presents valuable information about the second-largest ethnic group in the United States. Finally, throughout his narrative Schurz creates profiles of the famous men he met during his long and illustrious life, and these profiles give readers insights into the personalities of some of the men who controlled the destinies of nations during the second half of the nineteenth century.

BIBLIOGRAPHY

Schurz, Carl. *The Reminiscences of Carl Schurz*. 3 vols. New York: McClure, 1906–8.
———. *Speeches, Correspondence, and Political Papers of Carl Schurz*. 6 vols. New York: Putnam, 1913.
———. *Intimate Letters of Carl Schurz, 1841–1869*. Translated and edited by Joseph Schafer. Madison: State Historical Society of Wisconsin, 1929.
———. *The Autobiography of Carl Schurz*. New York: Scribner's 1961.
Easum, Chester Verne. *The Americanization of Carl Schurz*. Chicago: University of Chicago Press, 1929.
Fuess, Claude Moore. *Carl Schurz, Reformer, 1829–1906*. New York: Dodd, Mead, 1932.
Hogue, Arthur. "The Carl Schurz Memorial Foundation." *Indiana Magazine of History* 51 (1954–55): 335–39.
Neidle, Cecyle. "The Foreign-Born View America: A Study of Autobiographies Written by Immigrants to the United States." Ph.D. diss., New York University, 1962.
O'Brian, Marjorie. *Carl Schurz: Patriot Illustrated*. Madison: State Historical Society of Wisconsin, 1960.
Trefousse, Hans L. *Carl Schurz, a Biography*. Knoxville: University of Tennessee Press, 1982.

Tutt, Clara Little. *Carl Schurz, Patriot*. Madison: State Historical Society of Wisconsin, 1960.

Wade, Mary H. *Pilgrims of Today*. Boston: Little, Brown, 1927.

Wittke, Carl Frederick. *Refugees of Revolution: The German Forty-eighters in America*. 1952. Westport, Conn.: Greenwood Press, 1970.

MONICA SONE
(1919-)

Nisei Daughter

BIOGRAPHY

Monica Sone was born in Seattle in 1919. She is a Nisei, an American-born child of Japanese-born parents. Her father had studied law in Japan and emigrated to the United States in 1904 intending to continue his studies at the University of Michigan. Shortly after his arrival, however, he met and married the daughter of a Japanese Congregationalist minister in Seattle. The Sones remained in Seattle and ran the Carrollton Hotel on the city's waterfront.

Monica Sone led a life typical of many Nisei children. She attended both public school and Japanese school, and like the children of many immigrant parents she was exposed to the values of two often-conflicting cultures. For many Americans the bicultural experience has been enriching, but during the late 1930s anti-Japanese feelings, especially strong on the West Coast, forced the Sones to confront their ethnicity and racial prejudice firsthand.

After the Japanese attack on Pearl Harbor the Sones, as well as almost all of the members of the Japanese-American community in the Far West, were ordered to dispose of their property and prepare for relocation. The Sones were sent to Camp Harmony at Puyallup, Washington, and were later transferred to Camp Minidoka, Idaho. Near the end of the war Sone was released from the camp to the supervision of a Presbyterian minister in Chicago and shortly thereafter received a scholarship to Wendell College in Indiana. There she began to write seriously, using her experiences as a Nisei and as a prisoner in a relocation camp as the material for her work. In 1952 she published her recollections as an autobiography, *Nisei Daughter*.

THE AUTOBIOGRAPHY

Nisei Daughter describes the coming of age of a young woman caught between two cultures at war with each other, and although the narrative records a personal triumph, it does so against a backdrop of racism and discrimination. Sone opens her autobiography with a discovery:

The first five years of my life I lived in amoebic bliss, not knowing whether I was a plant or animal, at the old Carrollton Hotel on the waterfront of Seattle. One day when I was a happy six-year-old, I made the shocking discovery that I had Japanese blood. I was a Japanese. (3)

The discovery of identity is the main theme of many autobiographies, and *Nisei Daughter* records a search in which Monica Sone must first discover what is Japanese, then what is American, and finally what is Japanese-American. Perhaps Sone's greatest triumph is that she recounts her traumatic experience without apparent bitterness; her story records the dedication of a family and a community, and although her autobiography is personal and immediate, it is also a statement on behalf of an entire community.

While Sone adopts a pseudonym, Kazuko Itoi, in her narrative, she is clearly writing of her own experiences. In describing her early life Sone emphasizes the culturally diverse nature of her childhood: Her family ate both Japanese and American food, they spoke both Japanese and English, and Sone grew up playing both Japanese and American games. This peaceful coexistence of cultures ended, however, when Sone was sent to Nihon Gakko, the Japanese school. When her parents told her she must go, she protested that going to two schools a day would be unfair, but once she began attending Nihon Gakko, her protests increased, and they continue throughout the first half of her autobiography.

Sone depicts the Japanese schools as the symbol of Japanese culture, the antithesis of the American public school and the relative freedom of American culture. Sent by their Japanese-born parents, the Nisei children learned etiquette and language under the strict supervision of their teacher. Sone remembers:

As far as I was concerned, Mr. Ohashi's superior standard boiled down to one thing. The model child is one with *rigor mortis* . . . no noise, no trouble, no back talk . . . . As far as I was concerned, Nihon Gakko was a total loss. I could not use my Japanese on the people at the hotel. Bowing was practical only at the Nihon Gakko. If I were to bow to the hotel patrons, they would have laughed in my face. Therefore promptly at five-thirty every day, I shed Nihon Gakko and returned with relief to an environment which was the only real one to me. (24–28)

Sone recalls that the lessons of the Nihon Gakko seemed out of place in America, and she reinforces the idea of strangeness with her description of Mrs. Matsui, an older woman who has mastered the art of Japanese etiquette. Sone presents her as cold, distant, and overwhelmingly formal. Sone remembers that her mother often took her to visit the homes of other Japanese families, and she writes that she found the visits torture. After one particularly excruciating visit, complete with drinking scalding tea and eating brittle rice wafers, Sone recalls how she

staggered out at last into the frosty night, feeling tight as a drum and emotionally shaken from being too polite for too long. I hoped on our next call our hostess would worry less about being hospitable and more about her guests' comfort, but that was an impudent thought for a Japanese girl. (86)

Sone records two specific experiences that demonstrate her growing alienation from Japanese culture. The first is "Tenchosetsu," the celebration of the emperor's birthday. When her Japanese teacher announced that the entire class would attend the celebration, Sone's reaction was immediate and emotional:

I groaned. I thought it would be wasteful to spend a beautiful spring afternoon crowded into a dingy, crumbling hall and sit numbly through a ritual which never varied one word or gesture from year to year. But I knew there was no escape. (66)

Sone's language here, and in her other descriptions of Japanese school and social functions, is significant. Words like "numb" and "rigid" appear, and at the end of each passage the idea of escape or relaxation is often present. This tension between confinement and freedom is especially clear in Sone's second major example of alienation, her description of the family's trip to Japan.

Sone makes her distance from Japanese culture clear in her description of the family's visit. She describes her father's explanations of Japanese history, geography, and culture, but what she recalls most vividly is her desire to break away from the constant constraints of politeness and correct behavior. She remembers that at her grandfather's home in Takayama her alienation reached its peak when she was confronted by neighborhood children who first taunted her and then threw stones at her grandfather's house. Sone's visit to Japan taught her she was not Japanese, at least not Japanese enough for the Japanese. She rejects her Japanese heritage, with its rigidity and formality, but upon her return to the United States she learns that Americans refuse to accept her also.

Because the Sones lived within Seattle's Japanese-American community, Sone records little open prejudice in the first half of her autobiography. As the Japanese war in China continued, however, the family began to feel the effects of nativistic hostility. One summer the family attempted to rent a house near the ocean. They were turned away several times. Finally a woman told Sone and her mother that she wouldn't rent to "Japs." Sone, crying, turned to her mother and asked, "Is it so terrible to be a Japanese?" (114)

The most dramatic sections of Sone's narrative describe the events that followed the Japanese attack on Pearl Harbor. Hearing the news on the radio

Sunday morning, December 7, 1941, the family is shocked and confused. Previously Sone and her brother had criticized Japan's aggression in China and Manchuria, while her father and mother had argued against English and American prejudice against Asians, but after December 7 all political discussion ceased as the family began to realize the impact of the war.

Sone recounts the first weeks of the war quickly, remembering the stares of once-friendly storeclerks, the rumors of imprisonment circulating within the Japanese community, and visits by FBI agents. Finally, the moment the family dreaded arrived—relocation. With Executive Order no. 9066 the War Department authorized the removal of the Japanese, citizens and aliens, from the West Coast.

Relocation came quickly. General J. L. DeWitt of the Western Defense Command declared the West Coast Military Area no. 1 and ordered all Japanese removed. The army would take care of the relocation, and the Sones, along with thousands of other Japanese-Americans, received their orders:

Dispose of your homes and property. Wind up your business. Register the family. One seabag of bedding, two suitcases of clothing allowed per person. People of District #1 must report at 8th and Lane Street, 8 p.m. on April 28. (160)

Sone's account of her family's pilgrimage first to a temporary relocation center and then to Camp Minidoka in Idaho recaptures the dramatic contradictions faced by Japanese-Americans during the first years of World War II: citizens kept behind barbed wire, families forced to hand over such contraband items as knives, scissors, and hammers, and confiscation of all material written in Japanese, including the Bible. An even greater contradiction occurred later in the war. Sone recalls that one day a group of army officers appeared at Camp Minidoka and announced that the War Department was forming a special combat unit for the Nisei. The Nisei and their parents were astonished, wondering why, if they were loyal enough to fight, they had been interned in the first place. After initial misgivings, many of the young men, including Sone's brother, enlisted and left for basic training, leaving their families behind the barbed-wire fences.

By 1943 the War Relocation Authority was permitting Nisei to leave the camps if they had been cleared by the FBI and had proof of a job or had been accepted by a college. Sone was sponsored by a family in Chicago, and after a brief and unsuccessful stint as a dental assistant, she enrolled at Wendell College in southern Indiana, where she quickly immersed herself in college activities. During her second year there, however, she received a letter from her parents urging her to return to the camp for a Christmas visit. What she found when she returned shocked her; she had forgotten the armed guards. At the camp she found her parents older and more tired. They seemed to have given up something, Sone writes, but they remained hopeful for their children. Sone ends her autobiography with a depiction of her leaving the camp, her parents looking like "wistful immigrants," and she wonders when they would be able to leave. She, however, remains hopeful:

I was returning to Wendell College with confidence and hope. I had discovered a deeper, stronger pulse in the American scene. I was going back into its main stream, still with my Oriental eyes, but with an entirely different outlook, for now I felt more like a whole person instead of a sadly split personality. The Japanese and the American parts of me were now blended into one. (237–38)

While heartfelt, this concluding praise for America is out of place with most of the rest of *Nisei Daughter*. Except for the two short final sections, Sone's narrative is a chronicle of racism and prejudice—first Japanese and then American. The praise for democracy and America appears to be more an obligatory exhortation than a logical summation of the material that precedes it.

CRITICISM

Nisei Daughter appears to be a simple, straightforward narrative of success and perseverance in the face of prejudice and hostility, and a number of early reviewers suggested it as suitable children's reading. Recent readers, however, have discovered that Sone's autobiography is more complex. In her excellent study of Asian-American writers, *Asian American Literature*, Elaine Kim observes:

Upon closer examination within the context of Japanese American social history, however, the autobiography appears to be an account of the gradual suffocation by racial discrimination of everything that is creative and spirited or pugnacious in one *nisei* woman. (74)

Nisei Daughter suggests more than it says. Despite Sone's emphasis on her eventual successful assimilation into mainstream American culture, her book documents the isolating effects of institutionalized racism. It also shows the cost of assimilation. Sone and others did move "deeper into America," but the move was preceded by the destruction of a flourishing Japanese-American community.

BIBLIOGRAPHY

Sone, Monica. *Nisei Daughter*. 1953. Seattle: University of Washington Press, 1979.
Daniels, Roger. *The Decision to Relocate the Japanese-Americans*. Philadelphia: Lippincott, 1975.
Hazeltine, Alice Isabel. *We Grew Up in America*. Nashville: Abingdon, 1954.
Hosokawa, Bill. *Nisei: The Quiet Americans*. New York: William Morrow, 1969.

Kim, Elaine H. *Asian American Literature: An Introduction to the Writings and Their Social Context*. Philadelphia: Temple University Press, 1982.

Kulkin, Mary-Ellen. *Her Way: Biographies of Women for Young People*. Chicago: American Library Association, 1976.

Ogawa, Dennis. *From Japs to Japanese: An Evolution of Japanese-American Stereotypes*. Berkeley, Calif.: McCutchan, 1971.

Peterson, William. *Japanese Americans: Oppression and Success*. New York: Random House, 1971.

Weglyn, Michi. *Years of Infamy: The Untold Story of America's Concentration Camps*. New York: William Morrow, 1976.

PIRI THOMAS
(1928-   )

Down These Mean Streets

BIOGRAPHY

Piri Thomas is, without a doubt, the best-known Puerto Rican writer in the United States. His work has been reviewed in such mainstream periodicals as *Life*, *Atlantic*, *Newsweek*, *Time*, *Harper's*, and the *New Republic*, and his work in Spanish Harlem is the subject of a film, *Petey and Johnny*. Because of his stature in both the Puerto Rican and Anglo communities, Thomas is an important figure in the Puerto Rican community in New York and a spokesman for Puerto Rican interests, both social and literary.

Thomas was born in New York City in 1928. He grew up in Spanish Harlem before his parents moved to Long Island during World War II. After less than two years Thomas returned to Spanish Harlem where he began to use drugs and commit crimes to support his habit. In 1950 he was convicted of attempted armed robbery of a Greenwich Village bar. He served six years in prison before returning to Spanish Harlem, where he worked in a rehabilitation center for drug addicts and became involved in the Pentecostal movement. Thomas' autobiography, *Down These Mean Streets*, appeared in 1967. He later wrote two additional autobiographical works, *Savior, Savior, Hold My Hand* and *Seven Long Times*. These three works chronicle Thomas' life in Spanish Harlem and in prison from the late 1930s to the 1960s. Thomas continues to live and work in New York City.

THE AUTOBIOGRAPHY

Thomas' most famous book is *Down These Mean Streets*, which chronicles his life through his release from prison. *Savior, Savior, Hold My Hand* continues Thomas' life story, but emphasizes his work as a lay Pentecostal missionary in Spanish Harlem. *Seven Long Times* is a straightforward prison narrative, describing the Comstock prison riot of August 1955, that Thomas

wrote in response to the Attica prison riots of 1971. While each book is part
of the overlapping narrative of the life of Piri Thomas, *Down These Mean
Streets* is the most complete and comprehensive of his three autobiographical
works.

Down These Mean Streets is a realistic description of ghetto life, a story of
crime and punishment, a captivity narrative, and a conversion story. In it Piri
Thomas exhibits the concerns of many other ethnic-American writers. He
dramatizes the problems of class, generational conflict, ethnic rivalry and hostility, poverty, and identity. But for Thomas, the pervasive issue of race influences all of the conflicts he faces. He creates an autobiographical self, a dark-
skinned Puerto Rican caught between two worlds, and in his search for identity
within a divided culture he raises serious issues about the multiethnic nature
of American society.

Thomas calls the first section of his narrative simply "Harlem," and in it
he creates a vivid picture of the urban environment and begins to develop
the conflicts he faces. Thomas depicts his father digging ditches for the WPA
while he roams the Upper East Side of Manhattan. The conflicts and hostility
found in a changing ethnic community are a central part of Thomas' narrative:

Sometimes you don't fit in. Like you're a Puerto Rican on an Italian block. After my
new baby brother, Ricardo, died of some kind of germs, Poppa moved us from 111th
Street to Italian turf on 114th Street between Second and Third avenues. I guess Poppa
wanted to get Momma away from the hard memories of the old pad.

I sure missed 111th Street, where everybody acted, walked, and talked like me. But
on 114th Street everything went all right for a while. There were a few dirty looks
from the spaghetti-an'-sauce cats, but no big sweat. Till that one day I was on my way
home from school and almost had reached my stoop when someone called: "Hey,
you dirty, fuckin' spic." (33)

In order to survive in the streets, Thomas has to prove that he has "heart"
by fighting, and he soon becomes known as a young man with courage.

In 1944 Thomas' father began working in an airplane factory and soon
moved his family out of the Barrio to Babylon, Long Island. It is there that
Thomas' identity crisis came to a head. Thomas recalls that his family was
accepted, but because he was the darkest member of the family, he became
an outcast. At school he was ignored or made the object of racial comments.
His white classmates considered him black, and one day he overheard one
of them say that he was only passing for Puerto Rican because he was too
dark to pass for white.

Thomas discovers that the racism and hostility he encountered in the ghetto
are deeply ingrained throughout American society and that his ability to
interact with people is determined not by his actions or character but by the
color of his skin. This lesson is reinforced when he leaves his family to return
to the Barrio. There he and a friend apply for jobs as door-to-door salesmen.
Thomas is not hired, but his "white" friend is. Thomas writes:

I didn't feel so much angry as I did sick, like throwing up sick. Later, when I told this story to my buddy, a colored cat, he said, "Hell, Piri, Ah know stuff like that can burn a cat up, but a Negro faces that all the time."

"I know that," I said, "but I wasn't a Negro then. I was still only Puerto Rican." (107)

After these lessons Thomas begins to identify with blacks, and to test this new identity he signs on a merchant ship sailing out of New York. As in the narratives of many newcomers to America, the movement away from the city is depicted by Thomas as a necessary part of coming to terms with the totality of American society. Thomas deliberately depicts his journey as a voyage of discovery. He plans to travel to the South, in his mind the geographic heart of American prejudice, to try to learn the causes of prejudice and understand it better.

Thomas' southern voyage leaves him bitter and angry. On ship and ashore he discovers a pervasive racist system that labels him black and keeps him in the most menial jobs and out of the places he wants to visit. On his return to New York, Thomas becomes a drug addict.

Thomas' description of his drug addiction is one of the most powerful and graphic sections of his autobiography. The inevitable progress from snorting heroin to skin popping to full-time addiction shows Thomas losing both his self-respect and self-control. Dealing drugs to support his growing habit, Thomas eventually ends up without either money or drugs, and strung out and broke he decides to kick his habit cold turkey. He writes about this experience in cold, bitter terms, emphasizing the pains of withdrawal.

After his recovery Thomas gets a job washing dishes but again confronts hostility and prejudice. He turns to crime and learns that this questions a man's heart, not his color. He joins a gang of thieves and is told by its leader, Danny, that the gang is a kind of league of nations: "Billy's a Polack, I'm Irish, Louie is a white Puerto Rican, and you, who the hell knows?" (208). Thomas is skeptical, but when he proves his courage by robbing a cigar store and is accepted by the others, he finally feels that he has found a group that accepts him for what he can do and not for what he looks like. He remains with the gang for over a year, robbing bars throughout New York City, until police pressure forces the gang to disband.

After a one-year hiatus, the gang regroups for another job, and Thomas' account of the attempted armed robbery of a Greenwich Village bar in February 1950 is a small masterpiece. He re-creates the sense of anticipation and the intensity, confusion, and horror of the action so effectively that the reader seems to be watching the robbery taking place. This particular job is the gang's one failure; the bar is too crowded, the patrons panic, and an off-duty policeman present shoots Thomas. He shoots back, wounding the policeman, and fails in his attempt to escape.

Thomas has structured the first part of his narrative as a literal descent into hell; he has descended through the levels of poverty, racial discrimination, drug addiction, and crime until he is finally stripped of everything, lying naked and wounded under guard in a hospital room. Out of the ashes of one life, however, another is made.

The conventions of the conversion narrative demand a contrast built around the conversion experience, and like others who have written about their conversion experiences, Thomas sets his conversion at the emotional center of his narrative, using it to turn his autobiography into more than a naturalistic look at urban street life. He depicts prison as a hell, a place of physical and emotional punishment, but it is also a place of purgation and potential rebirth. Thomas describes his feelings in prison succinctly:

One of the worst feelings I can imagine is to be something or someplace and not be able to accept the fact. So it was with me—I was a con in jail, but nothing in the world could make me accept it. Not the grey clothes, not the green bars, not the bugle's measuring of the time, not all the blue-uniformed hacks, not the insipid food, not the new lines on my face—nothing. (245)

While Thomas' accounts of the physical experiences of prison are important, he places his emphasis in the prison sections of his narrative on the effects of solitude and time. Both are crucial to him, for they compel him to begin searching for self-discipline as a way to avoid insanity. Solitude and discipline teach Thomas lessons about himself and his life; they teach him the need for reflection, and like many other writers, Thomas uses his time and reflection to put his life in a new perspective, a perspective that becomes the beginning of his autobiography.

In prison Thomas meets two men who provide direction for his transformation. The first is Kent, an educated white prisoner whose skillful use of language fascinates Thomas. Kent provides Thomas with more than an interest in words; he introduces him to the world of books and writing, lasting influences. The second person of influence is Muhammed, a Black Muslim minister who teaches him the need for pride and discipline.

Thomas converts; the dignity, stability, and discipline taught by the Nation of Islam provide him with the means of coping with life in prison. He learns, grows, and eventually reenters the culture, and although his religious conversion is only temporary, a real transformation has taken place in his life. Looking back on his decision to become a Black Muslim, Thomas writes:

I became curious about everything human. Though I didn't remain a Muslim after my eventual release from jail, I never forgot one thing that Muhammed said, for I believed it too: "No matter what a man's color or race he has a need of dignity and he'll go anywhere, become anything or do anything to get it—anything." (283)

The final chapters of *Down These Mean Streets* show Thomas' return to the streets of Spanish Harlem and, after a temptation to return to drugs, his turning from the Nation of Islam to Christianity and his continuing search for dignity and identity.

Down These Mean Streets is not a typical conversion narrative, although it does contain such traditional elements as the depiction of early transgressions, enlightenment in confinement, and good works after the conversion. And although Thomas does describe two religious conversions, his emphasis is on his search for identity and his discovery of his own sense of dignity and self-worth. He depicts religion as a means, not an end.

CRITICISM

Piri Thomas is an important figure in Puerto Rican–American literature. Unlike such earlier Puerto Rican writers as Jesus Colon and Pedro Juan Labarthe, Thomas has no personal connection with Puerto Rico, and English is his native language. His work is the first of the mainland Puerto Ricans, or Neoricans. In addition, Thomas captures urban street life effectively. As Wayne Charles Miller notes in *A Gathering of Ghetto Writers*:

Thomas creates in the autobiographical *Down These Mean Streets* a narrative that includes nearly all the elements of ghetto existence: the early gang wars, the early introduction to sex (in this case both heterosexual and homosexual), the early experiments with alcohol and drugs, the terrors of drug addiction, the early encounters with police and the later choice of crime as a means of getting the all-consuming American objective—money. (67)

Down These Mean Streets is a significant autobiography for a number of reasons. First, it is a compelling narrative of one man's struggle to overcome numerous social handicaps. Second, Thomas' autobiography details the impact of racial discrimination and describes the kind of response discrimination can bring forth. Finally, Thomas writes eloquently as a representative spokesman for America's fastest-growing minority, Hispanic-Americans, and his voice speaks of lessons that must be learned.

BIBLIOGRAPHY

Thomas, Piri. *Down These Mean Streets*. New York: Knopf, 1967.
———. *Savior, Savior, Hold My Hand*. Garden City, N.Y.: Doubleday, 1972.
———. *Seven Long Times*. New York: Praeger, 1974.
———. *Stories from El Barrio*. New York: Knopf, 1978.
Cordasco, Francesco, Eugene Bucchioni, and Diego Castellanos. *Puerto Ricans on the United States Mainland: A Bibliography of Reports, Texts, Critical Studies, and Related Materials*. Totowa, N.J.: Rowman and Littlefield, 1972.
Holte, James C. "The Representative Voice: Autobiography and the Ethnic Experience." *MELUS* 9, 2 (1983): 25–46.
Klau, Susan L. "The Use of Spanish and the Works of Piri Thomas." Ph.D. diss., University of Puerto Rico, 1977.

Miller, Wayne Charles. *A Gathering of Ghetto Writers*. New York: New York University Press, 1972.

Mohr, Eugene V. "Fifty Years of Puerto Rican Literature in English—1923–1973: An Annotated Bibliography." *Revista/Review Interamericana* 3, 3 (1973): 290–98.

———. *The Nuyorican Experience: Literature of the Puerto Rican Minority*. Westport, Conn.: Greenwood Press, 1982.

Wakefield, Dan. *Island in the City: The World of Spanish Harlem*. Boston: Houghton Mifflin, 1959.

BOOKER T. WASHINGTON
(1856–1915)

Up from Slavery

BIOGRAPHY

Booker Taliaferro Washington was born into slavery in Virginia in 1856. By 1895 he was the most influential black man in America, an advisor to Theodore Roosevelt and William Howard Taft, and confidant of Andrew Carnegie and John D. Rockefeller. He was not universally praised, however. W. E. B. Du Bois questioned the wisdom of his advice to American blacks, and William Monroe Trotter, the editor of the *Boston Guardian*, considered him a traitor to his race.

Booker T. Washington's life provides a perfect example of the success story of the self-made man in America. As a young child he had a desire to learn, and he gained the rudiments of education while working to help support his family in Malden, West Virginia. Later, with almost no money, he traveled to the Hampton Institute in Virginia to continue his education. After graduation from Hampton, Washington was selected to head a school for blacks in Alabama. As the head of Tuskegee Institute, Washington emphasized practical education, self-help, and cooperation with whites in "all things essential to mutual progress."

At the Cotton States Exposition in Atlanta in 1895, Washington delivered a celebrated address renouncing social equality and proposing that blacks pursue careers in agriculture, mechanics, commerce, domestic service, and the professions. By appeasing white supremacists and encouraging black moderation, Washington insured Tuskegee's continued success and his own position as leader of the black community in America. Although race relations did not substantially improve during the final years of his life and criticism of his positions continued, Washington continued to write and speak as the most powerful spokesman for the American black community until his death in 1915.

THE AUTOBIOGRAPHY

Up from Slavery, published in 1901, is a classic American success story that appealed to millions of readers. As a rags-to-riches story it ranks with the autobiographies of Andrew Carnegie and Edward Bok, but unlike the stories of those men, Washington's personal narrative confronts an issue more controversial than economic success—racial prejudice. *Up from Slavery* appealed to black readers because it provided a model, and it appealed to white readers because Washington asserted that blacks should not demand political or social equality, insisting instead that the black movement emphasize economic, intellectual, and moral development. Washington's autobiography is a conservative document. Not all readers now or then would agree with its thesis. Yet its power remains, especially as it documents the heroic struggles of one man to rise above the circumstances of his birth.

Washington opens his autobiography with a description of slave life on a plantation in Franklin County, Virginia. His mother was the plantation cook, and he never knew his father, who was rumored to be one of the white men who lived on a nearby plantation. He writes that he knew nothing else of his ancestry. Washington's description of slave life on the plantation is detailed. He includes examples of hard work, inadequate clothing and shelter, and the deliberate white decision to keep slaves ignorant. Surprisingly, Washington's recollection of his young life as a slave contains little bitterness. Both the whites and the blacks, he observes, were victims of the same institution, and after the Emancipation Proclamation the ex-slaves were as suited to begin life anew as their ex-masters. For the most part, neither masters nor slaves had acquired any particular skills, Washington asserts.

After the Civil War, Washington's stepfather moved his family to Malden, West Virginia, where he had secured a job in a salt furnace. In his description of his life in Malden, Washington establishes the two main themes of his autobiography, work and education. According to Washington, the two are equally important elements of self-improvement. For Washington, the need to work and the desire to learn complement each other. Washington provides his readers with the following example of his own desire to learn:

I had an intense longing to learn to read. I determined, when quite a small child, that if I accomplished nothing else in life, I would in some way get enough education to enable me to read common books and newspapers. Soon after we got settled in some manner in our new cabin in West Virginia, I induced my mother to get hold of a book for me. How or where she got it I do not know, but in some manner she procured an old copy of Webster's "blue-back" spelling book. (43)

Washington worked while he learned, first with his stepfather at the salt furnace and later in a coal mine. Work kept him from attending school regularly, but when he had the opportunity, Washington went to class in the school founded by the black families of Malden.

Having to work to help support his family and make time for his own education had a tremendous impact on Washington. After describing his early life in Malden he tells his readers the lessons he drew from his struggles. "I have learned that success is to be measured not so much by the position that one has reached in life as by the obstacles which he has overcome while trying to succeed" (50).

While working in the coal mine at Malden, Washington overheard two other miners talking about a "great school for coloured people somewhere in Virginia." The school was Hampton Normal and Agricultural Institute, and Washington's experiences there, as much as his early life on the plantation and in Malden, would influence his entire life and educational philosophy.

After traveling by foot and wagon to Hampton, the penniless Washington enrolled at the institute, working as a janitor to pay for his tuition and board. Washington writes that it was at Hampton that he learned the most important lesson of his life.

I learned what education was expected to do for an individual. Before going there I had a good deal of the then rather prevalent idea among our people that to secure an education meant to have a good, easy time, free from all necessity of manual labour. At Hampton I not only learned that it was not a disgrace to labour, but learned to love labour, not alone for its financial value, but for labour's own sake and for the independence and self-reliance which the ability to do something which the world wants done brings. At that institution I got my first taste of what it meant to live a life of unselfishness, my first knowledge of the fact that the happiest individuals are those who do the most to make others useful and happy. (68)

The two ideals of work and service permeate *Up from Slavery*. Washington measures his own achievements and the aspirations of others by these two standards.

Washington graduated from Hampton Institute in 1875 and returned to Malden to teach in the town's school for blacks. There he taught both a day school for children and a night school for adults, stressing self-improvement as well as "book education." He also faced hostility from members of the Ku Klux Klan, who had organized to "regulate" the lives of the blacks by burning churches and schoolhouses. In 1878 Washington returned to Hampton Institute as a teacher, working with a federal program to educate American Indians.

Washington interrupts his narrative prior to describing his work as a faculty member at Hampton to provide an overview of the Reconstruction period. He depicts it as a time of excesses on the parts of both blacks and whites. After describing the Klan activity, Washington recalls the enthusiasms that swept through the black community: the craze for Greek and Latin, the desire to hold office, and the call to preach. Each was a symptom of a failure to "form any proper conception of what education was about" (71). Washington places the fault on the federal government:

During the whole of the Reconstruction period our people throughout the South looked to the Federal Government for everything, very much as a child looks to its mother. That was not unnatural. The central government gave them freedom, and the whole nation had been enriched for more than two centuries by the labour of the Negro.... it was cruelly wrong in the central government, at the beginning of our freedom, to fail to make some provision for the general education of our people. (73)

Washington decries the longings for the trappings of an education and the failure to perceive what real education was. The ambition was praiseworthy, but without direction the results were often discouraging. Washington notes the widespread belief that a smattering of Greek or Latin would automatically make one a superior being. He describes how the ministry was the profession that suffered most. Washington writes that "in the early days of freedom almost every coloured man who learned to read would receive 'a call to preach' within a few days after he began reading" (72). For many, the call seemed a way to avoid the crushing manual labor that most blacks were compelled to perform. Politics seemed to offer another escape, but Washington observes with sorrow the fate of the black legislators of the Reconstruction. Most were either uneducated or partially educated, and as a result they made, in Washington's opinion, tremendous mistakes. He sees whites refusing to enfranchise blacks for fear of the repetition of those same mistakes, and believes that the rush to political office actually hindered black political activity.

Washington views all of these enthusiasms as failures to see education for what it is, training to work and serve. As he picks up his narrative with his work at Hampton and the establishment of Tuskegee, it is clear that he is contrasting his own beliefs about education with those popular during Reconstruction.

Washington's life work began when he was recommended by General S. C. Armstrong, the head of Hampton Institute, to take charge of a normal school to be established in Tuskegee, Alabama. Washington and the citizens of Tuskegee opened the new school on July 4, 1881, in a small shanty and church building that had been secured for the campus. Washington and Olivia Davidson, his future wife and a new instructor, immediately set out to make Tuskegee a center for practical education and an example of Washington's educational theories.

The students were making progress in learning books and in developing their minds; but it became apparent at once that, if we were to make any permanent impression upon those who had come to us for training, we must do something besides teaching them mere books. The students had come from homes where they had had no opportunities for lessons which would teach them how to care for their bodies. With few exceptions, the homes in Tuskegee in which the students boarded were but little improvement upon those from which they had come. We wanted to teach the students how to bathe; how to care for their teeth and clothing. We wanted to teach them what to eat, and how to eat it properly, and how to take care for their rooms. Aside from this, we wanted to give them such a practical knowledge of some one industry, together with the spirit of industry, thrift and economy, that they would be sure of knowing how to make a living after they had left us. We wanted to teach them to study actual things instead of mere books alone. (96)

Once Washington begins recounting his life and work at Tuskegee, *Up from Slavery* becomes a narrative of an institution as much as the story of one man. Washington's greatest achievement was the establishment, growth, and success of Tuskegee, and his pride in his work is evident in the autobiography. He recounts supervising the students who constructed their own buildings, planning home economics and hygiene classes, and raising funds to keep the struggling school alive. Throughout he uses the analogy of the Children of Israel; like the Israelites, Washington's students had been slaves or the children of slaves, and they had to learn to struggle for survival in their new-found freedom. Washington assumes the role of Moses, leading his people out of the bondage of ignorance and poverty, and at the Atlanta Cotton States and International Exposition in 1895 he delivered an address that made him the best-known and most respected black leader in the country.

Washington recognizes the importance of his five-minute speech in his life, and he includes it in his autobiography. His address summarized his attitudes toward education and the position of the black community in the South, and Washington used the forum offered by the exposition to reach a worldwide audience. The thrust of the address can be seen in the following passage:

Our greatest danger is that in the great leap from slavery to freedom we may overlook the fact that the masses of us are to live by the production of our hands, and fail to keep in mind that we shall prosper in proportion as we learn to dignify and glorify common labour and put brains and skill into the common occupations of life; shall prosper in proportion as we learn to draw the line between the superficial and the substantial, the ornamental gewgaws of life and the useful. No race can prosper until it learns that there is as much dignity in tilling a field as in writing a poem. It is at the bottom of life we must begin, and not at the top. Nor should we permit our grievances to overshadow our opportunities. (147)

Washington's call for moderation, his insistence on cooperation rather than confrontation, and his emphasis on opportunities rather than injustices were criticized by some black newspapers, but the general response was overwhelmingly positive. After the Atlanta speech, Washington became the confidant of presidents, capitalists, and educators. His advice was sought on all the major issues impacting upon black Americans.

The concluding chapters of *Up from Slavery* chronicle Washington's travels and meetings with other great men. This part of the autobiography shows the transformation that took place in Washington's life. After the Atlanta speech Washington became a public man, and the tone of his narrative shifts from personal history to public record. It ends on a note of hope, with Washington praising both blacks and whites of the South for the distance traveled together:

The outside world does not know, neither can it appreciate, the struggle that is constantly going on in the hearts of both the Southern white people and their former slaves to free themselves from racial prejudice; and while both races are thus struggling they should have the sympathy, the support, and the forbearance of the rest of the world. (204)

CRITICISM

Booker T. Washington and his program of racial cooperation and political accommodation were never universally popular. Moderate and conservative black leaders, as well as most of the white political leadership, welcomed Washington's refusal to encourage confrontation. There were, however, other voices. Perhaps the most articulate critic of Washington and his program was W. E. B. Du Bois, who argued that black Americans had to confront white power structures and demand both economic and political rights. Washington's reputation remains mixed; some view him as a successful leader, while others see him as a tool of white interests.

A similar critical split appears in commentaries about his writing. Recently, however, criticism has begun to examine the form of his writing. Stephen Butterfield, writing in *Black Autobiography in America*, argues that *Up from Slavery* is a carefully crafted narrative:

He [Washington] professes religious values for political ends to conciliate and gain support of a white reading public; the Protestant ethic is the basis on which he identifies with American culture; he condemns racism because of its effects upon the morals of the white man (Washington, 165–66); and he interprets the suffering of the Negro as a sign of special attention from God. In these respects *Up from Slavery* resembles a slave narrative. Its purpose is to further a program external to itself, and its values are constructed according to whether or not they serve that program. (113)

Up from Slavery also resembles the narratives of success of other ethnic-American writers. Washington records a dramatic rise from poverty to prosperity and speaks as a representative of an oppressed minority. His autobiography combines a number of narrative traditions, and it remains of interest to students of black literature and culture, ethnic studies, and autobiographical writing.

BIBLIOGRAPHY

Washington, Booker T. *Up from Slavery*. 1901. In *Three Negro Classics*, edited by John Hope Franklin. New York: Avon Books, 1965.

————. *Character Building*. Garden City, N.Y.: Doubleday, Page, 1902.

————. *Working with the Hands: Being a Sequel to Up from Slavery*. Garden City, N.Y.: Doubleday, Page, 1904.

————. *Selected Speeches of Booker T. Washington*. Garden City, N.Y.: Doubleday, 1932.

Butterfield, Stephen. *Black Autobiography in America*. Amherst: University of Massachusetts Press, 1974.

Flynn, John P. "Booker T. Washington: Uncle Tom or Wooden Horse." *Journal of Negro History* 54 (July 1969): 262–74.

Graham, Shirley. *Booker T. Washington: Educator of Hand, Head, and Heart*. New York: Julian Messner, 1955.

Hawkins, Hugh. *Booker T. Washington and His Critics: The Problem of Negro Leadership*. Boston: Heath, 1962.

Mathews, Basil. *Booker T. Washington, Educator and Interracial Integrater*. Cambridge, Mass.: Harvard University Press, 1948.

Scott, Emmett J., and Lyman B. Stowe. *Booker T. Washington: Builder of a Civilization*. Garden City, N.Y.: Doubleday, Page, 1916.

Spencer, Samuel R. *Booker T. Washington and the Negro's Place in American Life*. Boston: Little, Brown, 1955.

Thornbrough, Emma L. "Booker T. Washington As Seen by His White Contemporaries." *Journal of Negro History* 53 (April 1968): 161–82.

THEODORE H. WHITE
(1915–1986)

In Search of History

BIOGRAPHY

Theodore H. White was born in Boston on May 6, 1915. His father, David White, had emigrated from Russia in 1891, and after working as a pushcart peddler in Boston he attended the local YMCA and Northeastern University. He eventually became an attorney. White's mother, Mary Winkeller White, was born in Boston in 1891 to Jewish immigrant parents from Russia. Education was important to the White family. Theodore White was sent to both Boston public schools and Hebrew schools, and later he attended the famous Boston Latin School and Harvard where he studied history and languages.

After he graduated from Harvard in 1938, White became a foreign correspondent for *Time*. Stationed in China, White covered World War II, the fall of Japan, and the rise of Chinese communism. In 1946 he published the Pulitzer Prize–winning *Thunder out of China*, which was sharply critical of Chiang Kai-shek and the Nationalist regime. He lost his position with *Time* because of his comments. Later he served as a correspondent in Europe for the Overseas News Agency, and his observations there led to his second major book, *Fire in the Ashes: Europe at Mid-Century*.

Although White's early fame came from his writing about China and Europe, he became a nationally known figure for his work describing domestic politics. His series entitled *The Making of the President*, written for the 1960, 1964, 1968, and 1972 elections, was both popular and well received critically. *The Making of the President* books chronicled the inner workings of American politics in an interesting and intelligent manner and made White wealthy and famous. In 1978 his autobiography, *In Search of History: A Personal Adventure*, appeared. In 1982 *America in Search of Itself*, a concluding volume to his presidential series, was published. White died on May 15, 1986.

THE AUTOBIOGRAPHY

In Search of History is primarily a memoir, a traditional form of the autobiography, but one seldom written by ethnic-American writers. Most ethnic-
American autobiographies are highly personal narratives. Their authors, having experienced the trauma of immigration and assimilation into a strange
new culture, most often write confessional or conversion stories. The memoir
traditionally records great events or meetings with great people; the author
recalls his or her observations of others, and the resulting narrative says as
much about a particular period of history as it does about the autobiographer.

Theodore White was a professional observer his entire adult life and had
written about many of the men who shaped the course of history during the
twentieth century. His autobiography combines the elements of personal
narrative and memoir. While White provides illuminating profiles of such
figures as Chou En-lai, Douglas MacArthur, Dwight Eisenhower, and John
Kennedy, he also tells the story of how a young Jewish boy from the ghetto
in Boston moved into the mainstream of American culture and world affairs
so as to be able to record the making of history.

White calls the first section of his autobiography, which presents his life
in Boston from 1915 to 1938, an "Exercise in Recollection." It is both the
most personal section of White's narrative and the one that examines ethnic
material most closely. White looks back to his youth, focusing his attention
on his family, his neighborhood, and his schools, to establish his identity and
to chart the distances he has traveled in his life. The first section of the
narrative also creates a personal voice, a distinct point of view that enables
the reader to understand many of the observations made in the following
sections of the autobiography.

White begins his autobiography with a specific reference to ethnicity and
the promise of America:

I was born in the ghetto of Boston on May 6, 1915.
   No one ever told me it was a ghetto, because the Jews who settled there, like my
father and my grandfather, had left the idea of a ghetto behind in the old country.
   America was the open land. Though they carried with them the baggage of the past
they could not shed, a past that bound all the exploring millions of Jewish immigrants
together, they hoped America would be different, and yearned that it prove so. (27)

White describes his family's life in Boston as part of an "ethnic ballet," a slow
but certain movement of ethnic groups through the neighborhoods of the
major American cities. His family's house on Erie Street was in the middle
of the ballet; it connected him with the New England past of Whittier, Emerson,
and Lowell, had been part of an Irish neighborhood before Jewish families
moved in, and later became a black ghetto. White describes the house itself

as a microcosm of the immigrant experience in America. Bought by his grandfather for $2,000 in 1912, it had two floors and eight rooms. His grandfather, grandmother, and unmarried uncle lived upstairs, while he and his family lived downstairs. Yiddish and Orthodoxy reigned upstairs, while English and socialism ruled downstairs. White grew up at home in both worlds.

As it had for countless other ethnic-American children, school played a major role in White's life, and the early part of *In Search of History* becomes a story of the education of Theodore White. Education was important to his mother; she wanted her children to have "good" jobs. Her children were going to be educated people, and White recalls the several systems of education available—the Hebrew school, the street school, and the public school.

The decision to send White to Hebrew School was made by his grandparents and his mother. Hebrew school began after public school ended, and White recalls that he came to love it. Hebrew school was based on memorization, and while White studied Hebrew, history, and Zionism, he developed skills that would make him an excellent student of languages. Erie Street was his street school, and on it he learned the value of the neighborhood, the interaction of Irish, Italian, and Jewish families, the necessity of hard work, and urban ethnic politics.

White remembers that during his childhood his family came first, then the street, and finally school. The Boston public school system absorbed White, as American public schools had millions of other immigrant children. White was a good student, especially fascinated by history, and public education became his avenue into the mainstream of American culture. With the encouragement of his elementary school teacher and his mother, White enrolled in Boston Latin School, the school of Franklin, Adams, and Emerson. White was on his way toward assimilation, and after Boston Latin his next step was Harvard.

White's depiction of his years at Harvard combines memoir and personal narrative. The memoir sections include short profiles of famous classmates—Rockefeller, Roosevelt, Kennedy, Morgan—and a general description of a college transforming itself into a university. In addition to this nostalgic look at his old school, White provides a portrait of his own awakening intellectual maturity. His primary interests remained history and languages, and White felt himself confortable in English, Latin, French, German, Yiddish, and Hebrew. At the end of his freshman year White selected Chinese history and language as his field of concentration and began a course of study and observation that would take him around the world.

These sections of the narrative prepare the reader for the Chinese chapters that follow and form the core of *In Search of History*. White describes his growing fascination with Chinese history and culture and his increasing self-assurance as an observer of world affairs. In 1938 White graduated summa cum laude and received a $1,500 fellowship that enabled him to travel to

China. In addition, he secured a position as a foreign stringer for the *Boston Globe*. In September 1938 White left Boston for China, where he would see and describe a world in the middle of war and revolution.

More than any other experience in his life, White asserts, living in China molded him, and White makes his China adventure the center of his autobiography. When White arrived in China, he discovered a country in turmoil. The Nationalist government was at war with Japan and had declared an uncertain truce with the Chinese Communists. White recalls that immediately upon his arrival he was contacted by the government and asked to serve as an advisor to the minister of information. He accepted and was flown over the Japanese lines to the interior wartime capital of Chungking. From there White was in a position to observe the thoughts and actions of men making history, and in these sections of his narrative White moves away from personal recollection of the early chapters and becomes a chronicler of great events.

The personalities and politics of four men dominate White's description of wartime China. The first is Chiang Kai-shek, a man White learned to respect and then to despise. White's portrait of Chiang reveals a leader more concerned with posture than performance; although Chiang was depicted by most contemporary journalists and politicians as the masterful supreme warlord of China, White portrays him as an ineffectual commander often out of touch with the events surrounding him. White's most telling example of Chiang's refusal to accept facts is his narration of the Honan famine of 1943, in which over five million people were starving. White reported the famine for *Time* and noted the failure of government relief. Chiang, however, denied that the famine existed and demanded an apology from *Time*. White considers Chiang's ultimate defeat by Mao Tse-tung, his second major character, a matter of perception as much as politics.

White depicts Mao as the opposite of Chiang. Unlike the distant Chiang, Mao appeared to understand the nature of the struggle against both the Japanese and the Nationalists. In addition, Mao was revered by his followers. White describes Mao as a man who had reverence and respect which he

earned in battle, where he had swum rivers, crossed mountains, led riflemen; earned by his sorrows, which had embittered him—his first wife and his sister executed by the Nationalists, both brothers killed, the younger one strangled to death in 1943.... But above all, the reverence arose from his authority as a teacher. He had been the man who had been right when all others had been wrong. (257)

White believed that Chou En-lai and Joseph Stilwell also played crucial roles in China, and he includes profiles of them as well. Observing the war in China, White came to know and admire both men, one the intellectual leader of the Chinese Communists and the other the American commander there. White valued their honesty and integrity, and his characterizations of the two men are equally warm and personal.

In 1946 White broke with *Time* and its publisher Henry Luce over White's response to Chiang and the Nationalists. In the same year his first book, *Thunder out of China*, became a best-seller. White recalls that he looked around for another large story to cover, and in 1948 he left for Europe to cover the Marshall Plan for the Overseas News Agency.

White writes that it was in Europe that he learned one of the most important lessons of the twentieth century, the power of global politics and money. In his autobiography he defines that lesson as the idea of command:

Whatever else money is, it is a medium that can translate one kind of command into another kind of command, up to the command of armies.

What was novel about the Marshall Plan was that the command quality of money, used on such a scale between nations, was being used for the first time not to kill but to heal; money provided the energy for a field of magnetic force, like electricity, in which things happened. (362)

As he did with his story of wartime China, White fills his narrative of the American resurrection of Europe with profiles of people. He describes the architects of the plan—Marshall, Truman, Acheson—but he saves his most detailed and intimate portrait for Dwight Eisenhower. White first knew Eisenhower as commander-in-chief of NATO and then as a potential presidential candidate. From watching Eisenhower White began to learn political lessons he would find useful later.

I had made the mistake so many observers did of considering Ike a simple man, a good straightforward soldier. Yet Ike's mind was not flaccid; and gradually, reporting him as he performed, I found that his mind was tough, his manner deceptive...that the tangled rambling rhetoric of his off-the-cuff remarks could, when he wished, be disciplined by his own pencil into clean, hard prose. (453)

The idea of command, or power, continued to fascinate White, and after reporting on the Marshall Plan, he returned to the United States to observe the most powerful nation on earth and to prepare to watch other presidential candidates.

The tone of *In Search of History* changes as White describes his return to America in 1954 and his own cold war struggles. White writes of an America caught in the grip of McCarthyism, of State Department investigations of himself and others who had served in China, of feeling like an outsider in his own country. White survived, but the pain of the period is clear in his prose. The autobiography changes again, however, as White describes how he decided to write a book about a presidential campaign, a book that would become White's most famous, *The Making of the President, 1960*.

The final sections of White's autobiography are about John Kennedy—the campaign, the presidency, and the assassination. White has written about these events before and well, and in this book he is content to provide highlights—

the primary campaign against Hubert Humphrey and Lyndon Johnson, climaxing in West Virginia, the debates with Richard Nixon, the Cuban missile crisis, Dallas. Next to the introductory chapters of the autobiography, this is the most personal section of White's book. White here is more than a mere observer; he was devoted to Kennedy, and his devotion comes through his narration clearly.

In his depiction of Kennedy and the presidency, White stresses the rise of ethnicity in politics and brings his narrative full circle. Describing Kennedy's Irish Catholic support reminds White of his own Jewish Boston background and the distance he has come in his life. The one-time newspaper boy has become the friend and confidant of the president, and he realizes that his autobiography is, in a very real sense, a success story.

White did not intend *In Search of History* to be a rags-to-riches success narrative, but despite the autobiography's collection of portraits of the great and the powerful, the real hero of the narrative is Teddy White. Although *In Search of History* is structured as a memoir and is full of observations about others, the life that White describes that best illustrates the potential for success in America is his own. While writing about patterns of world history and the problems of power, White has included as a central theme the story of how an outsider moved into the mainstream, how the son of immigrants moved to the center of power in the United States.

CRITICISM

Writing after White's death in 1986, Clifton Daniel observed in the *New York Times* that White "taught the American people more about politics than any writer of his generation." White was, Daniel asserted, a very good reporter, a fine historian, and most importantly, an effective storyteller. These qualities can be seen throughout White's work. His early nonfiction, *Thunder out of China* and *Fire in the Ashes: Europe at Mid-Century*, were popular studies of foreign affairs that Richard Rovere in the *New York Times* called "superior to anything else to come out of those years of agony and promise." White also wrote two novels. The first, *The Mountain Road*, was based on his experiences in China, and the second, *The View from the Fortieth Floor*, was about his work at *Collier's*.

Although his early writing was successful, *The Making of the President, 1960* and his subsequent studies of presidential elections made White a national celebrity. One of the few criticisms of his work was that White may have let his affection for American political institutions get in the way of objective analysis.

A similar comment marked the publication of *In Search of History*. Writing in the *New Republic*, R. J. Myers noted that White's "view of America as the land of opportunity with a capital O, his vision of political heroes dominating history, and his commonplace ideas about the role of accident in history are not the grist of complex political and social analysis." *In Search of History* is not, however, a complex political and social analysis; it is an autobiography of an ethnic-American writer who had the good fortune to be close to some of the dramatic social and political events of the century. White's view of America as "the land of opportunity with a capital O" may not be that of an objective historian, but it is one that appears throughout ethnic-American writing.

BIBLIOGRAPHY

White, Theodore H. *Thunder out of China*. New York: Sloane, 1946.
————. *Fire in the Ashes: Europe at Mid-Century*. New York: Sloane, 1953.
————. *The Mountain Road*. New York, Sloane, 1958.
————. *The View from the Fortieth Floor*. New York, Sloane, 1960.
————. *The Making of the President, 1960*. New York, Atheneum, 1961.
————. *The Making of the President, 1964*. New York, Atheneum, 1965.
————. *The Making of the President, 1968*. New York, Atheneum, 1969.
————. *The Making of the President, 1972*. New York: Atheneum, 1973.
————. *Breach of Faith: The Fall of Richard Nixon*. New York: Atheneum, 1975.
————. *In Search of History: A Personal Adventure*. New York: Harper and Row, 1978.
————. *America in Search of Itself: The Making of the President, 1956–1980*. New York: Harper and Row, 1982.
————, ed. *The Stilwell Papers*. New York: Sloane, 1948.
Adler, Gerry. "The Man behind the Scenes." *Newsweek* 107 (May 26, 1986): 64.
Daniel S. Clifton, "Joyful Journalist." *New York Times* (May 16, 1786): A1.
Ephron, Nora. "The Making of Teddy White." *Esquire* 84 (August 1975): 20+.
"Liberalism and Theodore H. White." *Commentary* 74 (September 1982), 38+.
Myers, R. J. "Brief Reviews." *New Republic* 179 (September 9, 1978): 46–47.
Peretz, Martin. "Turbulent Priests." *New Republic* 195 (July 14, 1986): 43.
Rovere, Richard. "Making of the Historian." *New York Times Book Review* 83, (August 6, 1978): 1+.
Sheed, Wilfred. "Brass Bands and Raspberries." *New York Review of Books* 25 (November 9, 1978): 6+.
"Theodore White RIP." *National Review* 38 (June 20, 1986): 62–63.
Thomas, Evan. "A Reporter in Search of History." *Time* 127 (May 26, 1986): 62.

JADE SNOW WONG
(1922-   )

Fifth Chinese Daughter

BIOGRAPHY

Jade Snow Wong was born on January 21, 1922, in San Francisco. Her father, Hong Wong, was a clothing manufacturer who owned and operated a series of small factories, which also served as the family's homes, in San Francisco's Chinatown. Jade Snow Wong grew up in Chinatown, receiving a solid public school education as well as an evening school education in Chinese language and culture before attending San Francisco Junior College and Mills College, where she received her B.A. degree in 1942.

From 1943 to 1950 Wong worked as a secretary and as a proprietor of a ceramics gallery in San Francisco as she revised essays she had written that would become chapters of her autobiography, *Fifth Chinese Daughter*. In 1950 her autobiography was published and was well received by both critics and the general public. In the same year she married Woodrow Wong, and in 1957 she and her husband became co-owners of a travel agency.

In addition to her autobiography, Wong has written numerous feature articles and a second full-length work, *No Chinese Stranger*. An award-winning ceramic artist as well as a writer, Wong received an honorary doctorate in humane letters from Mills College in 1976.

THE AUTOBIOGRAPHY

When *Fifth Chinese Daughter* appeared in 1950, reviewers responded enthusiastically to Wong's narrative of a young Chinese-American girl's coming of age. In her autobiography Wong sets out to provide detailed and accurate information about Chinese-American life to a primarily Anglo reading audience. Written and revised during a period in which American culture celebrated ethnicity in the face of a world war and a cold war, *Fifth Chinese Daughter* is a carefully written, nonjudgmental work that attempts to bridge

the distance between Chinese and Anglo cultures. As she describes her growing awareness of herself as a Chinese-American, Wong defines both Chinese
and American cultures and sees herself as a moderator between them.

Wong begins her autobiography by establishing both her setting and her
theme:

Chinatown in San Francisco teems with haunting memories, for it is wrapped in the
atmosphere, customs, and manners of a land across the sea. The same Pacific Ocean
loves the shores of both worlds, a tangible link between old and new, past and present,
Orient and Occident. (1)

For Wong, Chinatown is a microcosm of East and West, an example of the
melting pot in action. Her maturation and her movement from a totally
Chinese environment to a clearly Anglo one become examples of correct
ethnic reaction to mainstream Anglo culture. *Fifth Chinese Daughter* is a
narrative of transformation.

Wong writes that for the first five years of her life her world was almost
totally Chinese. She never questioned her mother or father, and she never
addressed an older person by name. She writes that her "life was secure but
formal, sober but quietly happy.... respect and order were the key words"
(2). When she turned six, however, her world began to change when she
began her education at an American public grade school.

Although located in Chinatown and taught by Chinese-American teachers
for Chinese-American students, the public school provided Wong with her
introduction to mainstream culture. She learned English, of course, and American history, but more importantly, she learned a less formal and more dem-
onstrative way of behaving, and she describes finding Anglo familiarity more
comfortable than Chinese formality.

Shortly after Wong's father enrolled her in public school, he enrolled her
in Chinese evening school, where she was encouraged to study Chinese and
correct calligraphy. Chinese school reinforced her family training while public
school offered her alternatives, and throughout the early sections of her
autobiography Wong recounts the often contradictory lessons she was
learning.

In the early 1930s the Wong family was forced to come to grips with the
larger American environment. Because of the Depression, the family clothing
factory was idle for half the year, and the family could no longer afford the
street-level, storefront factory-apartment and was forced to move business
and family into a two-story basement. Wong, who was ten in 1932 when the
family moved, took over her mother's duties as housewife so that her mother
could work full-time, and a number of the family relatives who were employed
by Wong's father were forced to go on relief.

Wong describes this period of her life with pride. She presents a detailed
account of the family's transformation of a damp basement into a comfortable

apartment and working factory. She is even more careful in her reconstruction of her duties as housewife, providing specific examples of meals she cooked and how she managed to cook them.

At the same time as Wong assumed more obligations for her family, she graduated from grade school and entered junior high school. Most of her classmates went to a local school with a mixture of Italian-Americans, but Wong's father believed that it was an inferior school and refused to send his daughter there (65). Instead she was sent to a junior high school farther away from home in which she was the only Chinese-American student. There she discovered American racism for the first time.

Wong recounts with surprise how she was taunted one day as she was leaving school by a student who threw an eraser at her and then danced around her gleefully singing, "Look at the eraser mark on the yellow China-man. Chinky, Chinky, no tickee, no washee, no shirtee" (68). Wong's response is illuminating. She writes that

Jade Snow thought that he [her tormentor] was tiresome and ignorant. Everybody knew that the Chinese people had a superior culture. Her ancestors had created a great art heritage and had made inventions important to world civilization—the compass, gunpowder, paper, and a host of other essentials. She knew, too, that Richard's grades couldn't compare with her own, and his home training was obviously amiss. (68)

When confronted with prejudice, Wong responds by assuming superiority of Chinese culture and the inferior education and upbringing of the prejudiced classmate. Ironically, through most of the remainder of her narrative Wong will move farther and farther away from the Chinese culture she puts so much faith in and closer to mainstream American culture.

Throughout her life Wong had been taught that education is the path to freedom. After finishing high school she decided that she wanted to be more than a stenographer or secretary, and she resolved to go to college, but that decision forced her to confront her situation as a Chinese-American girl. When she asked her father for help in meeting college expenses she was told:

You are quite familiar by now with the fact that it is the sons who perpetuate our ancestral heritage by permanently bearing the Wong family name and transmitting it through their blood line, and therefore sons must have priority over the daughters. ...Jade Snow, you have been given an above-average Chinese education for an American-born Chinese girl. I must still provide with all my powers for your Older Brother's advanced medical training. (108–9)

Wong recalls that she felt herself "wrapped in a mesh of tradition" (110). For the first time in her life she felt that her Chinese background and upbringing were hindering her development in America. Wong decided that her father's attitude was wrong and that somehow she would put herself through college.

The remaining chapters of *Fifth Chinese Daughter* record Wong's successful efforts to balance work and education as she puts herself through San Francisco Junior College and Mills College. In addition, they recount Wong's introduction to and adoption of elements of American culture.

Wong's description of her life at Mills College shows how much she has become part of the mainstream culture. She recounts immersing herself in the life of the college and finding it a welcome relief from her Chinese upbringing. In summarizing her first year at Mills College, Wong writes:

The happy living and stimulation from liberal academic thinking of a wholly Western pattern were the most significant rewards of this year's schooling. Eager to protect them as fully as possible, she clung to the campus except for infrequent visits home. (168)

Life at college becomes an introduction to both freedom and Western culture, and in her rush to experience both Wong sees her own family as a limitation.

Wong does not, however, reject her Chinese identity completely. In the final sections of her autobiography she records her growing awareness of herself as a Chinese-American, a woman capable of acting as an intermediary between two diverse cultures. She finds that her grades in English courses are better when she writes about her experiences in Chinatown, and as a result she begins to rediscover and come to appreciate the unique elements of Chinese-American culture. She continues to write about her upbringing and to explore the situation of other Chinese-Americans. The result of this exploration and reevaluation was both a success at Mills College and the encouragement to turn her her college literary efforts into the narrative that became *Fifth Chinese Daughter*.

CRITICISM

Early reviewers of *Fifth Chinese Daughter* stressed the humor and entertainment found in Wong's narrative. As Elaine Kim observes in *Asian American Literature: An Introduction to the Writings and Their Social Context*, during the World War II era readers and editors were interested in the exotic customs of Chinese-Americans, and they also expected certain stereotypical images in books about the Chinese in America (66). Wong's autobiography, which accepts the dominance of the mainstream culture and chronicles a successful assimilation, was well received. Like Mary Antin's *The Promised Land*, *Fifth Chinese Daughter* was so successful in praising education and the public school system as the avenue for assimilation into mainstream culture that it became a textbook itself.

Elaine Kim's examination of Wong's autobiography in *Asian American*

Literature provides a detailed, contemporary analysis grounded in the context of ethnic-American literature. Kim notes that the most significant aspects of the autobiography are its "documentation of her often enraged struggle to attain individual definition apart from her family and her acceptance of attitudes popularly ascribed to the Chinese American minority during her era" (66). Kim considers *Fifth Chinese Daughter* a valuable document of Asian-American social history that reflects the author's complex attitudes to her own sense of ethnicity and identity more than actual Chinese-American history.

Fifth Chinese Daughter is a more complex work than early readers perceived. Even though many libraries catalogue it as a children's book, Wong's narrative is a complex literary document. In recreating her childhood for an essentially white, middle-class reading audience Wong has filtered her experience through her middle-class education, and as a result, her autobiography is both a touching, humorous account of growing up as a Chinese-American girl during the 1930s and a more complex documentary of the uneasy position of an ethnic narrator standing between two cultures.

BIBLIOGRAPHY

Wong, Jade Snow. *Fifth Chinese Daughter*. New York: Harper and Row, 1950.
————. *No Chinese Stranger*. New York: Harper and Row, 1975.
Arbuthnot, May Hill. "Transitions from Juvenile to Adult Reading." In *Children's Reading in the Home.*Glenview, Ill.: Scott, Foresman, 1969.
Chun-Loon, Lowell. "Jade Snow Wong and the Fate of Chinese American Identity." In *Asian-Americans: Psychological Perspectives*, edited by Stanley Sue and Nathaniel N. Wagner, 125–35. Palo Alto, Calif.: Science and Behavior Books, 1973.
Evans, Ernestine. "A Chinese-American Girl's Two Worlds." *New York Herald Tribune Book Review* 27, 6 (September 24, 1950): 4.
Geary, Joyce. "A Chinese Girl's World." *New York Times Book Review*, October 29, 1950, 27.
Kim, Elaine. *Asian American Literature: An Introduction to the Writings and Their Social Context*. Philadelphia: Temple University Press, 1982.
Wyatt, E. V. R. Review of "Fifth Chinese Daughter." *Commonweal* 53, 7 (November 24, 1950): 182.

RICHARD WRIGHT
(1908–1960)

Black Boy

BIOGRAPHY

Richard Wright was born on September 4, 1908, on a plantation near Natchez, Mississippi. His father abandoned the Wright family five years after Wright was born, and his mother worked as a housemaid and cook to support her children until she became unable to work when Wright was twelve. Wright lived with a number of relatives in Jackson, Mississippi, and Memphis, Tennessee, while growing up. He attended school part-time, eventually graduating from the ninth grade in Memphis in 1925.

Wright worked at a series of unskilled jobs in Jackson, Memphis, and Chicago, where he eventually obtained a position in the post office in 1929. While living in Chicago, Wright read voraciously and began writing poetry and short stories. His interest in writing led him to work for the Federal Negro Theater, the Federal Experimental Theater, and the Federal Writers' Project. In 1932 he joined the John Reed Club, and shortly after he became a member of the Communist party. In 1938 he published *Uncle Tom's Children*, a collection of fiction about the black experience in the South. In 1940 his powerful novel *Native Son* appeared; it won the Spingarn Award of the NAACP and shocked both Party members and middle-class white readers with its dramatic depiction of racism, sex, and violence. In 1945 Wright published his autobiography, *Black Boy*, which increased his popularity.

In 1947 Wright moved to Paris, where he lived for the rest of his life. He continued to write, lecture, and travel. Much of Wright's later work is concerned with the problems and policies facing the developing third-world nations in Africa and Asia. He died of a heart attack on November 18, 1960.

THE AUTOBIOGRAPHY

Richard Wright remains one of the major American writers of the twentieth century. Although he was a prolific writer, his reputation rests on two books,

Native Son and *Black Boy*. *Native Son*, which documents both the emotional and economic impact of segregation, is a powerful novel that transcends the social realism of much of the fiction of the 1930s. *Black Boy* is equally powerful and transcendent. In describing a childhood and adolescence of poverty and violence, Wright does more than tell a story of his own life; he creates a document that speaks for an entire group of people. *Black Boy* is Richard Wright's manifesto, and in it he writes eloquently of the stultifying effects of racism and segregation in the United States.

Wright begins his narrative with a vivid description of a winter morning when he was four. He was, he recalls, bored and restless after having been told to be quiet because his grandmother was sick. Wright describes arguing with his brother and then in boredom lighting the straws from a broom. He then put one of the straws to the curtains, setting fire to the house. Aware of what he had done and seeing the house fill with smoke, he became terrified and crawled under the house, where he believed he was safe. Wright recalls thinking that it was all an accident and hoping that he would not be punished. He was, however, found and beaten.

This is more than an account of an accident. Wright uses the fire and his reaction to establish some of the major elements of his autobiography: violence, fear, isolation. He builds on these as he describes his life, recording the destruction of his family, the impact of segregation on black society, and the failure of both the school and the church to provide emotional and intellectual support.

Shortly after the fire, Wright's father moved the family to Memphis, and this begins a pattern of movement that will continue throughout *Black Boy*. Wright's father abandoned the family, and after his mother found work as a cook, she began instructing her children about their new life: "She would call us to her and talk to us for hours, telling us that we now had no father, that our lives would be different from those of other children, that we must learn as soon as possible to take care of ourselves" (23). Wright learned to take care of himself: He learned to fight, he learned to steal, and he learned to curse, all necessary skills on the streets of Memphis.

Wright's life took another dramatic change when his mother moved the family to Elaine, Arkansas. Wright was joyous and remembers being excited, happy at leaving a "hated home, hunger, fear" (44). He soon learned, however, that Memphis was not the sole place of danger.

Before arriving in Elaine, the Wrights visited Jackson, Mississippi, to stay with Richard's grandmother. At first, Wright considered the visit a marvelous adventure. He and his brother had the run of a two-story, seven-room frame house, a place, Wright recalls, that he believed was the finest house in the world. In addition, Wright's grandmother boarded a schoolteacher to help support the household, and the teacher, Miss Ella, would read to Wright. Wright soon developed a love for stories, but when Ella was reading him *Bluebeard and His Seven Wives*, his grandmother discovered them and declared the story "Devil's work." She banned fiction and told Wright that because he liked the story he would "burn in hell."

Wright discovered that he would be punished much sooner when he later let some of the words he had learned on the Memphis streets slip while his grandmother was bathing him. His language convinced her of her grandson's depravity, and after Richard ran into the bedroom, his grandfather, a "tall, skinny, silent, grim, black man who had fought in the Civil War with the Union Army," came to fetch him for his punishment. Unable to tell his grandmother where he had learned the words, he again was beaten.

Jackson meant more to Wright than beatings and warnings, however; it meant the country, and freedom, and enough food to eat. Wright describes the positive aspects of life in Jackson in a long Whitmanesque catalogue that appeals directly to the senses. Life there, despite his grandmother, was good. It was natural, simple, and satisfying. And when the Wrights moved to Arkansas to stay with Aunt Maggie and Uncle Hoskins, who owned a prosperous saloon, it was summer, and warm, and Wright believed that he had found security.

At first, Elaine, Arkansas, seemed an extension of the best parts of Jackson, Mississippi. Wright recalls the warmth, the fields, the flowers, and especially the food. His uncle told him that he could eat as much as he wanted, and Wright recalls eating until he was stuffed and then putting biscuits in his pockets for later. He remembers thinking that the biscuits would disappear and he would wake up hungry and without food.

Wright's respite ended, however, when his uncle failed to return one day from his saloon. His aunt was frantic and prepared to go to the saloon, but later a messenger arrived and told her that her husband had been shot by a white man and that "white folks say they'll kill all his kinfolks" (63). The family fled Elaine that night. Wright describes that later he discovered that his uncle has been killed by whites who had threatened him several times and wanted to take over his profitable business. He then goes on to describe the flight—no funeral, no flowers, not even collecting the body. Wright's mother and aunt, shaken, returned to Jackson and Grandmother's house. For the first time in the narrative, white racism has impacted directly on Wright, and for the rest of his autobiography he describes how racism blights all that it touches. From this point in the text, Wright's vision moves beyond the family to the larger social units that affect the family.

Wright introduces institutionalized racism into his autobiography as he describes observing two strange groups of men. The first was a "wave of black men dressed in weird mustard-colored clothing" coming over a crest of a hill near his grandmother's house. When he was told that they were soldiers, he wondered why they would bother to learn to fight Germans who were so far away. Later he saw a chain gang at work, and after first thinking that the men were elephants, wondered why they were black. His grandmother told him that white people were harder on blacks. Both observations are important; they serve to broaden the context of Wright's recollections and move the narrative from a personal to a public level. Wright keeps the two levels working as he describes his religious, educational, and work experiences.

When Wright was twelve, his mother suffered a stroke and he became dependent upon his grandmother, an ardent Seventh-Day Adventist. Wright quickly discovered that he "was compelled to make a pretense of worshiping her God" (113). Wright was enrolled in an Adventist school, where he was taught by his aunt. There and at home the battle for his soul was joined.

Wright fought his grandmother, and *Black Boy* is not a conversion narrative. Wright presents religion as a confidence game. Preachers visit his house and stuff themselves on the family's food, religious school promotes obedience rather than education, and the family remains violent in spite of its faith. Wright juxtaposes his baptism, which he endures for the sake of family peace, with a confrontation with his uncle in which Wright holds off the old man at razor point.

Throughout his autobiography, Wright makes a distinction between school and learning. School, like his family, serves one function, to teach obedience and keep him in his place. This is true both in the Adventist school, where Wright is beaten for an infraction he did not commit, and the public school, where Wright, who was selected valedictorian of his class, is refused permission to read his own speech and given one by the principal instead. Wright realizes that both school and church reinforce segregation and subservience. Learning, however, is different.

Throughout *Black Boy* Wright provides examples of his love of learning. Three episodes illustrate this passion. First was his reaction to the *Bluebeard* reading. He discovered in stories what he lacked in his own life—adventure and freedom. The second was his ill-fated career as a weekly newspaper salesman. Wright sent away for papers and then sold them throughout his neighborhood. Although he made some money, his primary motivation was reading. The papers contained fiction, including a serialization of Zane Grey's *Riders of the Purple Sage*. Like his first taste of literature, this one was spoiled when he discovered that the paper was sponsored by the Ku Klux Klan. Wright's third experience was more successful. He wrote a story and had it published in a local newspaper. But even this triumph was tarnished when everyone in his family thought that he was crazy for doing something so foolish.

The final chapters of *Black Boy* depict Wright's confrontation with white society. The family, church, and school have all attempted to prepare him for what a young black man will face looking for work in the South in 1925, but Wright has not learned his lesson. The constant violence and intimidations he faces have not made him docile; on the contrary, he has grown more defiant.

Wright describes that he had a series of jobs the summer after he finished school. He lost each one. Finally, in desperation, he asks a friend if he knows where there is a job. His friend tells him yes, but he will lose it if he doesn't learn how to live in the South. He tells Wright to remember that he has to eat and that he can be himself with other blacks but he must be subservient to all whites if he wants to keep any job.

Wright worked for an optical company, a drugstore, and a movie theater, and in each job found it impossible to "keep his place." Each job he took required him to accept humiliation or face the threat of violence. Wright provides the illustration of working in an optical factory where the white workers pitted Wright and another black against each other, hoping to start a knife fight. On another occasion, Wright is put in a position where he must call a white man a liar. Each situation is dangerous and traumatic, and from each Wright learned lessons and the rules of the Jim Crow South:

The whites had drawn a line over which we dared not step and we accepted that line because our bread was at stake. But within our boundaries we, too, drew a line that included our right to bread regardless of the indignities and degradations involved in getting it. If a white man had sought to keep us from obtaining a job, or enjoying the rights of citizenship, we would have bowed silently to his power. But if he had sought to deprive us of a dime, blood might have been spilt. Hence, our daily lives were so bound up with trivial objectives that to capitulate when challenged was tantamount to surrendering the right to life itself. (251)

Faced with this continuing dehumanization, Wright, like tens of thousands of other black Americans, headed north, looking for a different life. Wright ends his autobiography on a note of optimism, believing that "life could be lived with dignity, and the personalities should not be violated, that men should be able to confront other men without fear or shame, and that if men were lucky in their living on earth they might win some redeeming meaning for their having struggled and suffered here beneath the stars" (285).

CRITICISM

In *Black Autobiography in America* Stephen Butterfield argues that "Richard Wright's *Black Boy* is the autobiography most worth reading of all the works of its kind in American literature, whether black or white" (155). In addition to that praise, Butterfield asserts that *Black Boy* is representative of the entire genre of black autobiography because it "includes the identity crisis, the alienation, the restless movement, and the views on education, knowledge, and resistance that were demonstrated to be traditional in black autobiography as a whole" (155). These same elements make *Black Boy* representative of much ethnic-American writing. Keneth Kinnamon, in *The Emergence of Richard Wright*, praises Wright for his vivid and accurate depiction of black life in Chicago, and Edward Margolies, in *The Art of Richard Wright*, calls attention to Wright's insightful presentation of black nationalism.

Richard Wright's position as a major American writer is secure, and a large body of criticism and scholarship exists. *A Comprehensive Bibliography for the Study of American Minorities* provides a useful summation of the material available.

Black Boy is both a personal and a public work. Wright tells more than his own experiences of growing up in the South in the early part of the century. His experiences are representative ones; they suggest the experiences of a large number of Americans, and in doing so they become a public indictment of a social and political system. Wright himself was aware of this, of course. The structure of his autobiography, alternating description with commentary and building toward an escape to the North, is based on the pattern of slave narratives. In using this form in the twentieth century, Wright asserts that the economic, social, and psychological consequences of slavery still exist. In addition, Wright's autobiography provides an example of the development of a concrete personality in the midst of a realistic social background, and that has always been the mark of an outstanding autobiography.

BIBLIOGRAPHY

Wright, Richard. *Native Son*. New York: Harper, 1940, 1957, 1966, 1969; New York: Modern Library, 1942; New York: New American Library, 1961, 1964.

———. with Paul Green. *Native Son: The Biography of a Young American*. New York: Harper, 1941.

Wright, Richard. *12 Million Black Voices: A Folk History of the Negro in the United States*. New York: Viking, 1941; New York: Arno, 1969.

———. *Black Boy*. New York: Harper, 1945; New York: New American Library, 1963; New York: Harper and Row, 1964, 1966.

———. *The Outsider*. New York: Harper, 1953; Harper and Row, 1969.

———. *Savage Holiday*. New York: Avon, 1954; Universal Publishing and Distributing, 1965.

———. *Black Power*. New York: Harper, 1954; London: Dobson, 1956.

———. *The Color Curtain*. Cleveland: World, 1956; London: Dobson, 1956.

———. *Pagan Spain*. New York: Harper, 1957; London: The Bodley Head, 1960.

———. *White Man Listen!* Garden City, N.Y.: Doubleday, 1957.

———. *The Long Dream*. Garden City, N.Y.: Doubleday, 1958; London: Angus and Robertson, 1960; Chatham, N.J.: Chatham Bookseller, 1969.

———. *Lawd Today*. New York: Walker, 1963; New York: Hearst Corp., 1963.

Abcarian, Richard, ed. *Richard Wright's Native Son: A Critical Handbook*. Belmont, Calif.: Wadsworth, 1970.

Bakish, David. *Richard Wright*. New York: Ungar, 1973.

Baldwin, James. "Alas Poor Richard." In *Nobody Knows My Name*. New York: Dial, 1961.

———. "Richard Wright." *Encounter* 16 (1961): 58–60.

Bigsby, C. W. E. *The Second Black Renaissance: Essays in Black Literature*. Westport, Conn.: Greenwood Press, 1980.

Bone, Robert A. *Richard Wright*. Minneapolis: University of Minnesota Press, 1969.

Brignano, Russell Carl. *Richard Wright: An Introduction to the Man and His Works.* Pittsburgh: University of Pittsburgh Press, 1970.

Butterfield, Stephen. *Black Autobiography in America.* Amherst: University of Massachusetts Press, 1974.

Davis, Charles T. *Richard Wright: A Primary Bibliography.* Boston: G. K. Hall, 1982.

————, and Michel Fabre. *The Unfinished Quest of Richard Wright.* New York: Morrow, 1973.

Fishburn, Katherine. *Richard Wright's Hero: The Faces of a Rebel-Victim.* Metuchen, N.J.: Scarecrow, 1977.

Gayle, Addison. *Richard Wright: Ordeal of a Native Son.* Garden City, N.Y.: Doubleday/ Anchor, 1980.

Gibson, Donald B., ed. *Five Black Writers: Essays on Wright, Ellison, Baldwin, Hughes, and LeRoi Jones.* New York: New York University Press, 1970.

Hakutani, Yoshinobu, ed. *Critical Essays on Richard Wright.* Boston: G. K. Hall, 1982.

Kinnamon, Keneth. *The Emergence of Richard Wright.* Urbana: University of Illinois Press, 1972.

McCall, Dan. *The Example of Richard Wright.* New York: Harcourt, 1969.

Macksey, Richard, and Frank E. Moorer, eds. *Richard Wright: A Collection of Critical Essays.* Englewood Cliffs, N.J.: Prentice-Hall, 1984.

Margolies, Edward. *The Art of Richard Wright.* Carbondale: Southern Illinois University Press, 1968.

Miller, Wayne Charles, ed. *A Comprehensive Bibliography for the Study of American Minorities.* New York: New York University Press, 1976.

Negro Digest 18 (December 1968). Entire issue devoted to Wright.

Ray, David, and Robert M. Farnsworth, eds. *Richard Wright: Impressions and Perspectives.* Ann Arbor: University of Michigan Press, 1973.

Reilly, John, ed. *Richard Wright: The Critical Reception.* New York: B. Franklin, 1978.

Studies in Black Literature 1, 3 (1970). Entire issue devoted to Wright.

Turner, Darwin. "The Negro Novelist and the South." *Southern Humanities Review* 1 (1967): 21–29.

Webb, Constance. *Richard Wright: A Biography.* New York: Putnam, 1968.

Bibliographical Essay

Writing in "The Cycle and the Roots: National Identity and American Literature" (*Toward a New American Literary History: Essays in Honor of Arlin Turner*. Durham, N.C.: Duke University Press, 1980), Robert Spiller, whose *The Cycle of American Literature* and *Literary History of the United States* defined American literature for a generation of university students and scholars, calls for a reexamination of the national literature that would take into consideration ethnic and immigrant writing. He calls attention to the limitations of traditional literary approaches and notes that

> we have only touched on the problem of multiethnicity, as the movement of migration lost its westward direction but remained nonetheless active, and the evolutionary process became more and more the overlay of one culture on another, rather than the movement of a mature culture into a primitive environment as it had been in the days of steady frontier movement. (15)

Spiller then calls for continued study of those literatures that parallel traditional mainstream writing.

Spiller's comments here reflect the change in attitudes among students of American literature. The relationship of "marginal" to "mainstream" writing and considerations of race, sex, class, and ethnicity in American literature are now some of the accepted methods of approaching the study of American writing. The second edition of *The Norton Anthology of American Literature*, for example, not only includes examples of the work of a relatively large number of ethnic and women writers but also encourages the study of American writing from a pluralistic perspective.

The study of ethnic writing is a rapidly growing area of intellectual inquiry. Writers continue to create new texts, and scholars discover forgotten manuscripts. In addition, there are materials now available to help students in the field. The two most important general sources for the study of ethnic life and literature in the United States are Stephan Thernstrom's *The Harvard Encyclopedia of American Ethnic Groups* (Cambridge: Belknap Press, 1980) and Wayne Charles Miller's *A Comprehensive Bibliography for the Study of American Minorities* (New York: New York University Press, 1976). *The Harvard Encyclopedia* is an exhaustive overview of ethnic life and culture, while *A Comprehensive Bibliography* provides both overviews in essays and annotated bibliographies for nearly all American ethnic groups. In addition to these comprehensive sources, students interested in general studies of immigration and ethnicity should consult the following excellent studies: Louis Adamic's *A Nation of Nations* (New York: Harper, 1945); Henry Steele Commager's *Immigration and American History: Essays in Honor of Theodore C. Blegen* (Minneapolis: University of Minnesota Press, 1961); Nathan Glazer and Daniel Patrick Moynihan's *Beyond the Melting Pot: The Negroes, Puerto Ricans, Jews, Italians, and Irish of New York City* (Cambridge: M.I.T. Press, 1963; 2d ed., 1970); Oscar Handlin's *The Uprooted* (Boston: Little, Brown, 1951), *Immigration as a Factor in American History* (Englewood Cliffs, N.J.: Prentice-Hall, 1959), and *Children of the Uprooted* (New York: Braziller, 1966); John Higham's *Strangers in the Land: Patterns of American Nativism, 1860–1925* (New York: Atheneum, 1963); Andrew Rolle's *The Immigrant Upraised* (Norman: University of Oklahoma Press, 1968); and Carl Wittke's *We Who Built America: The Saga of the Immigrant* (1939; revised ed., Cleveland: Press of Case Western Reserve, 1964).

A number of collections of ethnic American writing are also available, and among the most useful are Charlotte Brooks's *The Outnumbered* (New York: Dell, 1967); Theodore Gross's *A Nation of Nations* (New York: Free Press, 1971); Gerald Haslam's *Forgotten Pages of American Literature* (Boston: Houghton Mifflin, 1970); Wayne Charles Miller's *A Gathering of Ghetto Writers* (New York: New York University Press, 1972); Katherine Newman's *Ethnic American Short Stories* (New York: Washington Square Press, 1972); and Myron Simon's *Ethnic Writers in America* (New York: Harcourt Brace, 1972).

Students of ethnic literature can also turn to any of a number of significant ethnic autobiographies not treated in this volume. There has been, for example, a growing interest in native American literature and culture during the past three decades. A number of native American autobiographies deserve further attention. William Apes's *A Son of the Forest: The Experience of William Apes, A Native of the Forest* (New York, 1831) is of interest to students of American literature in that it tells the story of a Pequot Indian who eventually became a Christian minister in Massachusetts. *Black Hawk: An Autobiography* (1833; Urbana: University of Illinois Press, 1955) contains accounts of his battles with other tribes as well as his final battle with the U.S. Army. Charles Eastman's two autobiographical works, *Indian Boyhood* (1902; New York: Dover, 1971) and *From the Deep Woods to Civilization* (Boston: Little, Brown, 1916), are both popular accounts of a young boy's coming of age and coming into contact with the white world. John Fire's *Lame Deer, Seeker of Visions* (New York: Simon and Schuster, 1972) is an account of a medicine man and worth reading in conjunction with *Black Elk Speaks. Geronimo: His Own Story* (1906; New York: Dutton, 1970) was dictated by Geronimo when he was imprisoned at Fort Sill, Oklahoma Territory, and is an important historical document. N. Scott Momaday's *The Way to Rainy Mountain* (Albuquerque: University of New Mexico Press, 1969) and *The Names* (New York: Harper and Row, 1974) are two excellent depictions of native American life from a contemporary native writer. Chief Luther Standing Bear has written three works: *My Indian Boyhood* (Boston: Houghton Mifflin, 1928), *My People, the Sioux* (Boston: Houghton Mifflin, 1928), and *Land of the Spotted Eagle* (Boston: Houghton Mifflin, 1933). In all of these works Standing Bear, chief of the Oglala Sioux, provides detailed information about the customs, history, and problems of his people, as well as giving a vivid account of his own life.

Another substantial subgenre of ethnic writing is the black autobiography. Considerable scholarship in the field exists and more appears every year as scholars continue to work in this once-neglected and provacative subject area. A number of excellent collections, especially of slave narratives, exist, including Arna Bontemps' *Great Slave Narratives* (New York: Macmillan, 1969) and Gilbert Osofsky's *Puttin' On Ole Massa* (New York: Harper and Row, 1969). Two works of criticism are especially useful for an understanding of black autobiography. The first is William L. Andrews' *To Tell a Free Story: The First Century of Afro-American Autobiography, 1760–1865* (Urbana: University of Illinois Press, 1986). In his analysis of the slave narrative Andrews not only provides insightful commentary on individual works but also uncovers the complexities within the genre itself. The second critical work is Stephen Butterfield's *Black Autobiography in America* (Amherst: University of Massachusetts Press, 1974). Butterfield, in examining the writings of black autobiographers from the slave narratives to work produced in the 1960s and 1970s, argues that black autobiographers used the literary form to discover identities denied them by white society.

The slave narrative was the dominant form of black literature prior to the Civil War. Among the most influential and representative works of this genre are *Narrative of William W. Brown, A Fugitive Slave* (Boston: Anti-Slavery Office, 1847); *The Narrative of Sojourner Truth* (1878; New York: Arno, 1968); and *The Life of Frederick Douglass, an American Slave* (Boston: Anti-Slavery Office, 1845). Douglass is the most famous of these writers, and the most interesting as well since he rewrote his narrative three times; it appeared later as *My Bondage and Freedom* (New York: Miller, Orton, and Mulligan, 1855) and *The Life and Times of Frederick Douglass* (1892; London: Collier, 1962). A study of Douglass' revisions reveals a great deal not only about Douglass but also about the rhetorical strategy of the black autobiographer.

Many outstanding black autobiographies do exist, and in addition to the ones examined in the text, the following deserve special attention. Claude Brown's *Manchild in the Promised Land* (New York: Macmillan, 1965) is a strong narrative of coming of age in Harlem. Eldridge Cleaver's *Soul on Ice* (New York: McGraw-Hill, 1968) is a powerful prison narrative that charts Cleaver's conversion from apathy to political militancy. W. E. B. Du Bois's two autobiographical works are important documents of black American life. *Dusk of Dawn: An Essay toward an Autobiography of a Race Concept* (New York: Harcourt, Brace, 1940) chronicles Du Bois's life with an emphasis on his work with the NAACP and its magazine, *The Crisis*, which Du Bois edited. *The Autobiography of W. E. B. Du Bois* (New York: International, 1968) is an overview of Du Bois's life written when he was much older. Langston Hughes's two narratives, *The Big Sea* (New York: Knopf, 1940) and *I Wonder As I Wander* (New York: Rinehart, 1956) provide background about the life of the influential black poet. Claude McKay's *A Long Way from Home* (New York: Lee Furman, 1937) is a vivid depiction of the writer's life beginning in his native Jamaica and including his travels to the United States, the Soviet Union, and Morocco. Anne Moody's *Coming of Age in Mississippi* (New York: Dial, 1968) records the maturation of a young black woman from rural poverty to involvement in the civil rights movement. Paul Robeson's *Here I Stand* (London: Dobson, 1958) is a statement of the black singer's political and economic principles. Era Bell Thompson's *American Daughter* (Chicago: University of Chicago Press, 1946) describes the childhood of a black woman who became an editor of *Ebony*. Walter Francis White's *A Man Called White* (New York: Viking, 1948) is the narrative of the man who was the executive director of the NAACP for three decades.

A number of significant Hispanic autobiographies are available in addition to the well-known works of Piri Thomas, Richard Rodriguez, and Nicky Cruz. Jesus Colon's *A Puerto Rican in New York and Other Stories* (1961; New York: Arno, 1975) describes life in New York's Puerto Rican community in the 1930s and 1940s from a Marxist perspective. Ernesto Galarza's *Barrio Boy* (South Bend: University of Notre Dame Press, 1971) chronicles the assimilation of an Hispanic boy from a small Mexican village until he enters high school in Sacramento, California. Oscar Zeta Acosta's *The Autobiography of a Brown Buffalo* (San Francisco: Straight Arrow Books, 1972) is a wildly satiric narrative of coming of age in the West.

As Elaine Kim demonstrates in her outstanding study, *Asian American Literature: An Introduction to the Writings and Their Social Context* (Philadelphia: Temple University Press, 1982), Asian-American writers have left a body of literature describing their experience in the United States. Although Maxine Hong Kingston and Carlos Bulosan have had the widest audiences, Pardee Lowe in *Father and Glorious Descendant* (Boston: Little, Brown, 1943) and No Yong Park in *Chinaman's Chance* (Boston: Meador, 1940) provide examples of Chinese-American life. Manuel Buaken's *I Have Lived with the American People* (Caldwell, Idaho: Caxton, 1948), like Bulosan's *America Is in the Heart*, documents anti-Filipino racism on the West Coast. Takie Okumura's *Seventy Years of Divine Blessing* (Honolulu, Hawaii, 1940) is interesting because it chronicles Japanese life in the Hawaiian Islands prior to Pearl Harbor.

Jewish-American writers have had significant success in the twentieth century. Such critical works as Allen Guttmann's *The Jewish Writer in America: Assimilation and the Crisis of Identity* (New York: Oxford University Press, 1971), Solomon Liptzin's *The Jew in American Literature* (New York: Bloch, 1966), and Irving Malin's *Contemporary American-Jewish Literature* (Bloomington: University of Indiana Press, 1973) demonstrate the wide range of Jewish-American writing, and it is no surprise that a number of outstanding Jewish-American autobiographies are available. Among the large number of personal narratives deserving critical attention is Charles Angoff's *When I Was a Boy in Boston* (New York: Beechhurst, 1947), which is a well-written coming-of-age story. Abraham Cahan's *The Education of Abraham Cahan* (Philadelphia: Jewish Publication Society, 1969) is a translation of the first two volumes of Cahan's five-volume Yiddish autobiography, *Bleter fun Mein Leben*. It contains a great deal of information about Jewish immigrant life in New York at the turn of the century. Samuel Gompers' *Seventy Years of Life and Labor: An Autobiography* (New York: Dutton, 1925) provides firsthand information about the labor movement in the late nineteenth and early twentieth centuries.

Alfred Kazin's *A Walker in the City* (New York: Harcourt, Brace, 1951) is another well-written narrative of the maturation of a city boy. Pauline Leader's *And No Bird Sings* (New York: Vanguard, 1931) tells a different story, that of a deaf girl who had an illegitimate child and was sent to a reformatory. Ludwig Lewisohn has written three personal narratives: *Up Stream: An American Chronicle* (New York: Boni and Liveright, 1922); *Mid-Channel: An American Chronicle* (New York: Harper, 1929); and *Haven* (New York: Dial, 1940). In all three volumes Lewisohn uses the personal narrative to provide criticism and commentary on literature and life. Norman Podhoretz' *Making It* (New York: Random, 1967) is another autobiography of commentary on life and literature, but Podhoretz focuses on the intellectual life of New York. Marcus Eli Ravage's *An American in the Making* (New York: Harper, 1917) is a popular narrative of the Americanization of a Rumanian immigrant. Finally, Lillian D. Wald's *The House on Henry Street* (New York: Holt, 1915) provides the details of Wald's settlement house in New York.

Writers from almost every generation of every ethnic culture have left records of their experiences. Some have been popular, some have become best-sellers, and some have been forgotten. The life stories provided by these writers, whether published by major houses or circulated in manuscript, present images of America that cannot be duplicated. Autobiography captures a moment in time from a specific perspective. It makes no demands for objectivity; it requires a willingness to look at events and circumstances from different perspectives. Perhaps it is inevitable, then, that in a culture formed from a variety of backgrounds and traditions we would have such a large number of stories telling us what it means to be an American.

Index

About the Author

JAMES CRAIG HOLTE is Associate Professor of English at East Carolina University in Greenville, North Carolina. He is the editor of *The Modern Essay: Writing from Experience*, and Associate Editor of *A Comprehensive Bibliography for the Study of American Minorities*.